THE TURNING POINT IN AFRICA

Lagos, 1944. Arthur Creech Jones, dressed as a Yoruba chief (seated), flanked by the veteran nationalist Herbert Macaulay on the left and J.O. Balogun of the 'Nigerian Farmers' on the right.

THE TURNING POINT
IN AFRICA

British Colonial Policy 1938-48

R. D. Pearce

Lecturer in History
St Martin's College, Lancaster

FRANK CASS

First published 1982 in Great Britain by
FRANK CASS AND COMPANY LIMITED
Gainsborough House, 11 Gainsborough Road,
London, E11 1RS, England

and in the United States of America by
FRANK CASS AND COMPANY LIMITED
c/o Biblio Distribution Centre
81 Adams Drive, P.O. Box 327, Totowa, N.J. 07511

British Library Cataloguing in Publication Data

Pearce, R.D.
    The turning point in Africa.
    1. Africa – Politics and government
    2. Great Britain – Colonies – Africa
    I. Title
    325'.341'096   JQ1875.A1

    ISBN 0-7146-3160-4

Typeset by John Smith, London
Printed and bound in Great Britain by
A. Wheaton & Co. Ltd, Exeter

For Joni and Leonard

Contents

Herbert Macaulay, Arthur Creech Jones and J. O. Balogun   *frontis.*

Acknowledgments   ix

List of Abbreviations   x

1   Introduction: Complacent Trusteeship of the
    Inter-War Years   1

2   The Re-definition of Imperial Principles in
    International and National Politics   17

3   Lord Hailey and Colonial Office Thought on
    African Policy   42

4   African Governors and the Making of Policy in
    Africa   70

5   Creech Jones and the Labour Government's
    Imperial Attitudes and Impact   90

6   The Making of African Policy in the Colonial Office,
    1945-48: The End of Indirect Rule and the
    Planning of Local Government   132

7   Planning the Transfer of Power   162

8   Reform at the Centre Overtakes Reform in Local
    Government   185

9   Conclusion   205

Bibliography   211

Index   219

Acknowledgments

This book is a revised and shortened version of my doctoral thesis, written at Balliol College, and I should like to record the debt I owe to the supervisor of this piece of research, Professor Ronald Robinson, and also to A. H. M. Kirk-Greene and Professor A. G. Hopkins. Dr Michael Lee kindly allowed me to read the typescript of his book, written with Martin Petter, *The Impact of War on the Colonial Office*. I should also like to thank the following for their permission to quote copyright material: the Earl Attlee, the Earl of Swinton, the Master and Fellows of Churchill College, the Librarian of Rhodes House, Diane Hayter of the Fabian Society, Mr Carol Johnson, the Librarian of the British Library of Political and Economic Science, Mrs T. Parsons, the Librarian of Sussex University, and the Master and Fellows of University College, Oxford.

One of the great pleasures and rewards of studying very recent history is the possibility of meeting those men and women who were personally involved in it, and I am indebted to the following for answering numerous questions, providing fresh insights, and in some cases for affording excellent hospitality: Ivor Bulmer-Thomas, Sir Alan Burns, Sir Sydney Caine, Sir George Cartland, Aiden Crawley, Hugh Elliott, Lord Listowel, the late Lord Ogmore, Sir Frederick Pedler, Dame Margery Perham, and Professor Kenneth Robinson. My thanks go to the many librarians and archivists who have made research such a pleasant undertaking and also to D. G. Graham, B. P. Wolffe, and William Golant for their friendliness and encouragement of my historical efforts. Lastly, for their kindness and moral support, I especially thank Martin Anthony, Jilly Hayman, Roger Butler, and Sheila Ardern.

Saint Martin's College, Lancaster   R. D. PEARCE

Abbreviations

ACJ	The Arthur Creech Jones Papers
CAB	The British Cabinet Papers
CD&W	Colonial Development and Welfare
Cmd	Command Paper
CO	Colonial Office Papers
CPP	Convention People's Party
FCB	The Fabian Colonial Bureau (Papers)
JAA	*The Journal of African Administration*
NA	Native Authority
OFC	Overseas Food Corporation
UGCC	United Gold Coast Convention

1

Introduction: Complacent Trusteeship of the Inter-War Years

> 'I suppose one mustn't talk about a plan', Rudbeck says.
> 'Oh, no, no, no. They'll take you for a Bolshy.'
>
> – Joyce Cary, *Mister Johnson*

This book deals with the remarkable transformation that took place in British policy towards the empire in tropical Africa between 1938 and 1948, during which time a revolution occurred in the methods and purpose of British rule. In the following chapters attention is given to the parts played by the Colonial Office, the Colonial Service, and by African nationalists, while the effects of the Second World War for the African empire are also evaluated. Finally, emphasis is directed to the immediate post-war years, when a definite course was charted for the first time and a policy constructed that prepared the way for the decolonization of British Africa.

Yet it is important for the historian to consider not only the political – 'technical' – process by which a policy for Africa was formulated but also the changing conceptions and assumptions which underlay and conditioned official pronouncements. For despite the impersonal and objective tone in which government reports and White Papers were couched, policy was formed by human beings and was never an automatic reaction to circumstances. The climate of opinion in Britain did materially affect British policy and rule in Africa. This is not very surprising, since the decision-makers in Whitehall were inevitably imbued with British ideas, thought with British minds, and saw with British eyes.

By 1920 nearly every inch of the modern colonial empire was in the grip of Whitehall. Well-meaning, over-civilized men, in dark suits and black felt hats, with neatly rolled umbrellas crooked over the left forearm, were imposing their constipated view of life on Malaya and Nigeria, Mombassa and Mandalay. The one-time empire builders were reduced to the status of clerks, buried deeper and deeper under mounds of paper and red tape.[1]

The importance of Britain's cultural assumptions is especially clear in the inter-war years. The British empire reached its greatest territorial extent after the First World War which, ironically, helped to undermine the self-confidence upon which the empire rested. The security of Britain's overseas territories always relied less on physical force than on confidence and moral superiority, intangible qualities which could prove illusory. The Great War, with its mass slaughter on a scale hitherto unknown, paralleled the discoveries of Sigmund Freud by showing how thin and precarious was the veneer that covered man's animal nature. It also cast doubts upon the value of Western civilization itself:

> How senseless is everything that can ever be written, done or thought, when such things are possible. It must all be lies and of no account when the culture of a thousand years could not prevent this stream of blood being poured out ...[2]

As a result, the assurance of certain certainties was dimmed and many illusions which had served as the props of imperialism were destroyed. Of cultural assumptions before 1914 Arnold Toynbee has written:

> It was taken for granted by almost all Westerners ... that the Western civilization had come to stay. Pre-1914 Westerners, and pre-1914 British Westerners above all, felt they were not as other men were or ever had been. Westerners were 'civilized'; non-Westerners were 'natives' in the sense that they had no human rights.[3]

The events of August 1914 totally exploded these naive myths for him.

In the inter-war years Western civilization largely lost faith in itself. These were Eliot's 'Twenty years largely wasted, the years of *l'entre deux guerres*'. There was in intellectual circles a wholesale attack on all *a priori* values and an increase in pessimism, introspection, and fatalism. No longer could Britain's cultural superiority be taken for granted. Decolonization may well be seen as a product of Britain's cultural outlook in this century. Even Britain's racial superiority over the 'lesser breeds' began to be doubted.

Greater experience was modifying the old view of the Africans as a 'vaguely menacing black mass'.[4] The usual list of patronising adjectives[5] – which depicted the Africans as primitive barbarians or children and the Europeans as adults or gods – was slowly being abandoned. Racialist views were commonplace in the inter-war period but did not go unchallenged. In December 1933 Dr H.L. Gordon sparked off controversy in the columns of *The Times*. From an examination of 3,444 Kenyans he had found a 'consistent inferiority in brain capacity as estimated by head measurements and in certain physical and psychological attributes'. He argued that the average brain capacity of the adult male Kenyan was only 1,316 cubic centimetres, while that of the average European was 1,481. Therefore, Dr Gordon went on, European education would obviously be dangerous to the African. The consensus of opinion in the letters column, however, was unfavourable to these conclusions. Lord Haldane pointed out that the Eskimos were said to have a cubic capacity of 1,563 centimetres (and no one thought they were intellectually superior); Cyril Burt argued that it was impossible to measure intelligence by measuring the skull; Julian Huxley thought that the ratio of brain weight to body weight had to be taken into consideration. The Colonial Office inclined to the view that there was little substance in Gordon's theories, and an enquiry was resisted.[6] The Office decided that the view expressed in Lord Haldane's *African Survey* finally settled the matter.[7] Hailey argued that there was no existing mental test which could be used on populations differing widely in culture, and no results so obtained could form a basis for the determination of administrative policy.[8]

Britain's cultural malaise, together with the decline in the belief in her innate superiority, affected colonial policy. British economic conceptions were also clearly reflected in African policy. The inter-war years were a period of high unemployment, poor economic performance, and general depression in Britain. The traditional views of the Treasury and of Montagu Norman, Governor of the Bank of England, dominated government thinking. In a period of deflation and economic stagnation, it was held that expenditure should be reduced, budgets rigidly balanced, and a natural recovery of trade awaited. It is not surprising therefore that the colonies were expected to be economically self-supporting; and the 1929 Colonial Development Act, which made £1 million a year available to the dependent empire in order to boost the British economy, did not greatly affect this general principle.

The inter-war years were, on the whole, a period of very limited progress in the African territories. Emphasis was put on the prohibition of abuses rather than on more positive or constructive actions:[9] African society had to be safeguarded rather than developed. It is more fruitful to talk of 'courses of action' rather than 'policy' towards Africa in this period,[10] since the Colonial Office's role was simply that of the 'supervision of administration'.[11] One official argued in 1930 that the chief duty of the Office was 'to select the best man available for any particular job, and send him out to do it, and back him up'.[12] The Colonial Office did not make African policy: this was the preserve of the separate Colonial Governments, with the Secretary of State for the Colonies merely exercising a possible veto. Unless any fundamental principle were violated, the views of a Governor would normally be implemented. Nor was it thought practicable to have one policy that would apply equally in the very diverse and complex conditions of the numerous African territories. Nevertheless there were definite principles espoused by the Colonial Office, though these had only a negative effect in practice.

The official historian of the Office during the Second World War asked what the guiding principles of colonial administration were during the inter-war period. He was able to come to no definite conclusions.[13] It had been the traditional imperial practice, stemming from the Durham Report of 1839, to devolve self-government on white settlers whenever practicable. The burden of administration was removed from Britain's shoulders without regret. Cape Colony became self-governing in 1872, and Natal followed in 1893. In 1910 the Union of South Africa became a white Dominion, and in 1923 the settlers of Southern Rhodesia became self-governing. But by this latter date conceptions were changing. No longer could the 'natives' be seen by everyone as merely a superior form of ape, and, moreover, an influential pro-native lobby had grown up. Despite schemes of various kinds for permanent forms of white supremacy in Kenya and Northern Rhodesia, and in East and Central Africa generally, the British Government officially accepted the principle of Trusteeship.

Trusteeship was to become a quasi-theological doctrine and, as with the Trinity, it was tantamount to heresy to reduce it to comprehensible dimensions. Its very vagueness was its strength, in that it could appeal to all sorts and conditions of men for contrasting reasons. Its major effect in the inter-war years was not only to endow imperialists with a good conscience but to veto settler self-government. This negative contribution was its greatest achievement.

Trusteeship was written into Article 22 of the Covenant of the League of Nations:

> To those colonies and territories which as a consequence of the late war have ceased to be under the sovereignty of the States which formerly governed them and which are inhabited by peoples not yet able to stand by themselves under the strenuous conditions of the modern world, there should be applied the principle that the well-being and development of such peoples form a sacred trust of civilization ...

The tutelage of such people was assigned to the victors of the war. The Mandate system was in fact simply a convenient form of territorial aggrandisement – a 'carefully disguised act of conquest', as a Colonial Office official minuted.[14] Yet although the words of the Covenant applied only to the Mandated territories, the principle of Trusteeship was soon extended to cover the other parts of the African empire. In 1923 Lord Devonshire declared that

> primarily Kenya is an African territory, and His Majesty's Government think it necessary definitely to record their considered opinion that the interests of the African natives must be paramount, and that if and when those interests and the interests of the immigrant races should conflict, the former should prevail.... In the administration of Kenya His Majesty's Government regard themselves as exercising a trust on behalf of the African population, and they are unable to delegate or share this trust, the object of which may be defined as the protection and advancement of the native races.[15]

What applied to Kenya would, by implication, govern relations with the other African territories as well.

Yet although it was accepted in theory that Britain held the territories in Africa as a trustee for the native inhabitants, little changed as a result. The settlers merely tightened their grip. The attempt by Britain to make Trusteeship a reality in Africa might well have driven the settlers to sever relations with the Mother Country and to make common cause with the Union of South Africa. No British Government was willing to incur the odium of using troops against white settlers. Even the possibility of introducing a common electoral roll in Kenya engendered considerable settler dissatisfaction: in the words of Cosmo Parkinson, later the Permanent Under-Secretary of State, it 'may lead to trouble of the most serious kind. Possible "revolution" is not too strong a term to use.'[16] The Secretary of State, Lord Passfield, told the Cabinet as much, and the issued was dropped.[17] In Central Africa there was equally a position of stalemate. Settler self-government was vetoed by Trusteeship, but Trusteeship was vetoed by the reality of settler power.

It is thus scarcely surprising that, despite the holy glow cast over imperialism by Trusteeship, there was no commitment in any but the most nebulous terms to ultimate self-government for the colonies. The achievement of this was not ruled out, but it was an ideal for a vague and unspecified future. As Kenneth Robinson has written:

> If British policy was certainly not opposed in principle to any idea of eventual self-government it equally did not during the inter-war years conceive it to be part of its duty 'officiously to strive' to bring self-government into existence.[18]

If real self-government was to become a reality, it would only be in the course of centuries, and meanwhile no one troubled to define the criteria to be fulfilled before a dependent territory could become self-governing. The real rationalization for the British presence in these years was usually stated as being that the Africans simply could not stand on their own feet, and that the British were giving them good government.

Policy towards Africa was thus negative. The Colonial Office was in fact starved of information, receiving only that which the Colonial Governments chose to give. There was a certain complacency regarding the conditions of these territories. The Secretary of State in 1935 complimented the House of Commons on Britain's record.

> One of the greatest achievements of this Parliament is that generation after generation ... it has guided sympathetically and wisely, and, on the whole, successfully the affairs of the widest and most complex empire the world has ever known.[19]

There seemed to be no need for urgent change, or for any heart-searching. A widely accepted view in these years was voiced by Julian Huxley: 'The most important lesson of history for Africa is to go slowly.'[20] There were too many unanswered questions about the future of the colonies for an immediate clear-cut policy to be forged; solutions could only emerge with the passage of time. The founder of a united Nigeria, Lord Lugard, stressed the importance of not going too fast with the Africans,[21] and in 1937 one of his successors as Governor, Sir Bernard Bourdillon, showed that imperial thinking still followed the same lines. Bourdillon

> said he felt very strongly that they must not force the pace too much. They must lead, not drive; persuade, not compel; and they must not forget that persuasion could come very near to compulsion.... The detribalized native was a very difficult problem, and, although he might be much more prosperous than his tribal brother, he was seldom as contented as the man who was still part of an organization he understood and which had controlled his whole life. They would be on the right lines if they set out with the idea, not of making the native producer do something, but of making him want to do something. That, he was sure, was the only way of getting permanent results. That meant going slow.[22]

If 'administration' rather than 'government' was the concern of colonial officials in the inter-war years, one administrative policy which became pre-eminent was the doctrine of 'indirect rule'. This was defined by Margery Perham as 'a system by which the tutelary power recognizes existing African societies and assists them to adapt themselves to the functions of local government'.[23] The British consciously – though not always successfully – tried to locate and use the traditional native authorities as agents of local rule.[24] The fully-developed system was marked by 'four pillars': the Native Treasury, Native Courts, the Native Authority (NA) – the chief and his council – and the administrative supervision of a Resident and district Officer.[25] Indirect rule was first utilised as a practical necessity in Northern Nigeria by Lugard and was then applied elsewhere, even where the units of administration were too small or traditional leadership too weak.[26] Throughout the *Dual Mandate* Lugard continually emphasised

> the necessity of recognising, as a cardinal principle of British policy in dealing with native races, that institutions and methods, in order to command success and promote the happiness and welfare of the people, must be deep-rooted in their traditions and prejudices.[27]

He viewed the Africans as 'attractive children' and did not think that educated youths would be suited to posts of high administrative responsibility.[28] Indirect rule seemed to him preferable in every way to direct British administration. It was widely held that the 'native' should be made a good African rather than a poor imitation of a European; and indirect rule seemed admirably suited to this end. The chief could act as a 'shock absorber', shielding the African from too intense an exposure to the European presence.

Indirect rule was not merely an administrative technique but a philosophical doctrine. The fundamental hypothesis behind it was the conception of societies as living organisms, adapting themselves spontaneously to the environment. The indirect rulers wished to stop the disruption of tribal society by the European presence; and yet at the same time they wished to encourage tribal institutions to adapt to the new facts of life. There was a continuous conflict between these two incompatible features of the indirect rule tradition. Change was to be stimulated and yet somehow remain organic. This contradiction gave rise to the two varieties of indirect rule: 'interventionist' and 'non-interventionist'.[29] The latter regarded law and order and administration as ends in themselves and deprecated undue interference by the supervising officers. Even the staunchest upholders of indirect rule recognised that the system might lead to a stultification of native life. As it was a mistake for a parent to be over-protective with a child, so it was foolish to make indirect rule a fetish rather than a stepping-stone.[30] Indirect rule could preserve Africa as 'a sort of Whipsnade'.[31]

It was Sir Donald Cameron, with his doctrine of Indirect Administration, who 'shook the indirect rulers out of their dangerous state of self-satisfaction' and called for greater intervention by the administrative officers, for the stimulation of change, and the development of civilized standards of government.[32] It was this interventionist form of indirect rule which the British Government attempted to foster in the years before the Second World War.

Indirect rule was introduced into the mandated territory of Tanganyika in the 1920s by Cameron, and it was this interventionist form that was used as a model elsewhere. The example of southern Nigeria was also influential. Northern Nigeria, where the emirates were large and powerful and where government influence was limited, was certainly not a model. Towards the end of the 1920s Governor Thomas had wished to effect indirect rule in Nyasaland. Direct rule was imposing a great strain on European officials, as well

as occasioning excessive expense and delay. After a representative
had been sent to study the Tanganyikan system, it was decided in
1932 that

> the Natives are well fitted for the introduction of indirect rule on
> Tanganyikan lines, that official opinion is unanimously in favour
> of it and that the time is ripe for its gradual introduction.[33]

The Colonial Office regarded an extension of the powers of native
authorities as 'the most effective and permanent method of
economising Government expenditure'.[34] It was decided to re-
constitute the N.A.'s in Nyasaland in accordance with historical
precedents, its introduction being limited to one or two districts in
the first instance.[35] A new Governor, Sir Hubert Young, decided to
apply reform to almost the whole of the Protectorate, and in July
1933 the Native Authority Ordinance and the Native Courts Ordinance came into force. As a result the work of the administrative
officers was in fact increased 'by the necessity for instructing and
exercising incessant vigilance over the activities of the Native
Authorities'.[36] In 1938 the possibilities of the new system were
thought to be great: 'the Government of the country may one day
stand mainly on the foundations now being laid.'[37] Nevertheless
important reorganisations had to take place when it was found that
some chiefs occupied places for which they had no hereditary
right,[38] and progress was proving very slow.

In Northern Rhodesia there had been attempts to introduce
indirect rule from 1930 onwards. According to the Governor, it was
by 1934 proving itself a 'sound institution', but the local authorities
had no power to collect any taxation.[39] When Hubert Young left
Nyasaland to become Governor of Northern Rhodesia later that
year, he decided to introduce native treasuries and 'reproduce the
general lines of the Nyasaland system'.[40] The attempt to utilise
traditional indirect rule proved a difficult and disappointing task:

> In encouraging the development of native institutions the North-
> ern Rhodesian Government has, except in Barotseland, had to
> deal with tribal organizations which have already fallen into
> abeyance. There are 73 different tribes in the Territory, and so
> much intermixture has taken place between them that it is often
> difficult to distinguish even approximately the boundaries of
> tribal areas.... Years of direct rule have unfitted chiefs for the
> tasks which they are now called upon to perform. Apathy and

dislike of responsibility are widespread.... On present prospects few Treasuries are likely to have any large balances.[41]

Indirect rule in British Central Africa was therefore largely a failure. According to Robert Rotberg, 'these forms of colonial rule made little difference to the actual administration of rural areas' since the District Commissioners refused to transfer important functions to the chiefs.[42]

In Sierra Leone the need for reform became acute in 1934. Chief Bai Sherbro was found guilty of numerous crimes and deposed. The new Governor, Henry Moore, was advised that indirect rule was too 'indirect' altogether and did not exist in the strictly Nigerian sense.[43] Hence J. S. Fenton, a Senior District Commissioner, visited Nigeria and produced a system for the application of indirect rule, based on the model of southern Nigeria, to the Protectorate of Sierra Leone. This was not a matter of substituting indirect for direct rule but of improving 'and bringing into close conformity with Nigerian practice the existing use of native authorities'.[44] An experimental start was made in 1936 in a small number of selected chiefdoms.[45] Little progress was made in the next few years, and there was little sense of urgency. The Governor insisted on the need to go slowly, and the Secretary of State agreed that it was most important 'to advance gradually and not to rush the Africans'.[46]

Further evidence that when native administration was proving unsatisfactory the Colonial Office turned dogmatically to indirect rule is provided by the example of the Gold Coast Colony. We can also see from this case that officials enjoyed the illusion of 'indefinite time ahead'.[47] In 1930 Governor Sir Ransford Slater had recommended indirect rule on the Nigerian model for the Colony area, where continual Stool disputes and the attempt to impose direct taxation had produced chaos. In the absence of a suitable Native Authority Ordinance, there was no statutory provision for control and supervision by the Colonial Government and its administrative staff.[48] It was hoped that, after lengthy investigations, indirect rule would be implemented; but instead Governor Arnold Hodson recommended in 1936 that artificial councils, as seen in Kenya, should be set up. The colony area was the most advanced in West Africa, and Hodson believed that few of the chiefs there were 'at present capable of exercising executive powers', while their political outlook was far behind that of the people.[49] The presence of the educated elite also made traditional indirect rule an impossibil-

ity. The preconceptions of the Colonial Office were now ruffled.
The Secretary of State replied to Hodson that he saw

> no practical alternative to the development in the Colony of a
> system of indirect rule based on the existing chiefs. The alterna-
> tives would appear to be either direct administration which, apart
> from other considerations, must be excluded on financial
> grounds, or the development of a system of indirect administra-
> tion through local councils. Such councils have, I understand, no
> traditional basis in the Gold Coast Colony, and their establish-
> ment as the foundation on which to build up a system of indirect
> administration would violate one of the cardinal principles on
> which such systems have been established elsewhere ... namely,
> that they should be founded on the tribal institutions which the
> native peoples have evolved for themselves.[50]

This was not logical argument but dogma! Hodson was forced to
shift his ground: instead of openly defying the Colonial Office, he
adopted a conciliatory attitude – but still did not institute indirect
rule. He insisted that, of course, native administration had to be
based on traditional rule, but 'long and careful propaganda' would
be necessary before any action could be taken.[51] He was playing for
time.

   In theory the only difference between Hodson and the Colonial
Office was the tempo at which the change to indirect rule would take
place. Yet the officials realised that no real progress would be made
while this man remained Governor. Nevertheless it was thought
best to let him have his way: if he went too slowly, at least it was safer
'to err on that side if we are going to err at all'.[52] The Colonial Office
would appoint a Governor more favourable to indirect rule once
Hodson retired.[53]

   We can thus see that indirect rule, and the enthusiasm for it in the
Colonial Office, violated the celebrated British colonial characteristics of empiricism and expediency. Though it was not accepted or
fully implemented everywhere, it was an essential feature in a
period of general stagnation. Constitutionally, little important progress was made. There were no unofficial majorities on any of the
Legislative Councils of West Africa, and in East and Central Africa
Africans had no direct representation at all. There was no clear idea
of the future development of these territories. In fact the British put
the emphasis not on political but on economic progress. Historians
may have exaggerated the economic neglect and social stagnation of

tropical Africa at this time;[54] but in general progress was limited, and the British took an ambivalent attitude towards the economic development of Africa. No great attempt was made to develop the 'undeveloped estates'. Most colonial economies were dependent – dangerously so – on a single export crop, and as a result the Depression of the early 1930s had debilitating effects. The price of cocoa, so important for the Gold Coast and elsewhere, declined from £68 a ton in 1927 to £26 in 1930. There were general reductions in staff in all the African colonies: these had not been adequate before, commented one Member of Parliament, and now they were worse.[55] Colonial labour conditions regressed. Major Orde-Browne, the expert on the subject, commented in 1937 that 'the position is far behind that of 1930.'[56]

Partly as a result of this worsening of conditions dissatisfaction with the state of the colonies became widespread in Britain towards the very end of the inter-war period, as we shall see, but before that time it was confined to what was widely considered a lunatic fringe. Internationally, world opinion put the imperialist on the defensive. Hobson and Lenin had tied imperialism to exploitation, and it soon became the 'hate-word of world struggle against Anglo-Saxon domination'.[57] Europe was seen as a bloated capitalist – of the George Grosz variety, drawing on a fat cigar – exploiting the colonial proletariat. In Britain the inter-war critics of empire helped sap imperial morale and prepare for the changes in policy that were to occur during and after the Second World War. In 1935 Edward Grigg voiced a prophetic remark in the Commons:

> The attack on our position in Africa is not, in my opinion, coming from Africans or from anybody outside ourselves. It is coming from within our own ranks.... If that kind of propaganda goes on it will undermine the peace of the Colonial Empire, not because of its effects on Africa, but because of its great effect upon ourselves.[58]

He was referring to the writings of men like Hobson, Leonard Woolf, and Leonard Barnes. The last of these is here taken as an example.

After working for a time as an official in the Colonial Office, Barnes became a farmer in South Africa and there underwent what can only be called a conversion. He came to realize the importance of seeing colonialism in the light of poetic truth:

When you catch a momentary glimpse of it like that, you grasp once and for all how grossly deformed a thing it is and how disgustingly it exults in its deformity.... The people in Africa who need civilising are not the Africans, but the Europeans.[59]

Barnes began to see that the *bantu* was in no way inferior or backward. He admired their 'intimate co-working of brotherhood and solidarity, untainted by the egoistic competition that thrives by injuring one's fellows'. This was what the Europeans must have been like before degeneration set in.[60]

The moral absolutism of Barnes was complemented by theoretical views derived from Hobson and Lenin. He believed that economic motives had been foremost in the acquisition of the African colonies and that empire was incompatible with economic justice and therefore with the peace of the world. The First World War, according to Barnes, had been caused by competing imperialisms; and in the 1930s he contended that another war would result from the narrow, imperialistic economic policies of Britain and France.[61]

Barnes was an outspoken, and entertaining, critic of empire. He condemned imperialism *per se*, and drew attention to the fallacy that

the British raj (or for that matter the imperial rule of any country) is beneficial or injurious to the colonial peoples according as it is exercised by enlightened and progressive officials or by obscurantist and reactionary ones.[62]

The system itself was bad. Quite simply, there was 'no such thing as the fitness of one people to govern another'.[63] Hence he called not for the reform but the end of empire. He did wish to see an amelioration of conditions, and argued for a Colonial Magna Carta, to comprise free and compulsory education, freedom of speech, movement, and association, and a minimum level of labour and social legislation.[64] But above all he wished to see the demise of empire: he thought self-government could be achieved after twenty years' vigorous preparation. In 1938 he anticipated that African independence would follow about fifteen years behind Indian freedom.[65]

Indirect rule, Barnes argued, was being used 'not as a road to the democratic control of Africa by Africans but as a substitute for it'. The system was doomed to failure, however, since 'merely screwing down the stopper of a bottle which is already cracked at the base' would avail nothing. In his view the problem was not to preserve the unity of the tribe but to produce

> a new social unity, a final emancipation at a far higher productive level than tribalism can ever reach, on the farther side of class-divided society. The tribe must go, and it is well that it should; for in no other way can the ground for that final emancipation be prepared.[66]

Was the empire, then, an unmitigated evil? Barnes was not able to point to any positive features, though he did quote Bertrand Russell: 'Social life in Britain has remained comparatively free from the impulses that seem repulsive in German nationalism because the empire has been a cesspool for British moral refuse.'[67] A damning indictment indeed.

The African territories in the inter-war years, it can be said, provoked many question, but few answers were forthcoming. It was a period when positive policies were at a discount. Yet there seemed no reason why administration should not continue its unruffled course. Criticism seemed to be mounting at home, but there was no cause for alarm. Having acquired her colonies, Britain seemed to have no idea what to do with them. There was no real purpose in imperial policy. 'What is it for?' asked a disgruntled voice in the Commons, referring to the colonial empire. 'Why have we got it? It is easy to repeat ... the phrase about trusteeship, but I do not think that gets us very much further.'[68] No one realized at that time just how soon policy would be defined, or the empire lost.

NOTES

1. *The Collected Essays, Journalism and Letters of George Orwell*, vol. II. Edited by S. Orwell and I. Angus (Penguin, 1971), pp. 93-4.
2. *All Quiet on the Western Front*, E. M. Remarque (London, 1963), p. 172.
3. *Experiences* (Oxford University Press, 1969), p. 199.
4. *The Listener,* 28 March 1934. Article by Margery Perham.
5. See Lord Lugard, *The Dual Mandate in British Tropical Africa* (5th edn. London, 1965), p. 69: the negro is a 'happy, thriftless, excitable person, lacking in self-control, discipline, and foresight, naturally courageous, and naturally courteous and polite, full of personal vanity, with little sense of reality ...'
6. CO 822/72/46514. Minute by J. E. W. Flood, 9 Nov. 1936.
7. CO 822/85/46514. Minute by Mr White, 12 Dec. 1938.
8. *African Survey: A Study of problems arising in Africa South of the Sahara* (Oxford, 1938), pp. 38-40.

9. A.B. Cohen, *British Policy in Changing Africa* (London, 1959), p.18.
10. 'Colonial Development and Welfare', by Sir Bernard Bourdillon. *International Affairs*, July 1944. Bourdillon was Governor of Uganda from 1932 to 1935 and Governor of Nigeria from 1935 to 1943. I am at present writing his biography.
11. D. Goldsworthy, *Colonial Issues in British Politics, 1945-1961* (Oxford, 1971), p.47.
12. Ajayi and Crowder, (eds.), *History of West Africa*, vol.2 (London, 1974), 'West Africa 1919-1939: the Colonial Situation', pp.525-6.
13. Sir John Shuckburgh, 'Colonial Civil History of the War'. (Unpublished, no date, 4 vols.) There is a copy in the Institute of Commonwealth Studies in London. I am grateful to Dr J.M. Lee for drawing it to my attention.
14. CO 323/1398/6656 Pt.1. Minute by Mr Lee, 25 Jan. 1936.
15. *Indians in Kenya*, Command Paper, no.1922. 1923, p.9.
16. CO 8222/27/25473. Minute by Parkinson, 8 Apr. 1930.
17. *Ibid*. Conclusions of Cabinet Meeting, 9 Apr. 1930.
18. K.E. Robinson, *The Dilemmas of Trusteeship* (London, 1965), p.89.
19. *Parliamentary Debates* (Commons), vol.304, col.2047. 25 July 1935.
20. *Africa View* (London, 1932), p.16.
21. Lugard, *Dual Mandate*, p.198.
22. *The Times*, 27 Jan. 1937.
23. *Native Administration in Nigeria* (Oxford, 1937), p.346.
24. M. Crowder, 'Indirect Rule – French and British Style', *Africa*, July 1964.
25. A.H.M. Kirk-Greene (ed.), *The Principles of Native Administration in Nigeria* (Oxford, 1965), p.24.
26. Cohen, *British Policy in Changing Africa*, p.24.
27. Lugard, *Dual Mandate*, p.211.
28. *Ibid*, pp.70, 80.
29. M. Crowder, *West Africa Under Colonial Rule* (London, 1968), p.217.
30. Huxley, *Africa View*, pp.114, 131.
31. L. Amery, *Forward View* (London, 1935), p.260.
32. Kirk-Greene, *The Principles of Native Administration*, pp.25, 194-217.
33. CO 525/145/34212. Minute by Green, 22 June 1932.
34. CO 525/148/5342. G.F. Seel to the Sec. of the Treasury, 10 Apr. 1933.
35. *Ibid*. Secretary of State to the Governor, 2 May 1933.
36. The Senior Provincial Commissioner of Blantyre to the Chief Sec. at Zomba, 10 July 1935. ('Nyasaland' file at Rhodes House.)
37. CO 525/180/44104. Report of the Financial and Economic Commission, 1938.
38. *Ibid*. Governor to Secretary of State, 17 July 1938.
39. CO 795/72/25641. Governor to Secretary of State, 17 July 1934.
40. CO 795/77/45096. Minute by A.B. Cohen, 2 Nov. 1935.
41. CO 795/102/45173/3. 'Report of the Commission Appointed to Enquire into the Financial and Economic Position of Northern Rhodesia, 1938'. Colonial no.145. The authors, A.W. Pim and S. Milligan (introduction, xi), thanked Cohen for his assistance. This enquiry was vital for the development of Cohen's views. The mastercopy in this file is covered with his characteristically scrawly handwriting.
42. *The Rise of Nationalism in Central Africa* (Harvard, 1965), p.50.
43. CO 267/651/32097. Minute by Fiddian, 17 Sept. 1935.
44. CO 267/658/32097. Minute by O.G.R. Williams, 29 Oct. 1937.
45. CO 267/651/32097. Governor to Secretary of State, 27 Aug. 1935.
46. CO 267/658/32097. Governor to Secretary of State, 4 Mar. 1938; Secretary of State to Governor, 25 Mar. 1938.
47. Cohen, *British Policy in Changing Africa*, p.25.

48. CO 96/749/31228. 'Summary of Proposals in Connection with the Introduction of Indirect Rule into the Gold Coast Colony'. 19 July 1938.
49. CO 96/730/32228. 'Native Administration in the Gold Coast Colony', n.d.
50. *Ibid*. Secretary of State to the Governor, 30 Jan. 1937.
51. CO 96/767/31228. Governor to Secretary of State, 12 Apr. 1940.
52. CO 96/746/31352. Minute by Parkinson, 25 Mar. 1938.
53. CO 96/746/31096/4. Minute by Dawe, 12 Jan. 1939.
54. See Gann and Duignan (eds.), *Colonialism in Africa*, vol. II (Cambridge, 1970), pp. 15-16.
55. *Parl. Debates* (Commons), vol. 280, col. 1452. 14 July 1933. Mr Lunn.
56. 'Memorandum on Labour' by Orde-Browne. n.d. but 1937. (Copy in the Arthur Creech Jones Papers, Box 14, file 3, Rhodes House.)
57. R. Koebner and H.D. Schmidt, *Imperialism* (Cambridge, 1964), Ch. XI.
58. *Parl. Debates* (Commons), vol. 304, col. 2069. 25 July 1935.
59. Barnes, 'Radical Destination,' vol. II, p. 22. (As yet unpublished autobiography of Leonard Barnes.)
60. *Ibid*. pp. 15-16.
61. 'The Future of Colonies' (A Day to Day Pamphlet, 1936). Letter to the *Manchester Guardian*, 8 May 1939.
62. *Empire or Democracy?* (Gollancz, 1939), p. 257.
63. *Daily Worker*, 1 June 1944.
64. *Empire or Democracy?* pp. 170-4.
65. Barnes, 'Radical Destination', vol. II, p. 126.
66. *Empire or Democracy?* pp. 161-2.
67. *Ibid*. p. 84.
68. *Parl. Debates* (Commons), vol. 337, col. 147. 14 June 1938. Mr Pickthorn.

2

The Re-definition of Imperial Principles in International and National Politics

Isn't it better that whoever cannot do without
having slaves should call them free men?

– Albert Camus, *The Fall*

The stagnation and frustrations of the inter-war years came to a head
at the end of the 1930s in dissatisfaction and recrimination. No
longer was it possible to veil with glib platitudes the fact that
conditions in many parts of the colonial empire were deplorably
low. Research in Kenya revealed that of 650 individuals examined
570 had anaemia, 546 had haemic murmurs, 425 had malnutrition,
just over 300 had malaria, and 159 had tuberculosis. Each of the
Africans was an 'ambulant pathological museum'.[1] In July 1939 a
report on nutrition made its appearance.[2] Colonial diets were shown
to be insufficient in both quantity and quality; malnutrition was
responsible for many preventable diseases and for 'deficiency states'
which prevented the full enjoyment of health. But by far the greatest
trauma came from the West Indies.

A series of riots and disturbances in the Caribbean islands during
the second half of the decade severely shocked those in Britain who
took an interest in colonial affairs. In 1935 and 1937 alone 39
people were killed and 175 injured there.[3] Subsequent investigations gave publicity to the poor conditions which had caused the
trouble. Malcolm MacDonald, Secretary of State for the Colonies,
set up a Royal Commission under Lord Moyne to enquire into the
social and economic state of the West Indies. In the House of
Commons criticisms of Britain's record were extensive and outspoken. Lloyd George was 'perfectly appalled at the conditions' and
felt ashamed that this 'slummy empire' had been tolerated so long.
Arthur Creech Jones argued that the riots had 'rudely shocked'

British complacency. Aneurin Bevan asserted that the boast about Britain being a good colonizer was baseless: 'We are obviously incompetent.... This House of Commons ... is entirely not to be trusted with the stewardship of these areas.'[4]

The Cabinet, despite MacDonald's advice, decided not to publish the Report of the Moyne Commission, and only the recommendations were made available.[5] The Secretary of State was instructed to speak to the leaders of the opposition parties in order to forestall embarrassing criticism in the Commons. But if MacDonald acted on this advice, his action proved ineffectual. There were protests in the Commons against the secrecy surrounding the Report: yet, it was pointed out, even the recommendations were a sufficiently damning indictment.

The Commons debates from 1938 to 1942 reveal an atmosphere of widespread discontent, a readiness to censure past mistakes in moral terms. Throughout the war there were repeated calls for a more definite and progressive policy. In 1939 Noel-Baker was arguing that 'we need a re-organisation and re-orientation of our colonial policy'.[6] In 1940 Sir Richard Acland, whose Common Wealth party espoused the international administration of colonial areas, called for 'violent' changes in policy.[7] The year 1942 saw repeated calls for a definition of colonial policy. Creech Jones urged the formulation of 'a positive policy in place of a weak negative one'.[8] Captain MacDonald revealed that for years he had been trying to discover the long-term policy of the Colonial Office, but without success.

> The policy of the Colonial Office up to now has been nothing but make-shifts and expedients.... The time for a policy is now and the time for putting it into practice is immediately after the war is over.[9]

As official definition did proceed, recommendations from the Commons became more specific. In 1944, for instance, Dr Haden Guest argued the feasibility of laying down 'a general line of policy for tropical Africa' and called for a 'one-generation plan of twenty years'.[10]

There was a very definite determination in Parliament to avoid in future what Lord Samuel termed 'lethargy tempered by riots'.[11] In some quarters it was thought that a change of machinery was needed; and Samuel himself urged that Parliament should create a

Joint Select Committee on Colonial Affairs to 'investigate, report and recommend' but have no executive powers. Malcolm Mac-Donald was much attracted to this idea, but not so his permanent officials, and when MacDonald was replaced as Secretary of State the matter was dropped.[12] Yet the unwillingness of the officials to support this committee should not disguise the fact that the dissatisfaction seen in Parliament was present also in the Office.

In March 1939 Assistant Under-Secretary Arthur Dawe criticized the deficiencies in colonial policy and noted 'the lack of constructive thinking on important matters and the absence of sustained working towards definite objectives'.[13] He was willing to endorse the direct representation of the colonies in the Imperial Parliament, arguing that lessons could be learned from the French in this matter.[14] Dawe was also clear on where to lay the blame for the present unsatisfying position – on Parliament and the politicians.

> Civil servants are a machine for the execution of policy. If there is no clear policy for them to execute they cannot function effectively.... The conclusion which I cannot escape from is that the House of Commons ... has ... displayed the most disquieting deficiencies as an instrument for governing Colonies overseas. It has indulged in petty criticism without constructive purpose. It has interfered spasmodically without plan and without clarity of direction. It has displayed ignorance and facile emotionalism in the face of problems which demanded knowledge and statesmanship.[15]

The men of the Colonial Office were profoundly dissatisfied with the *status quo*. They wanted a more definite policy, and one that could actually be put into operation. But the lead for this would have to come from the politicians: civil servants were far from bent on contravening their political masters and positively wished for active guidance.

The first result of this new thinking at the Colonial Office occurred at the height of the period of dissatisfaction. The 1940 Colonial Development and Welfare Act has been called 'perhaps the first unselfish act in British imperial history'.[16] This Act was to operate for ten years and was to make available a maximum of £5 million a year for development and welfare projects in the dependent empire, together with £500,000 a year for research. These amounts were to be subject to review from time to time. Eleven million pounds of the £15 million debts owed by the colonies to

Britain were also to be remitted.[17] The new Fund was not to provide a permanent source of revenue, since the 'dole mentality' had to be avoided, but rather 'artificial respiration which is justified until the colonies can build up their own strength'.[18] These proposals had been boosted by the Moyne Commission which had recommended that an annual grant of £1 million be made available for twenty years for general social and economic improvement in the West Indies.[19] But in fact the origins of C.D. & W. went back to a Colonial Office committee appointed in June 1938 to decide how far the Colonial Development Fund, founded in 1929, could be used to help finance education.[20]

The advisory committee to this Fund had at first been strict in applying its terms of reference but soon began to interpret them more widely. Hence some of the money was in fact spent on social services. It was decided in 1939 that this state of affairs had to be regularized and also extended in order to finance a 'more forward colonial policy'. There were two main reasons given in the Colonial Office for a more vigorous policy:

> the one a desire to avert possible trouble in certain colonies, where disturbances are feared if something is not done to improve the lot of the people, the other a desire to impress this country and the world at large with our consciousness of our duties as a great colonial power.[21]

The corollary was that colonial policy had to be specifically defined in terms of content. Much research and discussion would be necessary, but the preparation for what was to be the post-war policy had begun.

The Colonial Development and Welfare Act of 1940 was a landmark not so much because of its effects on Africa during the war – by February 1945 only £1,037,575 had actually been spent there[22] – but because it made possible and indeed vital the preparation of a real policy. Lord Hailey became accustomed to think of 1940 as 'opening an entirely new chapter in colonial policy'.[23] It ended *laissez-faire* and called, in the words of Sir Charles Jeffries, for a 'revolution in official methods of thought and approach'.[24]

Colonial Development and Welfare was partly a continuation at an increased rate of pre-war methods. MacDonald argued that the proposals were not 'a bribe or a reward for the colonies' support in this supreme crisis.... They are part of the normal peace-time development of our colonial policy'.[25] The Bill had been in draft form before the Second World War started. Yet it required the impetus of Moyne's recommendations and of the ideological requirements of a war against Nazi Germany to jolt the Treasury from its habitual parsimonious stance. 'A continuation of the present state of affairs', wrote MacDonald, presenting C. D. & W. to the Cabinet,

> would be wrong on merits, and it provides our enemies and critics with an admirable subject for propaganda in neutral countries and elsewhere.... Moreover, it is, I feel, of the greatest importance that at the end of the war, when the colonial question is bound to be much discussed, we should be in a position to face with a reasonable measure of confidence any criticisms that may be made of our record as a colonial power.[26]

Presented in this manner, the scheme received ready assent in Cabinet. This policy certainly did have propaganda value: given their Second Reading at a time when the Germans were already overrunning France and Britain stood alone, the measures could be seen as a sign of Britain's selfless devotion to her imperial trust. Indeed the Second World War provided the ideological framework upon which imperial policy had to be constructed. Britain was basically fighting for her very existence rather than for any particular principles or specific war-aims; but for propaganda purposes a more positive conception was needed.

> There is a real need for the formulation of post-war aims in broad terms which will sustain the spiritual motive force of our own people, appeal to our supporters abroad (especially America) and counter the German conception of a new order.[27]

Colonial policy was formed against a background of total warfare – ideological as well as military.

Nazi raciulism and imperialism led to British attempts to liberalize the whole ethos of her empire and to cleanse the colonial stables. 'The Nazis with their false doctrine of the Herrenvolk', wrote the Colonial Secretary in 1941, 'have made it clear that there is no place in our conception of life for the doctrine that one race is superior to another.'[28] On one level, this was an argument about semantics. The Ministry of Information issued a list of 'Do's and Don'ts'.[29] The word 'imperial' was to be avoided altogether, while the phrases 'British Empire' and 'British Commonwealth' were to be used interchangeably. The Colonial Office had a special liking for 'British Commonwealth and Empire': 'It has the virtue of being capable of at least three interpretations.'[30] There was an attempt to abandon the word 'dependencies' in favour of 'territories', and 'colonies' also received censure.[31]

Britain did her best to defend the morality of having an empire. Winston Churchill, who had been the chief opponent of Indian political advance in the 1930s and who announced that he had not become Prime Minister in order to preside over the liquidation of the British empire, resolutely resisted his critics. 'I make bold', he wrote to the American President, '... to suggest that British imperialism has spread and is spreading democracy more widely than any other system of government since the beginning of time.'[32] But few besides Churchill, and perhaps not even he, believed that a defence of the *status quo* would be sufficient to cope with a changing world. Since it was unlikely that publicity of Britain's past record would yield dividends, it was decided in the Colonial Office that, for propaganda purposes, it would be better to say nothing of past achievements – such as they were – and concentrate on plans for the future.[33]

Britain also made the most of the contribution of the colonies to the war effort. African reactions to the war were on the whole favourable. In Nigeria a 'Club Hitler Club' was formed, together with a Win the War Fund, to purchase a Nigerian squadron for the Royal Air Force.[34] In Tanganyika £25,000 was raised to buy a small naval vessel. The Gold Coast provided a bomber squadron and fighter squadron.[35] The Colonial Office was generally concerned to ensure that gifts and sums of money received the maximum publicity. The novelty of Spitfires soon wore off, and it was decided that mobile canteens, which covered a lot of ground and could be seen by large numbers of people, would be the best bet. By mid-1941 the colonies had given money gifts of £14,353,034.[36]

The important part played by African troops, who acquitted themselves 'with distinction',[37] was also stressed. By May 1945 about 374,000 African troops were serving in regular military units. This was an encouraging picture; but colonial enthusiasm for the war did not extend uniformly over the empire, as the loss of Hong Kong, Malaya, Singapore, and Burma to the Japanese showed. 'Before our very eyes, in this spring of 1942, the empire disintegrates.'[38]

It was not so much the military capture of these places as the apparently willing acquiescence of their inhabitants which called for an explanation. In *The Times* Margery Perham noted that with the fall of Singapore the writing was on the wall for the British empire and that it was necessary to 'achieve a new and more intimate and generous relationship with its peoples'.[39] Events, however, do not of themselves presuppose a course of action: they first have to be interpreted in the light of the wishes and preconceptions of those concerned. The state of British opinion in 1942 would decide the effects of the imperial losses.

THE DEFINITION OF COLONIAL POLICY

Outlook on the future of the colonies was in fact very divided. Over the ultimate future of the non-self-governing parts of the empire there was a lack of clarity and consensus. Yet this was a question that had to be seriously considered during the war. In some quarters there was little doubt that a form of self-government would come eventually. 'What is the main purpose of the British empire?' asked the Colonial Secretary, Malcolm MacDonald, in 1938.

> I think it is the gradual spread of freedom amongst all His Majesty's subjects in whatever part of the earth they live.... The spread of freedom in British countries is a slow ... evolutionary process. The pace varies from place to place.... There may even, sometimes, be inevitable setbacks. But over the generations the evolutionary process goes on.... Even amongst the most back-ward races of Africa our main effort is to teach these peoples to stand always a little more securely on their own feet.... The trend is towards the ultimate establishment of the various colonial communities as self-supporting and self-reliant members of the great commonwealth of free peoples and nations. The object will be reached in different places at different times and by different paths.... But it will be generations, perhaps even centuries, before that aim is accomplished in some cases.[40]

This statement can be taken as implying Dominion Status as the goal for colonial territories; but in fact it is not an exact definition of policy and was not seen as a commitment. It is heavily qualified, is more concerned with the spirit than the exact aim of administration, and is couched very much in the terms of a personal opinion. The words used (especially 'freedom') demand further definition to be free of ambiguity.

In 1941 Lord Moyne, a new Secretary of State, warned the Cabinet of the dangers of assuming that the aim of colonial policy was necessarily the fostering of each colony as a separate self-governing unit.[41] Could it be possible that 35 colonial dependencies would all end up as new Dominions? 'May it not be that we have pursued the centrifugal tendency long enough and that the time has come to set in motion the centripetal?' After all, one of the lessons of the war seemed to be that small units could not survive alone. Moyne could conceive that responsible self-government was a possible, though not necessarily desirable, development in East Africa and perhaps in the larger West African territories, Malaya, and the West Indies; but it would clearly be out of the question in the smaller territories. Some other solution would therefore have to be sought.

I advocate great caution in applying terms like 'democracy' or 'the development of self-governing institutions' to the Colonial Empire. Our aim must be so to mould the institutions of each colony and so to fit them into the general Empire framework that they give to the people of that colony the best expression possible in its peculiar conditions to our conception of freedom.

Again the vague and philosophical term 'freedom' is preferred to more specific ones. Moyne's opinions were definite only on what he did not want, and here lay the weakness of his position. In a war against Nazi imperialism, Britain was being urged more and more to define her position as an imperial power as clearly as possible, and as far as possible from an 'imperialist' stance.

For a short time it seemed as though Britain had done just this; the right of the colonial peoples to self-determination seemed to have been conceded. A meeting between Churchill and Franklin Roosevelt at Placentia Bay in August 1941 resulted in the Atlantic Charter. In Article 3 the British and Americans made known that 'they respect the right of all people to choose the form of government under which they will live'. It was believed in some quarters that this declaration meant what it said and in fact applied to the whole world, including the British empire. Clement Attlee said as much to the West African Students' Union in London,[42] while Roosevelt publicly refuted the idea that the Charter applied only to Europe.

The Colonial Office was taken by surprise. So was Churchill, who had not been thinking in terms of the empire at all. At the Atlantic meeting he had had in mind, he said, primarily those nations under Nazi domination. On the future of the British empire His Majesty's Government had already made declarations

> which are complete in themselves, free from ambiguity and related to the conditions and circumstances of the territories and peoples affected. They will be found to be entirely in harmony with the high conception of freedom and justice which inspired the Joint Declaration.[43]

The Office was naturally relieved that it was not affected by such a generalized declaration of policy, and Lord Cranborne, who became Secretary of State in February 1942, was able to continue with the ideas that had attracted Lord Moyne. He asked fundamental questions: 'Are we to train Africans to govern themselves, or are we to incorporate them, on a basis of equality, in the British administrative system? ... What is the ultimate aim of our policy towards the Colonial Empire?'[44] Cranborne was asking these questions in the light of deadlock in India and loss of Burma, Malaya and Singapore.

There seemed to be two alternatives: Britain intended to stay in the empire permanently or would leave when the colonial peoples 'grew up'. Cranborne believed that the latter alternative had created a sense of impermanence.

> We have ourselves indicated that our control is merely temporary and preliminary to something better. In such circumstances, can we expect subject peoples to co-operate with us or even to respect us? They are merely impatient to get on to the next stage, when they get rid of us and govern themselves. If we want the British empire to endure, is it not essential that we should assume that it is to be a permanency, and that so far from teaching colonial peoples to govern themselves, we should do the contrary, and welcome their participation in our administration?

Cranborne was calling for the increasing participation of colonial people in the Colonial Service and for their exclusion from the councils of government. He was evidently thinking in terms of the permanence of British political control rather than the development of new self-governing Dominions.

One school of thought was obviously drawing the moral from the war that small nations could not stand alone and that there was therefore a future for institutions like the British empire. A relationship of permanent political subordination was envisaged, at least for a substantial part of the empire. Yet the opposite view was also held. Lord Hailey, rapidly becoming one of the experts on the subject, decided in 1940 that 'It is implicit in the declarations made on the objective of colonial policy that the dependencies shall be given a full opportunity to achieve self-government'.[45] Yet he was aware that not everyone shared his view:

> There are clearly many who ... have little belief that self-government can ever be realised in our African dependencies.... If they refrain from a more open expression of these views, it is because they believe that the conception of self-government is so idealistic, or at any rate can only become realisable at so remote a date, that it does not form an issue of any immediate importance.[46]

The vagueness of British policy could support mutually incompatible expectations.

This inexactitude is best illustrated by the activity in the Colonial Office following Churchill's assurance that British policy towards the colonies was covered by declarations in harmony with the Atlantic Charter. In response to this, Creech Jones asked in Parliament whether a White Paper composed of these past statements could be published, and Harold Macmillan, Parliamentary Under-Secretary of State, initiated the preparation of such a paper. This proved far more difficult than had been envisaged: not only was the recording machinery of the Office ill-equipped, but the declarations themselves did not seem worthy of the description Churchill had given them. As Macmillan put it,

> I do not think the P.M. can have realised the true nakedness of the land when he made the statement of September 9th, 1941.... The declarations are not complete in themselves, nor are they free from ambiguity. They are scrappy, obscure and jejune.... The P.M. must have written the declaration on his own.[47]

The Secretary of State, Lord Cranborne, agreed that the proposed White Paper would have to be dropped. 'Declarations on Colonial Policy seem to have been mainly conspicuous by their absence, and where any have been made, they are vague in the extreme.'[48] There was in fact no overall colonial policy, only differing conceptions of possible future developments. Yet at least there was now an awareness of the vacuum to be filled, and a start would be made towards a real and realistic policy. The first official addition to colonial policy, however, only added to the confusion. This was the doctrine of Partnership, first put forward by Hailey as 'a new ... and more constructive and a more beneficial interpretation of trusteeship'.[49] It was first presented to the House of Commons by Macmillan in the Estimates debate of June 1942. Some M.P.s were unable to grasp what the term actually meant, and Dr Haden Guest thought it was 'just a form of words, soft soap or soothing syrup, which means nothing'.[50] The most important aspect in Macmillan's mind seems to have been the concept of permanence (even though the duration of a partnership is not implied in the term). When questioned about the word, he replied that he had 'merely meant to emphasise ... that we have no intention of putting this affair into liquidation.... We are going on with the job.'[51] Nevertheless the term could be interpreted in several ways and achieved a transitory popularity for reasons not originally intended.

The Times argued that Partnership implied that henceforth Britain's dealings with her colonies would be governed 'not by what is deemed desirable in the interests of the colonial peoples, but by what they in fact desire....'[52] The Labour Party's spokesman, Creech Jones, endorsed the new term strongly. He wanted a relationship that conveyed the idea 'of equality and friendship, the idea of service and practical assistance and which expresses it in dynamic and constructive terms'. Above all, Partnership implied to him that everything possible would be done to accelerate the development of self-government, 'that the whole process of government is geared to the supreme purpose of fitting the colonial peoples for political responsibility'.[53] Here was a form of Partnership which, if put into practice, would most certainly not lead to permanence.

The general result of the new slogan was to give the impression of greater equality between Britain and the colonies (despite references to senior and junior partners).[54] Henceforth colonial policy appeared more liberal. It was hoped that the change in terminology would meet with approval in the United States. The American *Mercury* considered that Partnership was a typical example of 'diplomatic double talk',[55] but on the whole American approval was subsequently given to the term. The vagueness of the word meant

that it could appeal to different men for different, even contradictory, reasons.

The importance of the wish to appease American anti-imperialist
feeling can scarcely be exaggerated for British colonial policy during
the war. Britain and America co-operated with the aim of winning
the war, but this did not preclude considerable differences of opinion. As the war proceeded, it became increasingly obvious that
Britain was in many ways herself a dependent territory, dependent
upon American help. In 1941 the United States provided ten per
cent of the British empire's munitions; by 1944 the figure had risen
to 28.7 per cent. At this stage American munitions production was
six times as great as the British. American strength increased pro-
digiously during the war, while Britain's declined drastically. More
and more the United States could call the tune, and the British had
to learn to dance. During the war the Americans acquired bases in
Africa and the West Indies and were exerting considerable influence, so much so that rumours began to circulate that Britain was
quitting West Africa and the Americans were taking over.[56] The
empire was no longer solely a British affair: the views of her great
ally had perforce to be taken into consideration.

Creech Jones judged in 1942 that Americans as a whole were
profoundly suspicious of the British empire. Yet they were in fact
uninformed about British policy, while their view of Britain was
nearly a hundred years out of date.

> They love idealistic generalisations, glowing phrases, which
> ignore the actualities of the colonial situation and seem impatient
> of the practical approaches to policy making, so common with
> Englishmen.... The suspicion of British motives, the distrust
> of our colonial good faith, the apprehension of alleged selfish
> imperialism, the prejudice from our past relations with them, all
> create a serious factor in Anglo-American understanding that is
> deplorable in wartime.[57]

The American stereotype of Britain was of an exhausted power,
hidebound by class and tradition. One American writer wrote of the
'utter helpless decadence of the English – something that had been
apparent to even English intellectuals for twenty years'.[58] It was
believed that Britain cunningly wanted to use American might to
safeguard her anachronistic Empire. But, in the celebrated remark
of *Life* magazine: 'One thing we are sure we are *not* fighting for is to
hold the British Empire together.'[59]

The Americans in fact had an even lower opinion of the French and Portuguese empires, but the British came in for extensive criticism. President Roosevelt wished to see the empire liquidated. He drew on his personal experience in the Gambia at a press conference in February 1944:

> It's the most horrible thing I've seen in my life.... The natives are five thousand years back of us. Disease is rampant, absolutely. It's a terrible place for disease.... For every dollar the British, who have been there for two hundred years, have put into Gambia, they have taken out ten. It's plain exploitation of those people.[60]

With their own position seemingly secure, the Americans could indulge in an essentially moral attack on the empire.

With American attitudes a grave embarrassment to the British, conciliatory initiatives had to be taken. Stafford Cripps, a man renowned for his puritanical sense of morality, was sent in the spring of 1942 with the most liberal offer that had ever been made to the Indian nationalists. Despite the refusal of the offer by Gandhi and the Congress Party, American opinion regarded the offer as a reasonable compromise which should have been accepted. The offer seemed proof of the sincerity of Britain's new outlook.[61]

Criticisms of the colonial empire were countered in a variety of ways. There was the 'Tu Quoque' argument,[62] pointing out the skeletons in the American cupboard – especially the inferior positions of negroes and Red Indians. Lord Hailey argued that the real problem in many parts of the world was that of inadequate economic development, and this had little to do with political status. The British colonies were not poor because they were dependent territories; they had acquired a status of political inferiority because of their original poverty and backwardness. Hailey stressed that there were definite plans for economic development within the empire and that the ultimate political goal was the development of self-governing institutions. But moderation and orderly development were essential. There were no easy solutions to the problems that beset the colonies and other backward areas of the world. It would certainly not be in the best interests of the colonial peoples to press on in doctrinaire fashion with the granting of political 'freedom'.[63]

The major card Britain had to play was the new policy of Development and Welfare. Whatever had been the case in the past, it was urged, Britain was now expending money on the welfare of her colonial wards and doing her utmost to foster better conditions. American criticisms may have smacked of self-righteousness, but now Britain developed a brand of her own. No longer, it was argued, could there be any talk of exploitation: Britain's policy was not imperialism but 'good neighbourliness'.[64] Indeed possession of the empire had become 'a burden of responsibility and liability'.[65] Promises were now being made, and expectations aroused, which would comprise part of the background of post-war policy. The process of moral re-armament was going on; but at the same time Britain was making commitments which could prove difficult to fulfil.

Besides general propaganda about Britain's good intentions, there was also need for a political initiative on the colonial empire. Practical international necessity dispelled the clouds of 'indefinite time ahead'. The United States, and to a lesser extent Soviet Russia, could be satisfied with nothing less than an assurance that responsible self-government would be granted – and for a time it did not seem that even this revolutionary step would suffice. Yet if a commitment to self-government was the best way to appease the Americans, not everyone thought it was in itself desirable for colonial policy.

We have seen how the imprecision of British declarations, which spoke of 'good government' and 'freedom', allowed of interpretations which envisaged either the ultimate development of self-government or of some permanent relationship with control remaining in British hands. It was the wish to appease the allies which finally tilted the balance in favour of 'self-government'.

The British politicians were only too conscious of their ally's critical attitude to the empire. 'It is clear', agreed four senior Ministers, 'that there is a widespread and rooted feeling in the United States which regards the British Colonial Empire as equivalent to the private estate of a landlord preserved for his own benefit.'[66] Something had to be done to enlighten American opinion and to dispel the 'almost complete ignorance' of Americans regarding the actual conditions in the colonies. There were severely practical reasons to temper America's hostility:

... we must, if we can, endeavour to get the United States to express their willingness to enter some general defence scheme which would include the defence of colonial areas. It is also desirable to commit the Americans, if possible, to the principle that we and the other Colonial Powers should have the unquestioned right to administer our own colonies, Protectorates and Mandated Territories, including those which we have temporarily lost to the Japanese.

It was necessary for the ideological enemy of empire to lend support to its maintenance.

The Cabinet first considered making a unilateral declaration in order to stem the rising tide of American criticism. But soon a more promising proposal came from Cordell Hull, the American Secretary of State, in conversation with Lord Halifax, Britain's ambassador in Washington. He suggested the possibility of a Joint Declaration to be issued by the Americans, the British, the Dutch, and possibly the Chinese. It was strongly urged in Cabinet that Britain should seize this opportunity to win over American opinion. This way Britain would retain the initiative. 'We are afraid that if no response is made to Mr Hull's proposal we shall be faced, in the near future, with some American initiative of a less friendly character.'[67] The American Administration was under considerable pressure to issue a declaration on colonial territories, and the time would come when they would be forced to declare their attitude.

Whitehall was glad of this opportunity of paving the way to agreement with the Americans. It was thought that the process of coming to a mutually acceptable formula would obviously be difficult but that the rewards would outweigh any disadvantages incurred. Work was begun on a declaration which Halifax could then show to Hull. It was obvious from the start that Britain would have to adopt as liberal a position as she could: all speculation as to 'centripetal' forces and permanent political dependency would have to be dropped. After advice in Cabinet, from Halifax, and from the Dominions, a final British draft was written. It was presented to Cabinet on 19 January 1943. The text argued that the United Nations were fighting to defeat the present aggression and to render future aggression impossible. To this end there had to be security, prosperity, and equal opportunity for all peoples. Yet certain colonial peoples could not achieve these objectives themselves.

It is therefore the duty of 'Parent' or 'Trustee' States to guide and develop the social, economic and political institutions of the colonial peoples until they are able without danger to themselves and others to discharge the responsibilities of government.[68]

The wording of this sentence is in many ways cautious. There is no mention of the time-scale involved, while economic and social developments are given at least equal prominence with political. Yet there was now a commitment to eventual self-government – at least there was a willingness to make this commitment, for American agreement to the declaration had yet to be secured.

The British draft also called for 'the establishment in the future of a wider and permanent system of general security'. Here was the possibility, at least, of associating the U.S.A. with the defence of the empire. And lastly the declaration, while noting that Parent States would remain responsible for the administration of their territories, called for co-operation between nations and for the establishment of Regional Commissions. These bodies would be composed of the Parent States of a particular region and those States which had a major strategic or economic interest there. The Commissions were to 'provide effective machinery for consultation and collaboration, so that the States concerned may work together to promote the advancement of the colonial peoples and the general welfare of mankind'. Here again was a means of associating the United States with the security and development of the British empire, without giving away Britain's ultimate control.

Yet British official calculations were soon dashed. Britain had been prepared to give a cautious commitment to eventual self-government, and had consequently been prepared to compromise; but when an American draft of the Joint Declaration was received in London the full complexity of the attempt to reconcile British and American views became apparent. Despair was the first reaction in the Colonial Office:

> After reading the American draft two or three times, I am left with a feeling of complete hopelessness. I do not think it is possible to secure such amendment of the draft as would make it acceptable to us and, I would add, to the colonies.[69]

It was thought it might be better to abandon the Joint Declaration altogether and return to the idea of a unilateral statement.

The main criticism in the Office was that the Americans had placed far too much emphasis on the eventual independence of colonial territories. The title of their draft, 'Declaration by the United Nations on National Independence', set the tone of the whole document. The words 'independent' and 'independence' were used nineteen times, whereas the British had avoided them altogether. It was obvious that the American draft implied the multiplication of small national sovereignties, an idea which aroused the chagrin of the British.

Independence is a political catchword which has no real meaning apart from economics. The Americans are quite ready to make their dependencies politically 'independent' while economically bound hand and foot to them and see no inconsistency in this.[70]

Furthermore, the Americans wished to see the setting of target dates for full independence 'at the earliest possible moment', while the colonial peoples themselves were to have an obligation to 'prepare and equip themselves for independence'.

Not all of the draft met with British disapproval. The preamble was far too long; but there was a suitable, if idealistic, emphasis on social and economic development. Also of importance was that the Americans approved the recommendation for Regional Commissions. But they also provided for an International Trusteeship Administration to actually administer former Italian and Japanese colonies; and there was a possibility that British colonies, then under the control of the Japanese, would fall into this category.

Opinion in the Colonial Office varied on the possibility of making the American draft palatable by amending it. Lord Hailey was worried about the prospect that British territories under enemy authority might be put under international control, and he also disliked the idea of fixing target dates. Yet on the whole he did not think the problems insuperable. To substitute 'self-government' for 'independence' would in his opinion suggest 'a refinement which will be viewed with a great deal of suspicion in the U.S.A.' Altogether, Hailey was in favour of carrying on negotiations for a Joint Declaration: unilateral action designed to carry weight in the United States would be as difficult to devise as the Joint Declaration was proving to be.[71]

Other opinions were not as sanguine. Christopher Eastwood in particular was unhappy about the whole business. The fact is that he disapproved of even the British proposals. Cabinet initiatives and international considerations were having an effect not welcomed by many Colonial Office officials. Eastwood did not share Hailey's views about 'independence':

It seems to me utterly wrong to set up independence as the

general goal for the greater number of the colonies and even if we have said something of this sort in the past (which I do not think we have) it would be a great mistake to say it again. I do not think that the phrase 'self-government' is really much better. I suppose it does leave a loop-hole for arguing that what we really mean is only local self-government, but that would not be a very honest interpretation of the phrase. Myself I believe that 'independence' and 'self-government' both imply substantially the same goal, namely fifty different self-contained sovereignties, which would be disastrous. The sooner we start emphasising the importance of solidarity and *inter*-dependence' the better. Something like self-government may be possible for one or two colonies (e.g. Ceylon) and for federations of other colonies, but even so it should be limited by their responsibilities to larger units, both to their neighbours (hence the value of the 'regional' idea) and the British Empire as a whole.[72]

At this stage the Colonial Office was being taken further than it wanted to go by the politicians.

The American draft was substantially modified in the Office, all mention of independence and target dates being removed, as was the possibility of any international control of British territories. The American proposals were altered with a vengeance; but Britain had not repudiated her cautious and qualified commitment to self-government. This was the major change that had occurred in British colonial policy since the beginning of the war and it constituted the only hope of some form of Anglo-American agreement. But Secretary of State for the Colonies Oliver Stanley decided that the proposals for a Joint Declaration would not bear fruit, and he called a halt to the search for an acceptable formula. 'Stanley stood at the helm of British colonial policy and steered a course away from Anglo-American collaboration and towards freedom of British action.'[73] In July 1943 Stanley used Britain's new liberal policy of fostering self-government to convince Americans of the sincerity of British intentions and to impress critics everywhere in what was, in effect, a unilateral declaration. He shrewdly presented his policy to the Commons:

> The central purpose of our colonial administration has often been proclaimed ... we are pledged to guide colonial peoples along the road to self-government within the framework of the British Empire. We are pledged to build up their social and economic institutions, and we are pledged to develop their natural

resources. Those objects have often been proclaimed, and for me to proclaim them today would be one more speech in a world where speeches are rather at a discount and it is deeds that count ...[74]

Stanley then went on to stress the vital necessity of solid social and economic foundations for political advance. Now that self-government was the admitted goal, an emphasis on economic and social development as a prerequisite became a commonplace. Towards the end of the debate he introduced the idea of regional colonial commissions, which would promote consultation and collaboration between states but would not interfere with Britain's administrative responsibility.[75] In other words, Britain's colonial declaration had now been made.

Stanley had in fact used the phrase 'self-government' in his speech rather than anything more definite, such as 'responsible self-government', for precisely the reasons stigmatised by Eastwood as not very honest. The Secretary of State thought that only the larger colonies could ever reach Dominion Status, and as a loop-hole was using the ambiguity of the term.[76] Yet the word was generally understood as meaning responsible self-government, with perhaps defence and one or two other governmental functions being reserved for the control of the Imperial Parliament. This is what the Americans believed, and the Cabinet, negotiating for a Joint Declaration, had understood as much.

Stanley's presentation of policy in 1943 is worthy of note. His assertion that he was not breaking new ground should not be taken literally. It is belied by the significance the Colonial Office gave to his speech, a copy of which was sent to all Colonial Governments.[77] By presenting colonial policy in this way, refusing to admit the novelty of his position, Stanley was not only gaining credit for a liberal objective but also helping to justify and exonerate the past, which had attracted so much criticism. British policy could now be seen as a unity, while ideas of permanent political subordination could be conveniently forgotten. The 'past' was in fact being changed: soon a simplistic meaning could be imposed on the whole history of the empire, and it was a meaning whose clarity distorted an original confusion. Events and motivations were brought to a focus which subjectively clarified but objectively distorted them. The very vagueness and ambiguity of previous British policy allowed the possibility of this process: there was just enough evidence to make Stanley's version of British colonial designs in the past credible. In fact, a moral rationalization was in 1943 transformed into an avowed objective. Henceforth the whole imperial process could be seen solely as the fostering of self-government. The past was being interpreted to meet the needs of the present.

Stanley's statement in Parliament did indeed achieve its objectives. *The Times* correspondent was taken in:

> That the constitutional goal throughout the colonial empire is responsible self-government needs by this time no emphasis. In his liberal and forward-looking speech in the House of Commons yesterday Colonel Stanley took it for granted, and addressed himself to the larger question of fostering in the colonies the growth of communities who can make self-government a success.[78]

He was thus credited with a liberal policy, and the past was to an extent vindicated. He had also, by using the ambiguous term 'self-government', left himself with a loophole – but misunderstandings create expectations, and to all intents and purposes Britain was committed to creating 'responsible self-government'.

American opinion was placated by the new tone of British policy, at least in some quarters.[79] The negotiations for the Joint Declaration were dropped, but not with any legacy of bitterness. It was now obvious that the war was coming to an end, and any statement on the future of colonial territories would be linked with the inauguration of a new World Organisation. The negotiations that followed between Britain and America, and other Powers, on the future of the Mandates, the principle of accountability, and the new United Nations Organisation, were important for the international aspects of post-war colonial policy. But the central point for this present work was the British espousal of the policy of granting self-government. The events of 1944 and 1945 produced only minimal changes.[80]

Britain could now afford to be less submissive in her relations with the United States since American attitudes gave evidence of a growing spirit of imperialism. According to Oliver Stanley, the whole colonial question was viewed in America

> entirely in relation to the occupation by the United States after the war of the Japanese islands. For this purpose, the one thing that matters is that the United States, while occupying the islands,

should not appear to have a theoretical sovereignty over them (for that would be Imperialism).[81]

In fact this view was an over-simplification, since American thinking was amazingly diverse. Plans were drawn up for control of the entire Pacific Basin, and the U.S. Navy wanted to make the Pacific into their lake, calling for full sovereignty over the Japanese Mandated islands (the Marianas, Carolines, and Marshalls). Yet the State Department wished to press for acceptance of the doctrine of trusteeship, which to their minds meant accountability to international control.[82] Britain countered by arguing that accountability, whether to a world organisation or to regional commissions, would impede progress to self-government, while the colonial peoples themselves would prefer to have to deal with a single Parent State.[83] International accountability was the *bête noire* of the Colonial Office;[84] and rather than extending the Mandates system, Britain's spokesmen wished to end it altogether.

Churchill and Stanley, in their abhorrence of the principle of accountability, would give way to neither the State Department nor Australia and New Zealand. Only because of a misunderstanding at Yalta in February 1945 did Britain agree to place her existing Mandates under the new trusteeship system: Churchill was misled by an American official who told him that trusteeship would apply only to the Japanese Mandated islands. The Prime Minister had been 'innocently bamboozled'.[85] Despite Eden's posturings that, since no one knew what trusteeship meant, Britain was committed to nothing, and despite protests from Tanganyika,[86] the Colonial Office was forced to acquiesce in the transformation of the Mandates into Trusteeship Territories – though no new territories would voluntarily be placed under the new arrangements.[87]

Several aspects of the Colonial Settlement of 1945, such as the power of the Trusteeship Council to receive petitions and despatch missions, met with the disapproval of British officials. Yet on the whole Britain emerged from the war-time colonial controversy remarkably unscathed. In negotiations for the Charter of the U.N.O., Britain and the United States agreed that Parent States would 'develop self-government in forms appropriate to the varying circumstances of each territory'. The aim of the system of trusteeship was, in their eyes, to be

to promote the political, economic and social advancement of the

trust territories and their progressive development towards self-
government in forms appropriate to the varying circumstances of
each territory.

They agreed that the General Assembly and the Trusteeship Council were to

consider reports submitted by its administering state, to accept
petitions and examine them in consultation with the administering state, to make periodic visits to the respective territories at
times agreed upon by the administering state.[88]

Not only did the Americans forego the proposal for target dates and
come to separate the idea of trusteeship from that of independence,
but their proposals for accountability had been drastically watered
down. Their main concern was that areas of strategic interest, and
particularly the Japanese islands, should be associated with the
Security Council rather than the General Assembly.

Those ideas from which the Americans had departed were now
put forward by the Russians. They wished to see trusteeship equated
not merely with the fostering of self-government but with 'self-
government and self determination with active participation of
people of these territories with the aim to expedite the achievement
by them of full national independence'.[89] They also called for a fuller
measure of accountability. After lengthy negotiations, the final form
of words agreed upon for the International Trusteeship System of
the U.N.O. laid down that the system aimed at promoting the
progressive development of the trust territories towards 'self-
government or independence as may be appropriate to the particular circumstances of each territory and its peoples and the freely
expressed wishes of the people concerned'.[90]

Britain had come through the war with her empire intact and with
her sole administrative rights confirmed. No great concessions had
been made on the international front. Few of those involved could
have expected such a comparatively unchanged position to have
resulted after almost six years of warfare. And yet changes there had
been. According to *The Times*, 'a revolution in the concept and
purpose of colonial administration has been quietly carried
through'.[91] Self-government was now the avowed aim and purpose
of Britain's presence in the colonies, whilst instead of colonial
self-sufficiency the doctrine of Colonial Development and Welfare
had been accepted. The political lead which the civil servants had

wanted had now been given them; the outline had been drawn into which the details could be inserted. African policy was constructed in the light of this re-definition of colonial principles.

NOTES

1. *Parl. Debates* (Commons), vol.324, col.1115. 2 June 1937.
2. *Nutrition in the Colonial Empire*. July 1939. Cmd.6050.
3. *Parl. Debates* (Commons), vol.332. col.804. 28 Feb. 1938.
4. *Ibid*. Vol.337, cols.151-2, 165, 14 July 1938; vol.332, cols.848-9, 28 Feb. 1938.
5. CAB 65/5. WM 42(40) 1. 15 Feb. 1940.
6. *Parl. Debates* (Commons), vol.348, col.544. 7 June 1939.
7. *Ibid*. Vol.361, col.115. 21 May 1940.
8. *Ibid*. Vol.380, col.2046. 24 June 1942.
9. *Ibid*. Vol.380, col.2026.
10. *Ibid*. Vol.400, col.1283. 6 June 1944.
11. *Parl. Debates* (Lords), vol.125, col.388. 12 Dec. 1942.
12. CO 323/1848/7318. Minute by C. Parkinson, 25 Nov. 1941.
13. CO 323/1695/7318. Minute by Dawe, 27 Mar. 1939.
14. CO 323/1695/7318/A. Minute by Dawe, 16 Oct. 1939.
15. CO 323/1847/7263. Minute by Dawe, 27 Feb. 1942.
16. P.S. Gupta, *Imperialism and the British Labour Movement* (Macmillan, 1975), p.248. Gupta errs in saying that the Act was passed while Oliver Stanley was Secretary of State.
17. *Statement of Policy on Colonial Development and Welfare*. Feb. 1940. Cmd.6175.
18. *Parl. Debates* (Lords), vol.115, col.992. 20 Mar. 1940. Moyne.
19. *West India Royal Commission, 1938-39: Recommendations*. Feb. 1940. Cmd.6174.
20. J.M. Lee and M. Petter, 'The Impact of War on the Colonial Office'. p.40 of typescript version of forthcoming book. I am grateful to Dr Lee for letting me read his typescript.
21. CO 323/1695/7318. 'The Method of Financing a More Forward Colonial Policy'. Memo. by G. Clauson, 1939.
22. *Parl. Debates* (Commons), vol.407, col.2078. 7 Feb. 1945. Stanley.
23. Hailey to Jeffries, 20 Oct. 1963. Hailey Papers.
24. CO 583/262/30519. Minute by Jeffries, 7 Oct. 1942.
25. *Parl. Debates* (Commons), vol.361, col.42. 15 Feb. 1940.
26. CAB 67/4. WP (G) (40) 2. Memo. by Secretary of State for the Colonies. 13 Feb. 1940.
27. CAB 66/13. WP (40) 444. 'Propaganda Policy'. Joint memo. by the Minister of Information and the Minister of Economic Warfare, 15 Nov. 1940.
28. CO 323/1858 Pt. II/9057. 'The Constitutional Future of the Colonial Empire'. Memo. by Secretary of State, Sept. 1941.
29. Copy in CO 323/1875/7094.
30. CO 323/1875/7064. Minute by Clark, 8 June 1943.
31. *Ibid*. Minutes by Cohen, 10 Apr. 1944, and Eastwood, 3 May 1944.
32. *Roosevelt and Churchill: Their Secret Wartime Correspondence* (London, 1975). Churchill to Roosevelt, 21 May 1944.

33. CO 554/133/33738. Minute by O.G.R. Williams, 14 Oct. 1943.
34. CO 323/1865/13204/11A. Bourdillon to Secretary of State, 2 Aug. 1941.
35. Minutes in CO 323/1865/13204/15.
36. *Parl. Debates* (Commons), vol.372, cols.1071-2. 25 June 1941.
37. *The Colonial Empire (1939-47)*. Cmd.7167. p.9.
38. Rita Hinden, *Tribune*, 3 Apr. 1942.
39. *The Times*, 14 Mar. 1942. Reproduced in Perham, *Colonial Sequence, 1930-49* (London, 1967), p.231.
40. CO 847/20/47139. Speech at Oxford. See also his speech in the Commons, vol.342, cols.1246-7, 7 Dec. 1938.
41. CO 323/1858 Pt.II/9057. 'The Constitutional Future of the Colonial Empire'. Memo. by Moyne, Sept. 1941.
42. *Daily Herald*, 16 Aug. 1941.
43. *Parl. Debates* (Commons), vol.374, cols.67-8. 9 Sept. 1941.
44. CO 554/128/33629/A. Minute by Cranborne, 12 May 1942.
45. Hailey, 'Native Administration and Political Development in British Tropical Africa', unpublished report of 1940-42, p.49. Copy in Rhodes House.
46. *Ibid*. p.50.
47. CO 323/1848/7322. Minute by Macmillan, 1 Sept. 1942.
48. Ibid. Minute by Cranborne, 4 Sept. 1942.
49. *Parl. Debates* (Lords), vol.122, col.919. 6 May 1942.
50. *Parl. Debates* (Commons), vol.380, col.2107. 24 June 1942
51. *Ibid*. Col.2122.
52. *The Times*, 23 June 1942.
53. *Parl. Debates* (Commons), vol.380, cols.2042-3.
54. *Parl. Debates* (Lords), vol.122, col.1095. 20 May 1942. Hailey.
55. *Mercury*, n.d. Copy in ACJ 15/1.
56 CAB 66/32. WP (42) 601. 'American Influence in West Africa'. Memo. by Secretary of State for the Colonies, 22 Dec. 1942.
57. ACJ 12/1 15. Creech Jones to Harold Macmillan, 17 Feb. 1942.
58. A. Turnbull (ed.), *The Letters of F. Scott Fitzgerald* (Penguin, 1968), p.92. Fitzgerald to Frances, 7 June 1940.
59. *Life*, 12 Oct. 1942. Quoted in Louis, *Imperialism At Bay*, p.198.
60. Quoted in Louis, *Imperialism At Bay*, pp.356-7.
61. *Roosevelt-Churchill Correspondence*, p.203.
62. A. Burns, *In Defence of Colonies*, (London, 1957), p.6.
63. *Parl. Debates* (Lords), vol.119, col.721. 9 July 1941.
64. ACJ 9/5 59. Text of an article for the *International Socialist Forum* by Creech Jones in 1943.
65. ACJ 14/4. 'Colonial Labour'. Undated article by Creech Jones.
66. CO 323/1858/9057B. 'Colonial Policy'. Memo. by Attlee, Eden, Cranborne, and Stanley. 5 Dec. 1942.
67. *Ibid*.
68. CO 323/1858/Pt.II/9057B. Memo by Attlee, Eden, Cranborne, and Stanley, 19 Jan. 1943.
69. *Ibid*. Minute by J.H.J., 27 Apr. 1943. For the American draft, see Louis, *Imperialism At Bay*, pp.177-9; for Foreign Office comment, pp.243-6.
70. *Ibid*. 'Comments on American draft' by Eastwood, 21 Apr, 1943.
71. *Ibid*. Note by Lord Hailey, 5 May 1943.
72. *Ibid*. Minute by Eastwood, 6 May 1943.
73. Louis, *Imperialism At Bay*, p.253
74. *Parl. Debates* (Commons), vol.391, col.48. 13 July 1943.
75. *Ibid*. Col.144.

76. CO 323/1858 Pt. II, 9057B. Stanley to Eden, 6 Jan. 1944.
77. C. R. Nordman, 'Prelude to Decolonisation in West Africa: The Development of British Colonial Policy, 1938-1947' (unpublished Oxford D.Phil.thesis), p.67.
78. *The Times*, 14 July 1943.
79. CO 847/23/47188. Speech by H.S. Villard, Asst. Chief of the Division of Near Eastern Affairs, 18 Aug. 1943.
80. For detailed discussion of these years, see Louis, *Imperialism At Bay*.
81. CAB 66/33. WP (45) 200. 'International Aspects of Colonial Policy'. Memo. by Stanley, 28 May. 1945.
82. Louis, *Imperialism At Bay*, pp.114, 267, 351-3.
83. CAB 66/59. WP (44) 738. 'International Aspects of Colonial Policy'. Memo. by the Armistice and Post-War Cttee, 16 Dec. 1944.
84. Louis, *Imperialism At Bay*, p.343n.
85. *Ibid*. p.460.
86. CAB 128/2. CM 64 (45) 4, 20 Dec. 1945.
87. CAB 65/50. WM 38 (45) 1, 3 Apr. 1945.
88. CAB 66/65. WP (45) 300. 'International Aspects of Colonial Policy'. Memo. by Secretary of State for the Colonies, 14 May 1945. Annex 1.
89. *Ibid*. Annex II.
90. The text is quoted in full in P.D. Curtin, *Imperialism* (Harper, 1971), pp.67-72.
91. *The Times*, 10 Jan. 1945.

3

Lord Hailey and Colonial Office Thought on African Policy

The will to a system is a lack of integrity
— Nietzsche, *Twilight of the Idols*

While the politicians were committing Britain to the development of self-government in the colonies, the Colonial Office itself was busy preparing for a definite post-war policy. Details had to be decided during the war so that afterwards there would be no delay in implementing positive proposals. A widespread feeling existed within colonial circles that the war would prove a turning-point in Britain's relations with her overseas dependencies. Sir Charles Dundas, the Governor of Uganda, had no doubt that the war would have important effects:

> Those of us who knew Africa before and after the last war saw great changes resulting therefrom, chiefly a remarkable awakening of the African.... It is my opinion that the present war will have an even more rousing influence, chiefly political and social, and it will be sheer blindness not to foresee the logical consequences. Unless we are prescient there is a danger that it will not be the Africans but ourselves who are backward and that our outlook and methods will be based on premises that since long have ceased to be valid.[1]

Expectations of a new world, which affected British domestic as well as colonial thinking, were vital for African policy. The Second World War was to form a crucial period in the transvaluation of imperial values and in the first policy for Africa which Britain had ever constructed. The man who dominated British thinking during the early years of the war was Lord Hailey, who first came to prominence with his monumental *African Survey* of 1938.

The idea of a comprehensive enquiry into the problems of Africa south of the Sahara was first put forward in the Rhodes Memorial Lecture at Oxford given by Smuts in 1929. A generous grant from the Carnegie Corporation of New York, later supplemented by the Rhodes Trustees, led to a seach for a 'superman'[2] to co-ordinate the research. Only when Sir William Marris and Sir George Schuster had refused the job, and the Colonial Office had used its influence to veto the choice of an American, was the candidature of Sir Malcolm Hailey proposed.[3] By July 1933 Hailey had definitely pledged himself to direct the enquiry when he left India in the autumn of the following year.

Hailey had already pursued a most distinguished career in India, serving as Governor of the Punjab from 1924 to 1928 and then as Governor of the United Provinces. In 1913 Edwin Montagu, a stern critic of the Indian Civil Service, described him as 'the best man in Delhi, and one of the best in India.... He is keen, industrious, popular, capable, definite, decided, well-educated ... he has everything, perhaps, but a little softness of outline'.[4] Later in his career he exercised influence over Irwin and helped persuade Gandhi to attend the second Round Table conference in London.[5]

The idea of an African Survey had originally been received in the Colonial Office with only a 'modified degree of enthusiasm', and the hope was expressed that there would be a minimum of criticism of the officers on the spot.[6] The work was begun in 1935 and published in November 1938. It was an authoritative piece of research, with its emphasis on 'the full statement of fact rather than ... the expression of opinion'.[7] The Colonial Office was greatly pleased by the result: it caught the imagination of the younger generation of officials[8] – curious in view of Hailey's own advanced age – and soon achieved a standing to rank alongside Lugard's *Dual Mandate*. One official wrote in 1939 that 'The Bible ... on practically everything relating to our administration in tropical Africa, is now Lord Hailey's African Survey'.[9]

The *Survey* had great effects on colonial policy, and it also remedied the dearth of information that beset Whitehall. It gave a boost to plans for Colonial Development and Welfare, and its recommendation for a special fund for research found its way into the 1940 Act. In a variety of ways the information it provided proved useful to the Office, but even more significant were the questions that Hailey asked. He argued that responsible self-government had been 'tacitly accepted as an ideal' of colonial policy:[10] but should, therefore, African representation on the legislative councils be progressively increased? In order to prevent a premature commitment to a course of action which might later be regretted, Hailey warned that questions such as this would 'before long demand an authoritative decision'.[11] There was especially need for clarification on native local self-government:

> Great Britain, in fostering the system of indirect rule, is promoting a widespread agency of local self-government for which a place will eventually have to be found in the political organisation of the colonies ... there is much that is difficult to foresee in the future of indirect rule; but possibly the most difficult problem of all, is to envisage the feasibility of integrating the system with the normal type of Parliamentary institutions.[12]

Native institutions would certainly have to be 'materially modified' if they were to fit into any scheme involving an elected Parliament.

Hailey presented a complex picture of native administration in Africa. He wisely noted that indirect rule, besides being a type of administrative device, was also a philosophy based on an appreciation of the needs of native life. Insofar as indirect rule aimed at cushioning the impact of Western civilization on the African, Hailey himself can clearly be seen as a philosophical indirect ruler: British policy, he wrote, should 'seek to moderate the pace of change, and allow full scope for the innate characteristics of the people to assert themselves in the conflict of forces that must ensue'.[13] Yet he was not uncritical of indirect rule, writing that it 'has not only its unsolved problems, but some noticeable points of weakness'.[14] There were many unanswered questions in regard to indirect rule. Should the expansion of the social services be left in the hands of inexperienced and inexpert Native Administrations? New duties would inevitably change the character of the NAs, and though Hailey was not averse to change he feared that some of these bodies might break down altogether. Would the imposition of new duties lead to chaos? On this important matter Hailey was cautious:

> There is not at the moment sufficient material on which to judge of this possibility, for not only do many of the present authorities owe their recognition to a comparatively recent progress of reorganisation, but there are also many of the older native administrations which have not yet been tested in their ability to undertake social services of a more than rudimentary type.[15]

He had introduced a note of caution, though not of alarm, and had prepared the way for further study of the problem. Another view he examined was that indirect rule was incompatible with the spread of education. Would there be a growing breach between the educated and the tribal elements? 'Here again', wrote Hailey, 'we have insufficient material on which to base a forecast.'[16] Disdaining hyperbole, Hailey's comments on indirect rule were cautious, exploratory, and non-committal. He provided fuel for its critics and supporters alike, giving himself the air of the wise, impartial arbiter. Yet he did provide the antidote to the Colonial Office conception of indirect rule as the infallible system to be applied automatically, almost regardless of circumstances.

Hailey's work presents several problems for the historian. There is the sheer bulk of material and also the fact that specific detail predominates over generalization. In his own words, he preferred the particular to the general, was conscious of the dangers of generalization in regard to Africa, and was pre-eminently an administrator.[17] Hence direct judgments are often lacking in his work, his phraseology was usually qualified and often couched in negative terms, while his arguments were so balanced as to provide convincing arguments for both sides of a case. This 'objectivity' and preference for individual instances rather than generalizations comprised what Hailey described to Frederick Pedler as his 'judgematic' approach.[18]

Small wonder therefore that Hailey had arguments with the classic theory of indirect rule as developed in Northern Nigeria. In a speech in December 1938 he argued that indirect rule has passed through three stages: first, that of a useful administrative device; then that of a political doctrine; and finally that of a religious dogma. 'We must not', he asserted, 'act as if the system had come to us graven on tablets of brass.'[19] But the same dislike of wide generalizations ensured that he did not condemn all aspects of indirect rule or call for its wholesale abandonment. In discussions at the Colonial Office he let it be known that, though he was not one who made a 'fetish' of indirect rule, he regarded it on the whole as 'sound in principle and successful in practice'. He called for the rule of the chiefs to be reformed under close supervision, but he also noted that indirect rule, like other British constitutional experiments, might be expected to develop naturally, 'carving out the course of its own flow'.[20] This metaphor reveals that Hailey obviously expected the experiment to be a lengthy one, and it also shows that his idea of 'natural' development did not preclude considerable outside interference – a characteristic contradiction in indirect rule thinking. These views had a considerable impact on Malcolm MacDonald, whose tenure of office as Secretary of State for the Colonies from May 1938 to May 1940 was particularly important in stimulating a new approach to African policy. At a meeting on 21 November, 1939, MacDonald said

> that he wished to see a 'seething of thought' in the African Division of the Office, and that even the most junior members of the Administrative Staff of the Division ought to be given an opportunity of thinking in terms of policy and of putting forward their suggestions.[21]

The Secretary of State himself initiated a major discussion of future policy towards Africa at the Carlton Hotel in October 1939, the outcome of which was Lord Hailey's second survey of Africa. MacDonald himself was clear about the need for a clarification of policy:

> Where indirect rule is the recognised policy it is time we got a clear idea of what we are aiming at. We should also have a clearer idea of how the development of Native Authorities and of Legislative Councils was to be harmonised. Where there are important non-native communities, if we do not decide upon ultimate objectives, we may take a step in the direction of giving more power to the European immigrant communities which can never be retraced, but which would be out of line with a proper policy of self-government for the whole people of the colonies concerned. These questions are ripe for investigation.[22]

Discussions proceeded on these topics. The variety of opinion expressed shows the essential fluidity of British opinion during the war and illustrates how far there was to go before the crystallization of 1947.

Lord Lugard, whose unsurpassed experience in Africa meant that he could command an audience despite his advanced age, argued emphatically that the objective in indirect rule territories should be to federate the NAs to form Central Councils with legislative powers. Margery Perham was in broad agreement, pointing out that political life in Africa was on two planes, the tribes corresponding to reality and the state system having been artificially imposed from above. She advised connecting the two planes by setting up large

regional councils of NAs to educate the chiefs and to 'head off the
intelligentsia from the state system'. Hailey agreed that, though the
ultimate objective was some form of self-government, this need not
necessarily be parliamentary: 'It might be better to try the alternative course of integrating the native administrations.'

It was the Colonial Office officials, in their comments on the
discussions of the experts, who showed a much greater willingness to
endorse western-style institutions for Africa.

> No matter what the Old Guard may say, you cannot turn Africa
> into Conan Doyle's 'Lost World', and I feel sure that British ideas,
> British institutions, and British laws are going to prevail. Indirect
> rule, to my mind, had much better be used as a means of educat-
> ing Africans to take their parts in these institutions than as a
> means of preserving them as interesting museum exhibits.

J. L. Keith made a similar point:

> In spite of our endeavours to revive and adapt what we are
> pleased to call native customary institutions the Africans them-
> selves are looking towards our own political institutions, however
> absurd they may be, as the goal for their own political ambi-
> tions.[23]

He did not believe it practicable or desirable to 'head off the intelligentsia from the state system', nor did he heed Lord Lugard's
'pontifical declaration that parliamentary institutions are not suited
to Africans'. Another official, O. G. R. Williams, drew attention to
Hailey's concern that he knew of no attempt to square native
administration with Parliamentary institutions. Williams pointed to
the Gold Coast method, first used by Guggisberg, of the indirect
representation of NAs on the Legislative Council by way of Provincial Councils. At that time this was by no means an obvious solution.
These Provincial Councils were performing so poorly that Governor
Hodson was seriously dissatisfied with them, while colonial officials
were increasingly impatient of their corruption and inefficiency, and
of the triviality of their discussions.[24]

The immediate outcome of the Carlton Hotel discussions was that
Hailey was commissioned to undertake an investigation in Africa
into native administration and political development, this time con-
fining himself to the British territories. MacDonald explained this to
Sir John Simon, the Chancellor of the Exchequer, who would have
to find the money for Hailey's expenses and for those of a Colonial

Office assistant, F.J. Pedler. His letter to Simon is worth quoting since it illustrates the problems and preoccupations of the time:

> If the war lasts for any length of time, it is certain to leave its mark on Tropical Africa, and some of the problems which have been facing us in recent years may become more difficult as the strain in each territory is intensified. The war is likely to create a demand in Africa for a quickening in the pace of the development towards self-governing institutions for Africans, as well as for the comparatively small but vocal and influential European communities there. Whilst proceeding cautiously, we shall be wise to anticipate this demand by having carefully thought-out plans for a proper advance in this direction. I ... am anxious that we should pursue a slowly but surely developing policy of training the Africans to look after their own affairs. This policy is being followed amongst tribal natives according to the principles of Indirect Rule, and we have reached a stage in which Native Authorities in various territories do control much of what in this country would be called local government. The question now arises, what next in those territories? Moreover, the problem is complicated by the existence in some colonies of large numbers of detribalised natives, living in towns or other centres of European influence. These are often represented on Legislative Councils. So the two different machines for native government exist side by side: and ... we are likely to end in difficulties unless we can think out very carefully now how they are to be co-ordinated in future developments.[25]

The primary purpose of Hailey's visit, therefore, was to examine the relationship between indirect rule and political advance to ensure that the NAs and the Legislative Councils did not develop on 'divergent lines with undesirable results'.[26] Yet his enquiry was not in fact defined in precise terms of reference,[27] and was in many ways a general survey. He was also entrusted with the secret mission of looking into the possibility of reconciling the native policies of Southern Rhodesia, Northern Rhodesia, and Nyasaland, and of closer union in Central Africa in the light of the Bledisloe Report.[28] The result of this tour of Hailey and Pedler was of seminal importance for the administration of the African colonies.

NATIVE ADMINISTRATION AND POLITICAL DEVELOPMENT

Hailey's report of 1940-42 was in many ways the bridge between pre-war and post-war ideas. The *Daily Telegraph* argued that this second survey would 'form the framework of our colonial policy at the end of the war'[29] – a view not fully justified by later developments. Yet the importance of the work cannot be doubted. The report is an extremely detailed, cautious account of the political and administrative situation in the British colonies, the contents of which defy a simple description. Hailey was true to his 'judgematic' approach: Pedler, jointly responsible for the report, was often encouraged to re-write passages in which he had been too outspoken and had failed to qualify statements meticulously.[30] The result was almost too technical and objective, as though Hailey lacked all personality. A useful corrective to this impression is provided by the diary he kept during part of his tour in 1940: this reveals him as being human after all. Here was a man dismayed by his failing powers – 'I cannot do half what I did then [in 1935]'; who greatly missed India and complained about the standard of African servants; who marvelled at the physical attributes of African women and wondered incredulously at chiefs called the Wum of Bum and the Bofo of Bamfe.[31]

Throughout the work Hailey stressed that every dependency in Africa had distinctive problems of its own. He was always aware of the multiplicity of varying conditions and needs. Yet he also saw the need for an overall strategy and for some idea of where British rule was leading, especially since pressure for an extension of self-government was likely to increase.

> Unless we have a clear view of the constitutional form in which self-government is to be expressed, the answer to this pressure will be ill-co-ordinated, and may lead to the adoption of measures which we may afterwards wish to recall.[32]

An element of planning was obviously essential, especially as the whole ethos of government was becoming more interventionist. Yet Hailey was certainly reluctant to indulge in it and even questioned the legitimacy of his work.

> It is indeed doubtful whether we are justified in attempting to

plan the political future of these populations when we have still so much to learn about their reaction to the new environment which circumstances are creating for them, and when we have yet made so few experiments in placing the African in situations where he must exercise initiative and final responsibility. At best we can for the moment only consider lines of advance which existing circumstances make possible for us.[33]

In view of this diffidence it is scarcely surprising that, although the report contributed to post-war policy, it did not itself provide the framework for that policy. Hailey did not think it justifiable to foreshadow the whole process culminating in self-government. 'The drama of Africa's political evolution', he wrote, 'is not of the type which can be handed ready-made by the playwrights to the actors. Its action will be largely developed by the actors themselves.'[34]

As we have seen from the international debate, Hailey believed that the primary need for Africa was economic, and he commented in 1940 that 'Good administration and well-conceived political institutions are only a means to an end'.[35] Self-government was not an immediate or short-term priority for Hailey, but he saw the need to plan in broad terms the direction of political advance. It was sometimes tacitly assumed that British political forms would gradually evolve in Africa, while Africans admittedly looked to the British model and strove to secure and increase African representation on the existing legislatures. But Hailey had his doubts. He had great sympathy with those who found difficulty in accepting that

> a form of institution which is so peculiarly the product of one section of the Western peoples, marked by strong characteristics of their own, is that which is best suited to peoples whose social and economic circumstances are so entirely different.[36]

For this reason he urged that Britain should take no step 'of which the logical conclusion must be the adoption of the normal form of parliamentary government';[37] and he argued against the concession of an unofficial majority on the legislature, since this would inevitably constitute a significant step in the direction of responsible government. He felt less strongly about the admission of Africans to the Executive Council[38] but later was to oppose this as well.

An alternative to the normal parliamentary institutions was the extension of indirect rule by way of the federation of the NAs. This had been strongly advocated at the Carlton Hotel and was still considered by many to be a practicable proposal. Nevertheless Hailey effectively quashed it in the report, though characteristically he in fact wrote that it was premature to give a final verdict on the issue. He did not think that effective self-government could be expected from a collection of small units, each possessing some form of independent authority and moreover not representative of the whole of a country. According to Hailey the NAs possessed no legal authority except that delegated by the Colonial Government and therefore their status was that of 'auxiliaries of the government';[39] and even when their functions and financial powers had grown, and control over them had lessened, still they would have this status of 'auxiliary or subordinate agencies'. He rebutted the idea that the NAs discharged functions appropriate to the central administration and were therefore not merely local government bodies. Hailey saw this as a fallacious argument since throughout the world the division of functions between central and local government had been determined not by principle but by historical accident or expediency. He also added that if the NAs were used as a means of providing representation in the central institutions of government, their use in this respect would be a matter of 'convenience, not of right'.

Hailey did indeed propose to use them in this role. Though having no wish to decide the final form self-government might take, he realised that there had to be some law-making body and that the NAs were a convenient source of representation. Yet they would not form the sole source. He wanted to see the formation of regional or provincial councils to be drawn from the NAs and township authorities; and these councils, together with the large municipalities, would send representatives to the legislature.[40] Such regional councils were to be based on similar organisations where these existed, as in the Gold Coast, and Hailey thought they might have an important future.

One advantage of Hailey's scheme was that this pyramidal structure of councils, with the NAs at the bottom and the Legislative Council at the top, would obviate the need for widespread elections, against which the localism and parochialism of rural Africans was a formidable bar. Hailey also believed that the regional councils, which at first would be merely consultative, might later be given powers of subsidiary legislation. If they were successful, considerable powers could be devolved upon them and the central legislature in each colony recast so as to deal with only a limited range of subjects. A legislature of this kind – or a Central Native Council, side by side with the Legislative Council – might well, thought Hailey, prove far more stable as an executive than that provided by the more normal type of parliamentary institution.[41]

Hailey gave great emphasis to the use of tribal institutions as an alternative to a system of direct election. Yet there were obviously certain educated groups of Africans who would disapprove of this method. Hailey expressed the view that the 'African intellectuals cannot at present compete with the Indian, and may never do so'.[42] Yet he also realized that the educated elite, though small, was of growing importance and was 'capable in certain circumstances of becoming of great political significance'.[43] He was aware of the view that the African middle class was a tiny unrepresentative minority and that Britain would do well simply to cement her alliance with the chiefs, who still attracted the loyalty of the mass of Africans; but he did not feel that any firm conclusion could be reached on this issue. 'The position is one on which it would be unwise to generalise'.[44] A typical Hailey statement! There seemed no sense in pre-judging the issue of whether eventually educated Africans would become more popular than the chiefs.

There seemed to be no danger in 1940 that African elites would challenge British supremacy. Though there had in the previous twenty years been a number of disturbances, especially over land rights and economic grievances, yet in relation to the areas involved these were few, and 'there has been little which points to widespread discontent or organised opposition to government policy'.[45] The troubles that did arise were capable of being dealt with 'by observance of the normal standards of good administration'.[46] Nor did there seem to Hailey at this time that there was any danger of nationalism arising in the African colonies. He was not one of those who believed that nationalism would arise in Africa in the course of nature. The political boundaries of British Africa were far too artificial for this. These dependencies

> for the most part represent only geographical units and not communities with any such natural ties or affinities as can form a basis for nationhood. ... People who are brought together by fate into one governmental unit – generally as a result of outside action – can of course be welded into something like nationality by the force of circumstances. ... But it is an historical process ... a matter of time, often of very considerable time.

It was a fantasy to suppose 'that we can create nations by giving a vote to everyone living within our artificially created units'.[47]

Of more serious concern to Hailey in 1940 was the possibility of the development of a 'general racial consciousness among Africans'.[48] He had no doubt that in the future a unity of sentiment among Africans would develop in response to alien rule, but there was very little evidence of it at that time. Yet Hailey warned against undue complacency. Dissatisfaction was bound to grow, he argued, and Britain would have to deal with it.

Having attempted to rule out substantial advances for educated Africans on the Legislative Council, Hailey pointed to the higher posts in the government services. 'It is in our readiness to admit Africans to such posts that they will see the test of the sincerity of our declared policy of opening to them the road to self-government.'[49] He strongly disagreed with the policy announced by the Government of Nigeria that Africans seeking employment in administration should look to the NAs, since the Administrative Service was a scaffolding which was to be dismantled.[50] Nor did he believe that tribal prejudice would veto the appointment of an African to a position of authority outside his tribal homeland. To facilitate the admission of Africans into the higher ranks, Hailey recommended the creation of an Intermediate Administrative Service, to be recruited locally in each colony.[51] This would provide a means of training Africans in administrative duties and of enabling them to take over more important tasks as they became available.

Another means of conciliating educated opinion would be to associate the middle classes with the Regional Councils: and on these bodies the concession of an unofficial majority would not have the same disadvantages as on the legislature. He also pointed out that educated Africans could be given greater influence in the institutions of local administration. An important section in Hailey's 'Native Administration and Political Development' is concerned with local affairs, and it is possible to interpret his work in several ways. He may be seen as a precursor of the local government policy inaugurated in 1947 or, alternatively, as a man whose regard for the chiefs and whose basic ideas of the possibility of African economic development, and whose fear of the ballot-box, label him an indirect ruler. Certainly Hailey had many arguments with the classic theory of indirect rule as developed in Northern Nigeria and he was an important figure in the development of the local government policy in that he helped to undermine the foundations of traditional native administration. Yet he himself did not construct any alternative scheme. Having helped to destroy one system, he did not want to help create another. He was always more interested in details than in slogans or neat generalizations. Hence his work on native administration left the future open to divergent possibilities – and only the future could give a final significance to his influence.

In his discussion of the NAs Hailey drew attention to the 'infinite variety of forms' of these institutions and called above all for flexibility in British policy.[52] The people of Africa varied widely in their political attitudes, some finding authoritarian regimes congenial and others guarding the rights of family or clan groups. The essential difference between the NAs lay in the variations of chiefly power. Hailey refused to believe that any one form was intrinsically superior to any other – the only criterion on which to judge being the success with which they operated in practice. He was concerned with what was best administered, with efficiency rather than uniformity. For more abstract values he had a pragmatic unconcern. Hence he did not find the unique position of Kenya, with its local native councils and appointed chiefs, at all disturbing and saw no reason for seeking to revive tribal institutions there. He also approved the use of appointed government agents in the coastal areas of Tanganyika. But overall he envisaged no wholesale change in the use of traditional NAs and was cautiously optimistic as to their future:

> Though the list of native authorities who have given evidence of any marked executive capacity is by no means a long one, there is a general disposition to feel that much improvement has already been shown. We are justified in looking forward to a progressive advance following the emergence of a younger generation of chiefs and elders. In many cases, also, the structure of the authorities is being adapted to meet the needs of the executive responsibilities now imposed on them.[53]

He was also moderately pleased with the recent changes that had occurred in native administration in certain areas: in particular the reorganization in Sierra Leone was certainly not without success.[54]

Yet despite this cautious optimism, Hailey did wish to see a radical shift away from old conceptions. He doubted whether the continued use of traditional authorities would be successful in certain areas of Nyasaland, Northern Rhodesia, Tanganyika, and Nigeria. He was clearly able to recognize that indirect rule had not been effective in these places – if it could be said to have been implemented at all – and that the wisest course was to abandon it. 'Respect for tradition', he wrote, 'should not be allowed to encumber any area with institutions which are incapable of adjustment to modern conditions.'[55] Where it was decided to abandon the native authority system, Government should choose between the use of appointed agents and a system of local native councils.

The changes Hailey envisaged were perhaps most significant in the traditional NAs themselves. He did not believe that adherence to tradition was in itself of great importance: it was useful only insofar as it helped secure the acceptance by Africans of those institutions on which the British relied. According to Hailey, 'acceptability is the essential quality' which NAs needed.[56] Sir Donald Cameron had earlier established the orthodoxy that traditional right and acceptability were both of importance in the proper composition of NAs; and in departing still further from the principle of tradition to the pragmatism of acceptability, Hailey was indeed levelling a crushing blow at indirect rule.

This departure was vital, Hailey argued, if non-traditional elements such as treasuries, federal councils, and group courts were to be successful. Tradition would stultify NAs and not allow of changes in their constitutions in the interests of middle-class or educated opinion, changes necessary to satisfy educated aspirations and to provide an impetus for social services. The composition of the chief's council was determined by custom and usage, but often the elders were out of touch with the younger and better educated elements, and it was in Hailey's opinion essential to associate these groups with the work of the councils. This was being done in some areas, but it did not seem in 1940 to be a general policy.[57]

Hailey thus gave great importance to securing changes in the composition of the local native authority councils. Referring to Tanganyika and Nyasaland, he wrote that 'It should be the duty of administrative officers to satisfy themselves that the council reflects local opinion. The inadequate recognition of educated elements will be fatal to native authorities...'[58] Similarly in Northern Rhodesia he called for the existence of 'strong councils' which would represent not only traditional leaders but also educated Africans.[59] Yet though advocating these reforms, Hailey hastened to add that he was not proposing 'anything in the nature of a reversal of the present policy'. He was simply making the native authority system more representative of the educated elements, and thereby guarding against attacks on it from this group, and also making the NAs more efficient instruments of social service by utilizing the ability of the intelligentsia.

Hailey was therefore reinvigorating the system of indirect rule; but at the same time, by aiming at a representative council, he was tending to undermine the position of the chiefs. This policy of making the councils more representative of the population at large, and particularly of the middle class and educated elite, was a means of changing the NAs slowly but surely. Hailey himself, in discussions at the Colonial Office, argued that 'The object to be aimed at was the conversion of Native Authorities into local Government bodies with members elected by the people'.[60] This aim, as we shall see, was well in line with the post-war local government policy. The election of representatives would introduce a change in kind and a new source of legitimacy, not derived from tradition or the central Government. Yet despite his correct prognostication of the end of indirect rule, his immediate proposals were of a minor character. 'The District Office,' he told the Secretary of State, Lord Moyne, in 1941, 'should be able to suggest to the Chief or other authority that they had better get some new element into their Council – a trader or teacher or the like – and this advice would usually be accepted.'[61]

The fact that Hailey urged the democratization of the NAs was an important contribution to official policy. But he was too cautious and pragmatic to devise any practicable method to bring about this objective. He gave primacy to the work of the NAs rather than their theoretical composition, just as he gave primacy to economic rather than political advance: and this meant that he did not work out in any systematic way the process whereby NAs could become local government bodies with elected members. Perhaps he was caught in the logical inconsistency inherent in interventionist indirect rule (though by the emphasis on acceptability rather than tradition he was moving towards a solution of the problem). On the one hand, he believed that Africa would decide her own future and stressed the importance of organic and natural development, while on the other he argued that the district officers had to intervene energetically and had to apply pressure for certain developments. Neither view was taken to its logical conclusion, and therefore Hailey does not seem to have considered other than piecemeal and informal methods of securing educated representatives on native authority councils.

Ideas of 'democratizing' the NAs were indeed commonplace during the Second World War. Several Colonial Governments were attempting to involve the educated Africans. In Nigeria Bourdillon attached great importance to the establishment of local village and district councils as one means of hastening the 'democratisation of the Emirs'.[62] In the Gold Coast Alan Burns was taking steps to make the local councils more representative.

> The only way I could do this was, I said to several of the Chiefs that this modern idea of finance is an awful bore and no really sensible people bother to fuss about a thing like that – why don't you appoint some educated young men as a sort of finance committee which would advise your council on financial matters – and that was accepted by several of them.[63]

However, these advisers did not constitute part of the NA itself and were in fact unpaid. Such informal methods were not likely to produce rapid results nor uniform change over a wide area.

Important sections of opinion in England also favoured the democratization of native administration. The Labour Party espoused the cause. Leonard Woolf wrote in 1941 that authoritarianism was no more attractive when exercised by chiefs or emirs in Africa than by Fuehrers or Duces in Europe. Indirect rule, he wrote, should not be used as an excuse for maintaining autocratic tribal rulers and for preventing the education and development of Africans.

> Indirect rule should be treated merely as a form of local government, as a method of integrating native institutions into the general government and administration; and where these institutions are undemocratic, steps must be taken to introduce into them the principles and practice of democracy.[64]

But the method of achieving the transition is again vague: 'District officers should be instructed to assist them to become democratic and efficient ...' Only at a later date did specific and detailed policies replace vague and generalized aims.

Hailey was thus not alone during the war in failing to work out a consistent scheme for the transformation of native administration. In fact it was never his intention to do so. He had performed a very useful task, providing an objective and detailed survey of the situation in the British territories and giving an account of recent developments, and had thus given the Colonial Office the material from which a policy could be constructed. His immediate impact on the plans of the Office is easy to see.

COLONIAL OFFICE PLANNING

The question of how definite and embracing colonial planning could be was a central preoccupation during the war. It was always necessary to strike a balance between the need for a general pan-African advance and the recognition of the tremendous variety of conditions in the individual colonies – between perception and intention. Sir Henry Moore wrote that there was danger

> in trying to over-simplify and generalise our aims. The Colonial Empire has grown up and been acquired in so haphazard a fashion and is composed of Colonies differing so widely in age, civilisation and development that any formula, drawn up in terms wide enough to embrace them all, is in danger of becoming otiose or mildly platitudinous.[65]

The most rigorous example of Colonial Office thinking on this issue came from Sydney Caine in August 1943.[66] He drew attention to the two snares in the formulation of policy. On the one hand, too much attention could be given to general principles which not only ignored individual circumstances but would fail to convince the administrators in the field. On the other hand, the Colonial Office might give such prominence to the requirements and demands of individual territories that no overall policy or strategy was defined. One of the major problems in colonial planning was that of power and authority: the Secretary of State and his advisers, though in theory responsible for the colonial empire, in practice did not have the power to implement their wishes except with the support of local officers. The need for central control and the susceptibilities of local power had thus to be finely balanced.

One of the first pieces of metropolitan planning carefully avoided treading on local toes and eschewed that precision of definition which would have ignored differing local circumstances. In the middle of 1943 O.G.R. Williams produced a 'Tentative Plan for Constitutional Development' in West Africa.[67] Several times Williams had noted the need to concert the political progress of the West African territories in order to avoid over-hasty concessions in one area which were likely to have repercussions in another. He wished to see a long-range policy into which concessions could fall as coherent parts.[68] Yet he was at pains to stress that his proposals were in no way a blueprint for constitutional advance. His original idea was that a programme of development should cover 'a period of years – no doubt an indefinite period'.[60] When the plan was drafted, he drew attention to the fact that there would have to be extensive modifications to fit the different West African dependencies, while there was no intention of forcing the programme on the Governors. The Secretary of State made it clear that the proposals 'were not intended to be anything more than suggestions which might form a basis of discussion'.[70] Nevertheless there was general accord with the plan in the Office, and Oliver Stanley thought it 'provided an admirable basis for long-term planning'.[71] General assent was also forthcoming from the Colonial Governments.

The memorandum was in fact largely drawn from Lord Hailey's report on native administration and political development in the West African territories. Not surprisingly, Williams found some difficulty in getting to the kernel of Hailey's recommendations; but he was in full agreement with the 'spirit' of his work – that irrevocable commitments should be avoided and room preserved for unforeseen future developments. The 'Tentative Plan' was based, according to its author, on two premises. The first was that political advance should proceed parallel with economic and social development and should, as far as possible, be dependent upon that development. There would thus be no hasty concessions to politically-minded Africans, who indeed were cut off and different in kind from the bulk of the population. The second was that 'when considering what to do in West Africa, no regard need be had to possible reactions in East Africa'. This is not to say that the scheme would in any way be applicable in East Africa, but only that the pace of development in the West was not to be slowed down by the situation in the East. These premises were well in line with Lord Hailey's thought. Williams only departed from Hailey's recommendations in that he considered further development of African representation on the Legislative Council to be necessary without delay, a concession necessary to secure the support of educated Africans. But this difference with Hailey he considered a matter of degree and not of principle.

The 'very rough tentative plan of political development' was divided into five stages which were not intended to be rigid and which would not be reached simultaneously in all four colonies. The details of the plan are of great importance in evaluating the state of Colonial Office thinking in 1943 on constitutional development and on native administration, and indeed on the degree to which planning from Whitehall was practicable. In Stage One there was to be increased African representation on the existing Municipal Councils by the addition of elected or nominated members, the ultimate aim being an African elected majority in councils with increased responsibilities. The NAs were also to be modernized, with the introduction of younger and better educated Africans and the gradual replacement of authoritarian regimes by authorities reflecting more fully the will of the community. Parallel with these developments in local government, Regional Councils were to be constructed: they were to cover suitable 'agricultural' areas and to be drawn from, or closely linked to, the NAs. Also in this stage, African representation in the Legislative Council should be increased: nomination should give way to election where practicable, though the aim at this time was not an African majority but a Council more fully representative of African interests.

In Stage Two the development of Municipal Councils would continue. The franchise should be widened and non-elected members eliminated, while the functions of the Councils would be extended and the Governor's overriding powers contracted. Meanwhile the Regional Councils would be given minor legislative powers, which could be increased in the light of experience. At this time African representation on the Legislative Council would be transformed, except in Municipal areas, by the substitution of representatives elected or nominated by the Regional bodies.

In Stage Three certain of the more important legislative powers were to be gradually transferred from the Central Legislature to the Regional Councils. In Stage Four African unofficial majorities, whether partly or wholly elected, should be introduced on the Legislative Councils of West Africa. This was a measure Hailey had strongly advised against, but Williams only recommended it after the central legislatures had been recast, and then with patent reluctance. The inclusion of this stage was, he wrote, 'very questionable'.

> Experience elsewhere suggests that unofficial majorities do not afford an education in self-government but merely a training in irresponsible opposition to Government. Paramount powers would have to be reserved to the Governor ... and the exercise of

these powers would be a frequent source of violent controversy.

Stage Five was simply labelled 'Towards Self-Government' and contained no details. There had been no mention of the admission of Africans to the Executive Council in the plan, and presumably this might occur in this final stage. But by that time there would be increasingly impatient demands by the Africans for self-government, and then would be the opportunity, after conferences between African 'interests' and British representatives, for the final form of self-government to be decided.

Williams realised that the political strategy he had outlined could help orderly progress in the West African colonies but he was not sanguine about future prospects:

> African opinion, unless it profits to a surprising extent by its period of probationary training during the first three stages, is likely to press for the fulfilment of its aspirations in ways which would be unlikely to be in the true interests of African communities.

He hoped that in time the common sense of the masses would temper the radical excesses of the few, and there was certainly plenty of time for this to happen in Williams' scheme. The doctrine of 'indefinite time ahead', which had vitiated colonial policy in the inter-war years, is still discernible at this late date. 'A good many years', wrote Williams, '(perhaps a good many generations though it would be impolitic to say so openly) must elapse before the possibilities of stages 1, 2 and 3 have been at all fully exploited.' A large, unspecified period would be necessary before active preparations could be taken to move definitely towards self-government.[72] This would not please everyone and there would obviously be agitation for the pace to be quickened: in many ways this would be a natural and healthy sign but, added Williams, 'it will raise problems of great difficulty'. There was nothing more he felt he could add.

Clearly Colonial Office planning had taken a step forward with these proposals. Never before had there been an attempt to plan in any way the future political development of a group of colonies. The cautious, 'judgematic' approach Williams adopted should not detract from this vital point. Indeed it was even coming to be realised by some of the younger officials that policy in West Africa could not be treated in isolation from the rest of the continent. Andrew Cohen noted that constitutional development in West

Africa could affect the issue of an unofficial majority in Northern Rhodesia.[73] He was well aware of the need for policies in different parts of Africa to be concerted and made complementary.

> It has been agreed that West Africa and East and Central Africa can be dealt with separately, but if the Gold Coast moves in advance of the other West African Colonies, it will make it more difficult to justify not allowing Northern Rhodesia to move in advance of Kenya. It was for this reason that I suggested ... that the proposed developments in the Gold Coast made it all the more necessary to press on in East Africa, so that something could be done in Northern Rhodesia.[74]

Here is an indication of the ideas which succeeded in 1947 in producing a scheme which embraced the whole of the British territories in Africa, though by 1943 Colonial Office policy had not advanced so far.

Lord Hailey expressed general agreement with the Williams memorandum, though observing that it went further than his own proposals.[75] He had two specific additional recommendations to make. Because of the difficulty of convincing educated Africans of Britain's intention of granting a real measure of political responsibility in West Africa, he urged that a general statement of policy should be issued analogous to that of 1917 in India, which laid down that Britain's policy was 'the increasing association of Indians in every branch of the administration and the gradual development of self-governing institutions with a view to the progressive realisation of responsible Government in India as an integral part of the British Empire'. This view did not, however, meet with the approval of the Secretary of State, who decided that any announcement should take the form of a despatch to Governors. Hailey's second suggestion was of greater significance. He put forward the idea that Africans should be brought into the Government itself, sitting in the Executive Council as heads of groups of departments. 'They would not of course be ministers but if and when the stage of full Parliamentary government was reached they would be turned into ministers.' This, he believed, would be preferable to granting unofficial majorities.

> We did not want to bind ourselves to the development of normal political institutions and then have to think again as we had had to do in India. The proposal which he had just made would have the advantage of associating Africans more closely in the Govern-

ment and enabling them to learn how to govern without committing us immediately to any line of political development.

In some ways Hailey's advice was prophetic, since semiministerial positions were later secured for Africans in the Executive Councils of British Africa. Yet his advice in fact lacked reality. Asked by the Secretary of State who precisely would be appointed to such positions, Hailey advised an Emir or some other chief. Since the aim of such appointments was to conciliate the educated elite, the move would scarcely have fulfilled its purpose. Stanley was certainly left in no doubt as to the inadvisability of the appointment of 'puppet heads of departments'. Yet it was thought possible that Africans could become advisers to departments, and Hailey agreed that this might be preferable. At any rate, some education in political responsibility was vital: 'If no steps were taken, the leading educated Africans would develop into a chartered opposition and suddenly administrative responsibility would be thrust upon them without their being ready to assume it.'

There can be no doubt that planning was thought vital so that after the war there should be no delay in pursuing a more forward policy. Yet the extent of the practicability of planning varied enormously. In West Africa the ground was relatively free of complications; but this was not the case in Central and East Africa, where the white settlers were an important factor. This is well illustrated by a comparison between the Williams memorandum, which though vague and cautious did at least contain some specific proposals, and one written on Central Africa by G.F. Seel in April 1943.[76]

The Bledisloe Commission, reporting on closer union in Central Africa in 1939, had argued that the three territories concerned – Southern Rhodesia, Northern Rhodesia, and Nyasaland – would become increasingly interdependent in their activities, and that this would lead in time to political unity. Yet it had recommended no immediate union because of the differing native policies being pursued, there being no prospect of any real form of self-government for the Africans of Southern Rhodesia. In 1940 Lord Hailey had added his weight to the view that there should be no amalgamation in the short term, since there were real divergencies of native policy, and these seemed likely to increase rather than diminish.

In 1943 the situation was confused: there were pressures, from America and elsewhere, against amalgamation, and yet the settlers were becoming increasingly restive. There was also the fact that the economic co-operation of the European community in Southern Rhodesia would promote economic development throughout the whole of Central Africa, while amalgamation of the British territories might also prevent the absorption of Southern Rhodesia into the Union of South Africa. Seel therefore cautiously argued that rather than reject amalgamation outright or shelve the issue indefinitely, it would be better to attempt to obtain agreement on the basis of a formula which would safeguard the position of Africans in Northern Rhodesia and Nyasaland. There should be a real effort to work out a statement on native policy acceptable to both sides. If this succeeded then the question of a political system to be employed in the combined territories could be considered; but this was not an immediate prospect, since there was little chance of Parliament's agreeing to an extension of complete self-government in that area simply because of a compromise on native policy. A federal arrangement at that time seemed unlikely, and Seel looked more favourably on the proposal that the Prime Minister of Southern Rhodesia should become the High Commissioner of Northern Rhodesia and Nyasaland, while at the same time an interterritorial council would be set up, without executive powers, to co-ordinate government services and frame plans for development. At the end of a period of years a review might be undertaken to see whether closer integration of the three territories was desirable.

It will be readily seen that in 1943 future policy had not been planned in Central Africa at all. Seel's tentative proposals depended on variables not under Britain's control. He received high praise in the Office for the quality of his work, but the response it got from the Governor of Nyasaland was 'a flat negative'.[77]

Other aspects of future policy were more straightforward and could receive detailed planning, as was the case with education. Two Commissions were set up and both reported in June 1945. The Asquith Commission on Higher Education in the Colonies urged the creation of new universities for those areas not already served by one: university colleges were recommended for the West Indies and a university for Malaya, while Makerere College in Uganda should be developed to university status. The creation of an 'Inter-University Council for Higher Education in the Colonies' was also advised: this should contain members of home universities and colonial institutions and was to foster the development of education in the empire. It was believed that only higher education could produce the men and women needed for rapid political, social, and economic progress.

In August 1939 the conference of West African Governors agreed that the creation of a West African university was an ideal at which they should aim, a decision endorsed by the Colonial Office Advisory Committee on Education in December 1940. Hence in July 1943 the Elliott Commission was appointed to investigate higher education in that area. The Majority Report recommended the development of three centres of study: a new college at Ibadan in Nigeria, an extension of Achimota College in the Gold Coast, and a reorganisation of Fourah Bay College in Sierra Leone, which was also to serve the Gambia.

These proposals were rejected by a minority of the Commission, including Creech Jones, Julian Huxley, and Margaret Read, who issued their own Report. They felt that the majority recommendations would diffuse what should be a concentrated effort.[78] They themselves were anxious to see quality rather than mere quantity and called for a comprehensive university college in Nigeria to serve the whole of British West Africa, together with a Territorial College for each of the three larger dependencies. These Colleges would be valuable centres for community education and would also serve as a means for training applicants to the University College.[79]

The minority proposals were unanimously preferred in the Colonial Office, and the Secretary of State informed the West African Governors of the fact. Britain now had a clear higher education policy for West Africa, but it was still theoretical and the attempt to make it a reality provoked many difficulties.[80] But this was not for lack of money. At the end of 1944 Oliver Stanley had applied to Cabinet for an extension of the 1940 Colonial Development and Welfare Act.

> I do ... feel that the Colonial Empire means so much to us that we should be prepared to assume some burden for its future. If we are unable or unwilling to do so, are we justified in retaining, or shall we be able to retain, a Colonial Empire?[81]

He went on to argue that Britain's financial burden could in the long run result in considerable economic benefit. Yet his real argument was that without the Commonwealth and Empire Britain could only take a minor role in world affairs: but generous aid to the dependent territories would set 'the Colonial Empire on lines of development which will keep it in close and loyal contact with us'.

Stanley wished to see the proposed new Act extending for ten years and giving payments totalling £150 million, annual grants increasing in total as the period progressed (from £10 million in 1946-47 to £20 million in 1955-56). But the Chancellor of the Exchequer, Sir John Anderson, approved neither the total expenditure nor the sliding-scale. It was finally agreed that £120 million could be spent over a ten-year period, with unexpended balances not, as hitherto, reverting to the Exchequer. With a general reserve for emergencies, £85 million could be allocated for schemes worked out by individual territories in accordance with ten-year development plans.[82] This new Colonial Development and Welfare Act was one sign that the Colonial Office intended to transform its theoretical planning into reality.

In response to increased planning and its more forward role, the Office itself was changing. As the unpublished official history puts it:

> The war-time history of the Office, in its domestic aspect, was one of progressive expansion and adaptation of administrative machinery to meet conditions that changed from day to day, and a pressure of work that was constantly on the increase.[83]

The proliferation of work is well illustrated by the fact that the number of despatches and telegrams sent and received in a calendar year increased from about 7,000 each way in 1937 to about 40,000 in 1944. Staff increased from around 400 in 1938 to 1,168 in 1947, during which time eight specialist advisers were added and the number of specialist, as opposed to geographical, departments rose from five to well over twenty.[84] There were also some minor, though significant, changes: in 1941 Ivor Cummings became the first coloured man to obtain a position in the Colonial Office,[85] while the Jamaican Dr Harold Moody, founder of the League of Coloured Peoples, was appointed to an Office committee in 1943.[86]

Whitehall was thus equipping itself for a much more extensive role in colonial affairs and was becoming an effective instrument for deciding policy. As the Office expanded during the war, so did the concerns of the civil servants. There was in fact a new attitude discernible among some of them, an attitude combining repentance and determination to make amends. This is best illustrated by the attempt, led by Andrew Cohen, to purchase the mineral royalties of the United Africa Company in Northern Nigeria, which had increased from £122,731 in 1937 to £155,898 in 1942. The head of the company, Lord Trenchard, had first broached the sale in a letter to the Secretary of State in August 1943, and the scheme was eagerly taken up by officials for essentially moral rather than economic reasons. The stumbling-block proved to be the parsimony of the Exchequer: the Treasury refused to pay even fifty per cent of the cost, while Cohen's idea of using C D & W money to compensate the United Africa Company was vetoed.[87] In January 1945 the matter was temporarily dropped.[88]

Yet despite the war-time changes in the Colonial Office – the extension of its duties, the reorganisation, and the new attitude of some civil servants – initiatives from Africa, from the 'man on the spot', were still important and in some areas vital. It was because of local power that Hailey's theoretical African planning never became a reality, and what might have been the beginning of a new volume proved to be merely the end of a chapter.

NOTES

1. CO 847/23/47177. Dundas to Secretary of State, 1 June 1942.
2. CO 323/1166/90033. Minute by S.J.F. Fidian, 14 July 1932.
3. *Ibid*. Minutes by Fidian, 17 June 1932, 14 July 1932, 20 July 1932, 4 Nov. 1932. CO 347/2/4204. Minutes by Fidian, 17 Mar. 1933, 23 June 1933.
4. E. Montagu, *An Indian Diary* (London, 1930), p.194.
5. Interview with Sir Frederick Pedler, 30 Mar. 1979.
6. CO 847/2/4204. Minute by Sir C. Bottomley, 12 Jan. 1934.
7. *African Survey* (Oxford, 1938), Introduction, v.
8. Interview with Sir Frederick Pedler, 25 Apr. 1977.
9. CO 847/13/47100 A.B. Cohen to Dr Provinse, 30 Nov. 1939.
10. *African Survey*, p.251.
11. *Ibid*. p.260.
12. *Ibid*. p.252.
13. *Ibid*. p.1281.
14. *Ibid*. p.573.
15. *Ibid*. pp.540-1.
16. *Ibid*. p.542.
17. Talk at Oxford, 2 Aug. 1950: Hailey Papers, Rhodes House. Hailey, 'Native Administration and Political Development in Tropical Africa', p.1. Unpublished report of 1940-42. Copy in Rhodes House.
18. Interview with Sir Frederick Pedler, 25 Apr. 1977.
19. Speech at Chatham House, 'Some problems dealt with in the African Survey'. Hailey Papers.

20. CO 847/13/47100. Note of Discussion between Hailey, Secretary of State, Tomlinson, Dawe, and Pedler, 5 Dec. 1938.
21. CO 847/15/47135. Minute by Pedler, 23 Nov. 1939.
22. CO 847/15/47093. Record of Discussions held at the Carlton Hotel, 6 Oct. 1939.
23. CO 857/17/47135. Minute by Bushe, 7 Nov. 1939. Minute by Keith, 3 Nov. 1939.
24. CO 96/749/31228. 'Summary of Proposals in Connection with the Introduction of Indirect Rule in the Gold Coast Colony,' 19 July 1938. R.L. Stone, 'Colonial Administration and Rural Politics in South-Central Ghana, 1919-51' (unpublished Cambridge Univ. Ph.D. Thesis, 1974), p.115.
25. CO 847/21/47100/1. MacDonald to Simon, 26 Oct. 1939.
26. Ibid. MacDonald to West African Governors, 18 Dec. 1939.
27. Hailey, 'Native Administration and Political Development', p.1.
28. CO 847/16/47100/1/Pt.1. Minute by Cohen, 6 Oct. 1939.
29. Daily Telegraph, 29 Oct. 1941.
30. Interview with Sir Frederick Pedler, 25 April 1977.
31. Diary for 8 Feb. and 9 Mar. 1940, Hailey Papers.
32. 'Native Administration and Political Development', p.50.
33. Ibid. p.54.
34. Ibid. p.56.
35. Ibid. p.62.
36. Ibid. p.51.
37. Ibid. p.58.
38. Ibid. pp.60-1.
39. Ibid. pp.43-4.
40. Ibid. p.55.
41. Ibid. p.56.
42. Diary, 19 Feb. 1940, Hailey Papers.
43. 'Native Administration and Political Development', p.12.
44. Ibid. p.13.
45. Ibid. p.5.
46. Ibid. p.7.
47. Hailey to G.C. Denham, 9 Apr. 1945. Hailey Papers.
48. 'Native Administration and Political Development', p.11. In the 1956 Revised edition of African Survey, pp.251-4, Hailey strongly recommended the term 'Africanism' rather than nationalism since it implied that African developments had indigenous connotations.
49. Ibid. p.47.
50. Margery Perham, Native Administration in Nigeria, p.361, argued that the Administrative Service would eventually disappear.
51. 'Native Administration and Political Development', p.48. This was not created.
52. Ibid. p.15.
53. Ibid. p.20.
54. Ibid. p.78.
55. Ibid. p.37.
56. Ibid. p.14.
57. Ibid. p.16.
58. Ibid. p.264.
59. Ibid. p.278.
60. CO 554/132/33727. Note of a Meeting in the Secretary of State's Room, 20 July 1943.
61. CO 847/21/47100/1. Note of Discussion with Hailey, 18 Mar. 1941.

62. CO 847/22/47100/1. Comments on Hailey's Report on Nigeria by Bourdillon, 30 Aug. 1943.
63. Typescript of Interview with Sir Alan Burns. Rhodes House.
64. Labour Party Imperial Advisory Committee. 'Draft Memorandum Formulating a Colonial Policy for the Labour Party after the War,' by L.S. Woolf. No.236, Sept. 1941. Reprinted in 1943 as 'The Colonies', p.3.
65. CO 323/1695/7318. Minute by Sir H. Moore, 16 June 1939.
66. Lee and Petter, 'The Impact of War on the Colonial Office' (typescript), pp.264-6.
67. CO 554/132/33727. 'Tentative Plan for Constitutional Development' (June or July 1943).
68. CO 554/131/33702. Minute by Williams, 2 Nov. 1942.
69. *Ibid*. Minute by Williams, 24 July 1942.
70. CO 554/132/33727. Note of Discussion with Secretary of State, 27 Oct. 1943.
71. *Ibid*.
72. *Ibid*. Williams minuted, 4 Sept.1943, that the Governor of Sierra Leone thought the plan implied change faster than desirable: 'I can only suppose that Sir H. Stevenson is thinking rather in centuries! I daresay he is right.'
73. CO 795/124/45170. Minute by Cohen, 16 Dec. 1943.
74. CO 96/782/31499. Minute by Cohen, 30 May 1944.
75. CO 554/132/33727. Note of Meeting in the Secretary of State's room, 20 July 1943.
76. CO 795/122 Pt.1/45014. 'Notes on future policy in Central Africa'. Secret. G.F. Seel. n.d.
77. *Ibid*. Minute by Gater, 1 May 1943.
78. *Report of the Commission on Higher Education in West Africa*. Cmd.6655. p.130.
79. *Ibid*. p.141.
80. CO 554/135/33599/7. Minute by K.E. Robinson, 28 Dec. 1946. Because of opposition to the Minority proposals in the Gold Coast and Sierra Leone, Creech Jones reluctantly agreed that Achimota should be developed into a university college.
81. CAB 66/57. WP (44), 15 Nov. 1944. 'Future Provision for Colonial Development and Welfare'. Memo by Stanley.
82. *Colonial Development and Welfare*. Cmd.6713. Dec. 1945.
83. Shuckburgh, 'Colonial Civil History of the War.' Vol.3, p.5.
84. Lee and Petter, 'The Impact of War on the Colonial Office', p.68 (typescript). Goldsworthy, *Colonial Issues in British Politics*, pp.45-6.
85. *Daily Telegraph*, 9 May 1941.
86. *Evening Standard*, 9 Feb. 1943.
87. CO 583/270/30568. Minute by Cohen, 19 Oct. 1944.
88. CO 795/133/45367. Minute by Cohen, 15 Jan. 1945. The mineral royalties were eventually acquired in Jan. 1950.

4

African Governors and the Making of Policy in Africa

'Once you stop being imperious with them,
they no longer think you're better than they are.'

– Dickens, *Our Mutual Friend* (Mr Boffin)

Most Colonial Governments experienced administrative changes broadly similar to those that affected the Colonial Office during the war. Yet this did not stem extensive criticism from some quarters. The more Lord Swinton, Cabinet Minister resident in West Africa from 1942 to 1944, saw of the Colonial Service, the more was he 'impressed with the number of misfits, or at any rate of men who just carry on because they are permanently in the groove'.[1] Lord Harlech, another former Colonial Secretary, believed that the promotions system in the Service discouraged the more worthy and pushed forward those men 'who can be trusted never to break an egg and so never make omelettes'.[2] The war had in fact imposed an excessive strain on the Colonial Service. In Africa twenty-five per cent of the administrative officers had been released for service with the armed forces, and those who remained were dissatisfied with salary scales, housing conditions, lack of leave, and overwork.[3] Swinton told the Cabinet that the administrative machine in West Africa might break at some important point.[4]

Despite the weaknesses within the Colonial Governments, and regardless of the more active role the Colonial Office was beginning to take, the impetus for change still lay with individual Governors. Of great importance during the war were the activities and proposals that emanated from the empire itself. Part of the significance of officials and politicians in London lay in the acceptance or rejection of policies which they themselves did not initiate. By the interaction of metropolis and periphery, the Second World War saw the

emergence of a much more clearly defined body of colonial doctrine, but only after the African Governors had largely destroyed
Hailey's theoretical African strategy.

The pressures on the Colonial Office were divergent and conflict-
ing. Despite the fact that pressure from the United States forced
Britain to adopt the goal of self-government for the African dependencies, the Union of South Africa, whose strength and importance
could not be ignored, was pushing in the opposite direction. The
Union called for the increasing association of Dominions with the
colonies in a particular area. General Smuts, who must rank with
Churchill and Hailey as one of the most trenchant upholders of the
British empire during the war, argued that the African colonies
should be grouped into large units, each under a Governor-General,
and that 'not a few' of them should be abolished as separate entities.[5]

South African influence during the war alarmed the Colonial
Office by its rapid and seemingly inexorable spread northwards. So
long as the loyalist Smuts remained in control in the Union, the
situation was not disastrous: but what if the nationalists were to
come to power? In the summer of 1940 it had seemed quite possible
that an Afrikaner Republic would be set up.[6] Britain's best policy
seemed to be to co-operate with Smuts and thereby foster the Union
war effort, and yet at the same time it was necessary to deflect the
expansionist danger. 'Should we not', asked the Colonial Secretary
in 1941, 'make our stand upon the Zambesi to safeguard the British
north?'[7] By the end of the war, however, the danger had receded.
Smuts began to call for co-operation in Africa by means of *ad hoc*
conferences rather than by means of amalgamation.[8] The main
demand of South Africa was now that South-West Africa should be
incorporated into the Union rather than become a Trusteeship
Territory.

In both East and Central Africa, Union influence was an important factor in these years. In East Africa official policy was clarified
to an extent during the war, a negative attitude from the Colonial
Office being its most important contribution. On the eve of the war
there had been no uniform policy:

> In Uganda we seem to be committed to work towards black
> supremacy: in Kenya we have declared that native interests are
> paramount and scared the whites into consolidating a position
> which is strong politically but precariously supported by a weak
> economic structure: in Tanganyika the whites are so few and the

blacks so backward that it is difficult to see how the relations between the races will develop; but the mandate seems to commit us to an ultimate future of black self-government.[9]

The main political issue during the war was the old one of closer union between the three territories. There were obvious economic and administrative advantages in such a proposal, but Tanganyika's mandated status and the differences in native policy were important obstacles. Colonial Office opinion in 1940 was that it would be unwise to proceed with closer union as a positive policy, though this did not mean it might not occur at a later date.

> East Africa is in an experimental stage. We have introduced to the country ... the wonders and horrors of European civilization and no one can tell how the experiment will turn out. Many enthusiasts profess to see clearly the road which should be trodden: but it may be unwise to surrender ourselves to these people. The fact is that the issues remain extremely doubtful.[10]

When Lord Cranborne took over at the Colonial Office, however, there was a resurgence of interest in the possibility of amalgamating or federating the East African territories and producing a new Dominion under settler control. In May 1943 the Governor of Kenya, Sir Henry Moore, submitted a plan for the amalgamation of Kenya, Uganda, and Tanganyika. The territories would be governed by a Governor-General, with one Executive Council and a legislature with an unofficial majority.[11] Only the departure of Cranborne and the dedication of some officials to the ideal of trusteeship meant that this scheme was not accepted. The Colonial Office's contribution had therefore been negative, but no less significant for that.

In March 1944 the Governors of the three East African territories agreed merely to support a high commission which would, after the war, take over the main functions of the Governors' Conference. It was to be a means for promoting economic co-ordination rather than political union. The possibility of the eventual self-government of each of the dependencies had thus been preserved. But there were few signs during the war that the doctrine of African paramountcy would have any positive effect. In the Commons Creech Jones urged that Africans should be assigned places in the Kenyan Legislative and Executive Councils[12]; but while it was admitted that there was force in his arguments, Colonial Office officials were also aware that 'the white settlers will not allow Africans to be put in a position where they might learn to challenge their political power'.[13]

Only in June 1944 was an advance made in Kenya, the Governor announcing that for the first time an African was to be nominated to represent native interests in the Legislative Council. E. W. Mathu, the product of a Kikuyu medicine man and Balliol College, was chosen.[14] The presence of settler minority groups meant that progress towards African self-government would inevitably be slow and tenuous: yet despite the settlers' veto of trusteeship, their presence and power guaranteed that future development would follow the British pattern. Self-government would be developed through an increase in the powers of the Legislative Council.

Hence Kenya did not justify what in the Colonial Office was called the 'Hailey philosophy'. The situation in Uganda seemed much more promising: it was the only territory in East Africa where there was a chance of developing on 'full native lines'[15], while the legislature was not the same focus for political attention as in Kenya.[16] The Office therefore vetoed the call of the Governor, Sir Charles Dundas, for the appointment of one European and one Indian, from amongst the members of the Legislative Council, to the Executive Council.[17] The next measure advocated by the Governor was much more in keeping with Hailey's ideas: he proposed to set up a Regional Council for the whole of the Eastern Province, and if this proved successful other such Councils could be established. The end result of these innovations could well turn out to be 'something in the nature of a native parliament or assembly representative of the whole territory.'[18] The issue of African representation on the existing Legislative Council was declared by the Secretary of State in 1942 to be unworthy of discussion 'until indications of post-war policy in these matters takes [sic] more definite shape'.[19]

By 1944, however, Dundas was pressing hard for the appointment of three or four Africans to the Legislative Council: such a measure he believed inevitable sooner or later.[20] The Africans would be selected from Provincial or Regional Councils. The selection process was therefore in harmony with Hailey's recommendations, but not so the new emphasis on increased African participation in the Legislative Council. It was on this latter point that opinion turned against Hailey. In 1945 Africans were for the first time admitted to the Ugandan Legislative Council. Even in Tanganyika, where there was a great paucity of suitable candidates, the Colonial Government stressed the importance of appointing two or three African representatives to the Council.[21] Two chiefs were appointed in 1945.

War-time developments in Central Africa illustrate a similar pattern to those in the East: tendencies towards closer union and amalgamation were combated, while the development of a system of Regional Councils prepared for an extended African representation on the Legislative Council. But much was uncertain during the war, and few clear-cut decisions could be made. The war gave an added impetus to settler demands for closer union, and there were calls for an unofficial majority on Northern Rhodesia's Legislative Council. The Colonial Office had to be cautious and wary: 'We are in the dilemma that the more we deny to them political power, the more we are going to force them into the arms of Southern Rhodesia, and to strengthen the demand for early amalgamation.'[22] There was also the danger that the concession of an unofficial majority in Northern Rhodesia would stimulate similar ambitions in East Africa, while if Southern Rhodesia were not appeased by some form of closer union then the consequences could be severe. 'We must have amalgamation or be absorbed by the Union', Prime Minister Huggins told Lord Lloyd in January 1941.[23] As if this were not enough, there were also calls for an increase in African representation in Northern Rhodesia: only the missionary Gore-Brown at that time represented the indigenous population, and Creech Jones argued in 1940 that two or three Europeans should be considered to represent African interests.[24]

The solution to the problem was found in granting an unofficial majority on the Legislative Council by increasing the number of nominated unofficial members from one to five, three of whom were to represent African interests. It was intended that as soon as possible Africans should be chosen to represent themselves. Once again settler influences had ensured that political progress would be through the development of the usual instruments. Provincial Councils had recently been established in Northern Rhodesia, the Secretary of State informed the Commons in October 1944, and once sufficient experience had been gained these would send delegates to an African Central Council. In due course this body would send African members to sit on the Legislative Council.[25]

A similar policy was taking shape in Nyasaland. In reply to criticism from Creech Jones that educated Africans were not being represented, Oliver Stanley insisted that British policy was to prevent educated and tribal Africans diverging in ideas and aspirations.

The councils of government would therefore contain representatives of both groups. He emphasized that Britain had

> a definite policy for the political development of Central Africa. We want to see Africans freely represented and we hope that educated Africans will be able to play their part.... we must be guided by the conditions in each Territory, and I am sure that it would be a mistake to upset the carefully thought out process of political development for Africans merely in order to make the political gesture of putting Africans on the Legislative Council straight away instead of waiting until the political institutions which have been established and which are projected for African representation have had time to develop. I do not wish you to get the impression from this that it is the intention of Governments to keep the process slow. On the contrary they will make it as fast as it is possible.[26]

A pattern was undoubtedly emerging, but the future was anything but certain. By March 1944 the Colonial Office had come down definitely against the amalgamation of the three territories. Creasy and Cohen drew up a memorandum, accepted by the Governors and presented to the British Cabinet, which argued that amalgamation could not be accepted then or for a number of years to come. Yet a completely negative attitude might well throw Southern Rhodesia into the arms of the Union.

> We should therefore aim at securing acceptance for the treatment of the three Central African Territories as Territories in close co-operation with each other on matters of common interest, but not amalgamated or federated. With this object we should be ready with concrete proposals for strengthening and making more formal the present machinery for co-ordination.[27]

In October the Secretary of State announced that there was to be a Standing Central African Council, under the chairmanship of the Governor of Southern Rhodesia, with a permanent Inter-Territorial Secretariat. 'The Council will be consultative in character and its general function will be to promote the closest contact and co-operation between the three Governments.'[28] It was hoped that this institution, and the fact that some form of closer union had not been ruled out for the future, would appease the ambitions and dissatisfactions of the settlers. Yet it was at this stage far from clear that they would acquiesce in these proposals.

It was in West Africa that the most important political develop-ments occurred. This was the area where Colonial Office planning, taking its lead from Lord Hailey, had gone furthest. There was to be Africanization of the administrative service, the modernization of the NAs, and the formation of Regional Councils, together with resistance to change at the centre. Initiatives from West Africa itself, and particularly from Burns in the Gold Coast and Bourdillon in Nigeria, killed the Hailey conception of political development and prepared the way for the post-war proposals. First there was a bitter tussle.

The argument between Hailey and the Governors was simple and yet crucial. Whereas Hailey believed that to develop the existing apparatus was to make a commitment to that machinery, the Gover-nors had no such qualms. In 1942 the upper echelons of the Colonial Office were firm supporters of Hailey. The idea that Britain was committed to fostering eventual unofficial majorities in Africa was repudiated by Arthur Dawe.

> There is a strong case against unofficial majorities in the central Legislatures in West Africa. All our colonial experience ... is, to my mind, against the idea.... Unofficial majorities in central Legislatures mean power without responsibility. ... They encourage petty criticism at the expense of constructive ideas and are the worst form of educating native peoples in the manage-ment of their own affairs.[29]

Here was plain speaking indeed from Dawe, and the Permanent Under-Secretary of State, Sir George Gater, agreed with him.[30] Yet this very proposal was soon to become official policy.

We have seen how the proposal to allow unofficial majorities found a place in O. G. R. Williams' tentative proposals for constitu-tional development in West Africa only with the utmost reluctance on the part of their author, while there was no mention of any change in the Executive Council. It was on this latter issue that the Colonial Office was first forced to concede defeat,[31] and thus the Whitehall proposals were in fact stillborn and a re-think from Hailey's position was essential. As early as 1930 the Governor of Nigeria – and his Acting Chief Secretary, Alan Burns – had called for the appointment of two Unofficials to the Executive Council, [32] and in January 1942 Burns, now Governor of the Gold Coast, made a similar request, asking Whitehall's approval for the appointment of two or perhaps three Unofficials to his Executive Council. Two of these would be

Africans, including one Paramount Chief. Reasonable Africans, argued Burns, would be pleased by such a measure and would feel that the Government was prepared to make reasonable concessions. But such a reform was bound to have political repercussions elsewhere, and while the Governor of Nigeria supported the proposal, the Governor of Sierra Leone was firmly against it.

Colonial Office opinion betrayed some sympathy with the desires of Governor Burns. Pedler and Talbot Edwards were in favour of appointing important chiefs. Williams argued that the proposals would in no way make for practical efficiency but that from the point of view of expediency – to his mind always the *summum bonum* – they should be accepted.[33] Unofficials on the Executive Council would be a nuisance but not a disaster[34] – therefore support the man on the spot. Naturally, it was Hailey who came out strongly against the idea of admitting Africans to the Executive Council. 'He thinks that we ought to avoid bringing in Africans at the centre too early and thus endeavour not to repeat the mistakes made in India.'[35] Hailey believed that concessions made at that time would increase rather than assuage the appetite of dissatisfied Africans: better to keep something in reserve so that if real agitation arose there would be reforms to call upon. This strategy was opposed by the alternative idea that only concessions given before agitation could insist on them would maintain the initiative of the Colonial Governments. Each side seems to have been drawing different lessons from the political deadlock that existed at that time in India, and both were reasonable (and 'imperialist') points of view.

In July 1942 the Secretary of State let it be known that he agreed with Hailey and refused to countenance the proposals put forward by Burns and supported by Bourdillon. Yet the matter did not rest there. We now see an excellent illustration of the pressure a Colonial Governor scorned could bring to bear, and of the importance of the 'periphery' for the decision-making process. Burns got his way because he and Bourdillon had political weight and knew how to use it. In July he returned to the fray:

> I am second to none in my admiration of Lord Hailey's ability and I recognise that he has had much more administrative experience than I have had, but he has not had such a long experience of Africans as either Bourdillon or myself: I have spent the greater part of my life in colonies inhabited by Negroes. Further, although Lord Hailey may be theoretically correct in his views

about Executive Councils, it is Bourdillon and I who have the practical responsibility, under your direction, for the administration of our two Colonies.[36]

Despite the high mutual regard Bourdillon and Hailey had for each other, this Governor also had the 'temerity' to challenge the Colonial Office adviser. Bourdillon had spent over nine years as a Governor in Africa and had frequently felt hampered by having no African on his Executive Council to advise him of native reactions to particular measures. If there were Africans 'sufficiently knowledgeable, impartial and trustworthy', he would welcome them to his Council.[37]

Burns – whose favourable impression of Unofficial Executive Councillors in the West Indies was partly responsible for his attitude[38] – put his case even more strongly, making intelligent use of the Colonial Office fear of the estrangement of African goodwill and the possible breakdown of law and order.

I assure you that I am not an alarmist, but each day I get fresh evidence of the increasing feeling of Africans against Europeans, and against the Government which Europeans represent. As I have recently returned to West Africa after an absence of eight years it is probably more apparent to me than to those who were here all the time, and could scarcely notice the slowly growing feeling. It would be disastrous for the future, and dangerous in existing circumstances, if we lose the goodwill of the Africans, which did exist and probably still does to some extent, by failing to make a gesture which I am convinced would have an immediate effect on public opinion. ... It would be too late to do any real good if we wait to make the concession until there is an organised agitation on the subject.[39]

Strong words indeed, and ones calculated to weigh with the Colonial Office and consequently to ruin the political strategy worked out by Hailey. Yet despite Burns' emphasis on African discontent, he was not reacting to pressure and indeed believed that his reforms were a surprise to the African.[40] In his own words: 'I believe in giving people what I think they would like, and should have, before they ask for it.'[41]

After the despatches of the Governors had been studied at the Colonial Office, the issue was studied anew at the beginning of September, and the decision went in favour of Burns and Bourdillon.[42] The Office gave little publicity to the admission of Africans to the Executive Councils of Nigeria and the Gold Coast, partly to avoid the impression that there would always necessarily be Africans on these councils.[43] Yet there can be no doubt that a move of some significance had been made. Not only were Africans admitted to the Executive Councils of the two larger West African dependencies, but in April 1943 two Africans – one chief and one creole, a typical ratio for this time – were appointed in Sierra Leone as well. Once a concession had been made in one area it became practically impossible to resist demands for a similar advance elsewhere.

Yet it should not be imagined that in 1942-3 Colonial Governments were consciously opening the door to decolonization or that they believed that the Executive Council would become a Cabinet. In 1943 Burns was proposing that the Executive Council be abolished and its place taken by four separate bodies: a Privy Council, a Civil Service Commission, a Social Welfare Committee, and an Economic Development Committee.[44] Nor did he believe that the Gold Coast would become independent in his lifetime but only after generations.[45] To the historically-minded, of whom Burns was one, it was quite obvious that the Legislative and Executive Councils were quite simply not equivalent to Parliament and Cabinet.[46] And yet Africans often treated them as if they were[47] (as did the white settlers in other parts of Africa), and the reforms of 1942 were corroborative evidence, giving an indication of future developments not intended by their authors.

Perhaps it was Lord Hailey who best understood what was happening. He had always argued that changes in African representation at the centre would form an irrevocable commitment to self-government with Western parliamentary institutions. Thus his consistent strategy for advance was ruined not by the adoption of an alternative plan which could take its place but by an expedient concession, a 'gesture,'[48] which was not part of any overall conception of political development. Hailey advised strongly against the admission of unofficials to the Executive Council, but the touchstone of his strategy was that there should be no unofficial majority on the Legislative Council. Yet after 1942 the battle had been lost and won, and by the end of the war unofficial majorities had been conceded with remarkable ease.

An unofficial majority was inaugurated in the Gold Coast by Sir Alan Burns, whom the experienced Lord Swinton considered the best Governor he had ever known.[49] In September 1943 the Joint Provincial Council of the Gold Coast Colony and the Confederacy

Council of Ashanti, together with African unofficial members of the Legislature, presented a Petition to the Governor calling for elected majorities in both Executive and Legislative Councils and for the appointment of an elected Minister for Home Affairs.[50] Burns himself thought these demands excessive, and moreover unrepresentative of local opinion, and he obtained authorization from London to proceed with negotiations with the chiefs and political leaders of the Gold Coast in order to frame a new constitution.[51] The main change which the Governor advocated was the introduction of an unofficial majority on the Legislative Council – the very measure which Hailey had thought it crucial not to concede. Burns evidently did not think it of such importance.

> I feel confident that the granting of an unofficial majority ... will be greatly appreciated by the people of the Gold Coast, and, although in some minor matters this may result in some unreasonable and irritating obstruction to Government measures, I do not believe that in the long run the country will be the loser. In major matters the proposed 'reserve powers' of the Governor are adequate, and I should not hesitate to use these powers should circumstances make it necessary.[52]

The constitution that emerged provided for an unofficial majority of twenty-four to eight. Of these twenty-four, six were to be nominated by the Governor, four were to be chiefs indirectly elected by Ashanti, and nine were to be indirectly elected by the Joint Provincial Councils. The remaining five were municipal members: two for Accra and one each for Cape Coast, Sekondi-Takoradi, and Kumasi. Burns also increased the number of Africans on the Executive Council from two to three, choosing them from amongst the unofficial members of the Legislative Council. The Gold Coast Government was encouraging the co-operation of chiefs and intelligentsia in the central councils.[53]

Developments in the Gold Coast meant that an unofficial majority could not be long delayed in Nigeria. Towards (and indeed after) the end of his Governorship, Sir Bernard Bourdillon submitted proposals for constitutional reform. Bourdillon believed that if the Emirs 'cannot see beyond the end of their own noses, they are doomed',[54] and he wished to shock the North out of its isolationist and reactionary outlook and produce a constitution which would eventually foster self-government for a united Nigeria. He therefore invited all his administrative officers to submit, quite informally, their views on constitutional progress – a scheme that was known as Bourdillon's 'prize essay competition'.[55]

Change in Nigeria was considered essential by some in the Colonial Office, not least by Andrew Cohen:

> Up to now Nigeria has been governed by a benevolent autocracy of officials. At its best this has taken the form almost of a squirearchy. At its worst it has tended to give too much weight to the rigid and rather inhuman outlook of the Secretariat. The day of such autocratic government is passing and more and more educated Africans have got to be brought into the administrative machine.[56]

Rather than introducing an unofficial majority, Bourdillon first proposed to abolish the distinction between unofficial and official members of the Legislative Council, allowing the latter to vote as they chose. When this was rejected, however, he did come down in favour of the alternative of the unofficial majority. Yet altogether his proposals failed to find support in London: they would not

> carry the ship very far towards self-government; they are more in the nature of a trimming of the sails and a slight alteration of course which will eventually shorten the journey.[57]

Bourdillon, though realising that change was vital, saw no undue cause for alarm and retained a pragmatic attitude: in his view ninety-nine per cent of the discontent in Nigeria was due to economic causes, while the loyalty of the mass of the peasantry was unquestionable.[58] He had helped to ruin Hailey's tentative strategy by insisting on changes in the Executive Council, as now by advocating reform of the Legislative, yet he did not believe it possible to try to forecast the precise form self-government would take in Nigeria 'within even the comparatively limited period of fifty years'.[59]

It can now be seen that the Colonial Office, having in effect been forced to abandon the Hailey model, was favouring new reforms. This is especially clear in the discussions that took place with Sir Arthur Richards before he left for Nigeria as Governor in 1944. Bourdillon, now retired because of ill health, had favoured unofficial majorities on both the central Legislative and also on the Regional Councils – the latter bodies having been widely accepted throughout British Africa. But there was also the need to regularize the position of the two unofficial members on the Executive Council, who were free to speak in debates against measures this body had accepted. By British standards, this was an important anomaly. Cohen put forward a possible solution, similar to the one mooted by Hailey in 1943:

> One possibility might be to attach the African unofficial members of the Executive Council to departments or groups of departments in which they would specialise and to which they would in a sense act as advisers. If such an experiment were successful, the number of Africans on the Executive Council might be increased and in this way a process of development would have been started under which Africans might eventually become heads of departments and, in the more distant future, ministers. If the constitutional reforms now being considered were accompanied by a step in that direction, however small, that ... might make them more acceptable to educated African opinion.[60]

Cohen was obviously future-oriented rather than historically-minded and was a systematizer, wishing to impose a pattern on the future rather than simply deal piecemeal with present difficulties. This attitude was paralleled by war-time plans for the reconstruction of Britain itself. This is not, however, to say that these ideas had much influence on the Richards constitution.

The constitution set up a Legislative Council that, for the first time, included representatives of the whole of the country.[61] Yet it was only at the insistence of the Secretary of State that an unofficial majority was conceded. The opposition of the Governor also had to be overcome to the maintenance of direct elections for Lagos and Calabar.[62] The new Council was to consist of sixteen officials and twenty-eight unofficials, of whom only four were to be directly elected, three for Lagos and one for Calabar. Of the remainder, most were to be indirectly elected by Regional Houses of Assembly.[63] The importance of the chiefs had increased dramatically.

Many in the Colonial Office were dissatisfied with the new constitution. F.J. Pedler had been particularly critical of the situation in the North and had wanted more radical change.

> In the Northern Provinces we have hitherto supported a conservative regime which is rapidly becoming reactionary. Though it is the home of the native authority policy, it is the place where that policy works worst. ... If the true state of affairs in Northern Nigeria were really known, I believe it would be more damaging to British Colonial prestige than any other situation in Africa.[64]

Adequate steps, it was thought, were not being taken to modernize the NAs. Colonial Office officials thought that one of the major lacunae in Bourdillon's constitutional proposals had been his failure to deal adequately with this issue. Bourdillon had agreed that the modernization of native administration was necessary but saw no need for this to form part of any constitutional proposals. His successor Richards was of the same mind.

SUMMARY OF THE CHANGES EFFECTED BY THE WAR

It can clearly be seen that during the war inroads were being made into indirect rule. In the Gold Coast Colony Burns introduced a form of traditional indirect rule, the issue baulked by Hodson, but only to give the Government greater control over the NAs.[65] Though there was no intention of abandoning traditional authorities as government agents in West Africa, there was an appreciation of the need for traditional forms to be modified to meet novel aspirations. The chiefs remained the centre and the pivot, though it was thought inevitable that in time their power and authority would dwindle, while that of the educated Africans grew inexorably. The new constitutions that were inaugurated in Nigeria and the Gold Coast soon after the end of the war were founded on the use of the NAs as the base of an electoral pyramid. But the use that would finally be made of the Native Authorities was still uncertain in 1945, as was the possibility of their democratization.

The war period had ensured that any advance at the centre would not have to wait on substantial developments in Regional Councils and native administration, or on the Africanization of the Administrative Service, as Hailey wished. It was also clear by 1945 that this advance would take place in the existing institutions, the Legislative and Executive Councils. Hailey had been overruled, though his idea of indirect election via Regional or Provincial Councils had received substantial assent, as had his stress on the importance of local administration as a training-ground in political responsibility.[66] A method of developing African responsibility at the centre had also been broached, though not accepted, and so had the fundamental dichotomy between the chiefs and the educated elite. An aim of policy at the end of the war was to prevent an unbridgeable breach forming between the two groups.

Lastly, the war had changed Britain's self-image. In the words of the official historian, Sir John Shuckburgh, the Second World War saw a

> 'new angle of vision' towards Colonial Problems as a whole, which, if it did not originate with the war, was greatly accentuated by war-time conditions and reactions. ... In the Mother Country there occurred what may be described as a complete change of heart on the part of the ruling race. The cult of 'Imperialism' was almost wholly extinguished; what had once been a high-minded political doctrine passed into a term of vulgar reproach. Britain, to all appearance, had lost all sense of pride in her Imperial position. The 'White Man's Burden' no longer made any appeal to the public imagination. The task of empire had come to be regarded as an incubus rather than an obligation.[67]

Indeed it was in the realm of intangibles, of ideas and confidence and imperial will, that the real change had occurred. Britain was certainly not planning to abandon her empire in Africa after the war, but the whole ethos of war-time propaganda had its effect. Innumerable politicians had made countless speeches to the effect that, to quote Clement Attlee, the British Commonwealth and Empire was in theory and practice 'the exact contrast to the Nazi conception of a world order', the one based upon the principles of Christianity, the other upon the creed of Antichrist.[68] The spirit of democracy and liberty, it was said, was the cement binding the majestic structure of the empire together.[69] What began as expediency ended as principle.

The war had seen very great fluidity in imperial thinking. The possibility of making imperial control permanent had been mooted with conviction and passion in some quarters, while the various attempts by settlers to achieve some form of closer union had only with difficulty been defeated. Yet liberal propaganda – and pressure from the United States – won the day, and by 1945 a degree of crystallization had occurred. The commitment to self-government was real, and some progress had been made towards it, especially in West Africa. But even here the initiatives that had been taken lacked consistency, and there was no overall conception of precisely where government was going. Bourdillon, in many ways an advanced Governor, believed that self-government was several generations in the future. His successor, Sir Arthur Richards, who disagreed with many of his policies,[70] was one with Bourdillon on this point. Even Sir Alan Burns thought in the early 1940s that it would take generations to achieve responsible self-government in the Gold Coast.

The years after 1945 did not of themselves produce all elements of the 1947 proposals – far from it. Yet they did produce a new sense of urgency and another revision of the time-scale, which had already foreshortened from centuries to generations during the war. They also provided an overall positive conception of political advance. Finally they gave a new and added emphasis to the educated elite and heralded attempts to transform native administration into English-style local government. War-time and post-war thinking fused to produce a strategy for the decolonization of the African empire.

We have thus seen that during the war the Colonial Office and Colonial Governments were concerned with constitutional reform, political advance, and native administration. Yet most of the thought devoted to these issues was merely speculative, and in fact far more attention was given to the economic mobilization and to the defence of the empire. In sharp contrast to liberal theory, Britain actually became more imperialist in her relations with the dependent territories. The Official History of the Colonial Office concentrated heavily on economic policy – control of imports, maintenance of essential supplies, stimulation of local production, colonial finance, control of the cost of living, and inter-colonial arrangements. It was on problems such as these that the bulk of official thinking and energy was spent. For the purposes of this present study it has been necessary to concentrate on other matters; but the economic history of the colonies was vital, and some knowledge of it is essential for an understanding of the post-war situation.

The main aim of the Colonial Office during the war was 'the mobilisation of all the potential resources of the Colonial Empire, both of men and materials, for the purpose of war'.[71] This was especially urgent after the loss of the Eastern territories, when ninety per cent of the world's rubber production and sixty per cent of tin production was lost to the Allies. Colonial imports and exports were strictly controlled, often at 'material economic sacrifice'. Yet many colonies actually gained from the experience of war. There were general increases in agricultural production, together with some economic diversification. The colonies' increased output could not be paid for wholly with goods, because of shortages, nor with paper money, as this would simply cause inflation. Instead many colonies accumulated considerable annual surpluses which were retained in Britain as 'post-war credits'. The imposition of increased local taxation during the war also aided the financial position of Colonial Governments. The extension of annual budgets was indeed remarkable. Between 1940 and 1945 local revenue in the West African colonies and in Kenya rose by a hundred per cent, while in many other territories it increased by over fifty per cent.[72] At the end of the war a relatively impoverished Britain was in substantial debt to her African colonies, a reversal of roles which complemented the policy of granting increasing measures of self-government.

In February 1942 Harold Macmillan was moved from the Ministry of Supply to aid the economic tasks of the Colonial Office,[73] and the Economic Section of the Office became a small supply department, under Creasy, Clauson, and Caine.[74] But economic policy remained inadequate in view of the intractable problem of African backwardness. The possibility of using Development Corporations in West Africa was discussed but with no definite conclusions. The Secretary of State himself dismissed the idea that the Native Authorities were sufficiently advanced to undertake industrial enterprises.[75] Economic development would nevertheless involve some disturbance of the established social institutions. A Colonial Office advisory committee recommended that all possible should be done to soften the impact of industrial development: yet 'substantial changes in the social structure must be accepted as a necessary cost of progress'.[76] Economic development would have political consequences: but Sydney Caine, for one, did not believe the inverse proposition was true. He did not think that administrative action was necessary for, or could make a great difference to, economic development. He quoted Britain and the U.S.A. as countries which had developed without government 'prodding'.[77] (He is today still of the opinion that political change could do little to increase the pace of economic progress.[78])

One of the main paradoxes of economic growth, and one likely to vitiate progress, was that it was indeed contradicted by political policy. As Gerald Creasy argued,

> Our dilemma appears to me to arise from the fact that, for political reasons, we seem to be driven towards taking measures which will make investment in West Africa less, and not more, tempting to private interests on whom we must rely, than it is at

present. Other things being equal, therefore, it may be expected that with our present policy, industrialisation in West Africa will be even slower than it would be had we not to contend with these political considerations.[79]

Thus despite Colonial Development and Welfare, and the possibility of Development Corporations, economic policy at this time lacked clarity and direction. Yet it was on economic progress that the rate of political development ostensibly depended. In the years following the end of the war this situation changed dramatically.

NOTES

1. Swinton to Stanley, 23 Mar. 1944. II 5/6. Swinton Papers.
2. ACJ 8/3 61-2. Harlech to Creech Jones, 5 Aug. 1945.
3. See R.L. Stone, 'Colonial Administration and Rural Politics' (Ph.D.Thesis), pp.187-96.
4. CAB 65/33. WM 16 (43) 4. 25 Jan. 1943.
5. Speech to the U.K. Branch of the Empire Parliamentary Association, 25 Nov. 1943.
6. N. Mansergh, *Problems of Wartime Co-operation and Post-War Change* (Oxford, 1958), p.76.
7. CO 847/23/47173/1. 'Most Secret: Expansionist Ambitions of the Union of South Africa'. March 1941.
8. *The Times*, 23 Mar. 1945.
9. CO 822/96/46523. Minute by Pedler, 28 Sept. 1939.
10. CO 822/103/46523. Minute by Dawe, 19 Jan. 1940.
11. Louis, *Imperialism At Bay*, pp.322-6.
12. *Parl. Debates* (Commons), vol.395, col.1909. 17 Dec. 1943.
13. CO 533/524/38032/A. Minute by Dawe, 29 Apr. 1943.
14. G. Bennett, *Kenya: A Political History* (Oxford, 1963), p.98.
15. CO 536/208/40099. Minute by Dawe, 13 July 1942.
16. CO 536/211/40020/6. Minute by Hailey, 6 July 1944.
17. CO 536/208/40099. Governor to Secretary of State, 9 Dec. 1942, and subsequent minutes.
18. CO 536/210/40293. Governor to Dawe, 10 Sept. 1942.
19. CO 536/211/40020/6. Governor to Gater, 12 June 1944, including quotation from despatch by Secretary of State, 7 Aug. 1942.
20. *Ibid.*
21. CO 859/122/12804/3. Deputy Governor to Secretary of State, 5 Feb. 1944.
22. CO 795/124/45170. Minute by Dawe, 2 Mar. 1943.
23. Lee and Petter, 'The Impact of War on the Colonial Office' (typescript), p.143.
24. CO 795/118/45170. Creech Jones to George Hall, 5 Nov. 1940.
25. *Parl. Debates* (Commons), vol.403, col.2365 *et seq*. 18 Oct. 1944.
26. CO 795/130/45170. Stanley to Creech Jones, 7 May 1945.
27. CO 795/128/45104. Memo. by Cohen and Creasy.
28. *Parl. Debates* (Commons), vol.403, col.2365. 18 Oct. 1944.

29. CO 96/770/31013/5. Minute by Dawe, 12 Jan. 1943.
30. *Ibid.* Minute by Gater, 15 Jan. 1943.
31. This issue, and the Burns and Richards constitutions, are well described in C. R. Nordman, 'Prelude to Decolonisation in West Africa: The Development of British Colonial Policy, 1938-47' (unpublished Oxford D. Phil. thesis, 1976).
32. CO 554/131/33702. Minutes.
33. CO 554/131/33702. Minute by Williams, 16 Mar. 1942.
34. *Ibid.* Minute by Williams, 24 July 1942.
35. *Ibid.* Minute by Williams, 16 Mar. 1942.
36. *Ibid.* Burns to Cranborne, 8 July 1942.
37. CO 583/255/30024/1. Bourdillon to Cranborne, 21 July 1942.
38. Typescript of Interview with Sir Alan Burns (Rhodes House). Interview with the author, 31 Mar. 1979.
39. CO 554/131/33702. Burns to Cranborne, 8 July 1942.
40. Typescript of Interview with Sir Alan Burns.
41. CO 96/779/31458. Minute by Burns, 13 Jan. 1945. He was writing specifically about advances in municipal government, yet the statement is also indicative of his wider attitude.
42. CO 554/131/53702. Note of a meeting between Secretary of State and civil servants, 1 Sept. 1942.
43. *Ibid.* Minute by A. Mayhew, 16 Sept. 1942.
44. CO 323/1871/4444. 'Memorandum on the Executive Council in the Colonies'. Burns, 21 Nov. 1943.
45. Typescript of Interview with Burns.
46. CO 96/782/31499/1. Burns took this view in his criticism of the Petition from the Joint Provincial Councils of the Gold Coast.
47. CO 583/261/30453. J. H. Carrow (Resident, Sokoto) to Bourdillon, 12 Feb. 1942: 'The African members, particularly the elected ones, more and more regard themselves as *Members of Parliament for Nigeria.*'
48. See the previous quotation from Burns. The word 'gesture' was repeated by Sir Alan Burns to the author, 31 Mar. 1979.
49. Swinton to wife, 9 Oct. 1942. Swinton Papers 3/3.
50. Copy in CO 96/782/31499/1.
51. CO 96/782/31499. Secretary of State to Burns, 15 June 1944.
52. *Ibid.* Burns to Secretary of State, 21 Aug. 1944.
53. D. Austin, *Politics in Ghana* (Oxford, 1964), p. 9.
54. CO 847/22 Pt. 1/47100/10. 'Comments on Lord Hailey's Report on Nigeria'. 30 Aug. 1943.
55. Interview with Hugh P. Elliott, 31 Mar. 1979.
56. CO 583/261/30453. Minute by Cohen, 14 Oct. 1943.
57. *Ibid.* 'Note on Sir Bernard Bourdillon's Proposals for Constitutional Reform'. n. d.
58. *Ibid.* 'Note of a meeting held in the Secretary of State's office', 22 June 1943.
59. *Ibid.* 'Note on Sir Bernard Bourdillon's Proposals for Constitutional Reform'. n. d.
60. CO 583/261/30453. 'Constitutional Development in Nigeria. Note for discussion with Sir. A. Richards'. n. d. A. B. Cohen.
61. Previously the North had not been directly represented.
62. See Nordman, 'Prelude to Decolonisation', pp. 202, 208, 215.
63. A. Burns, *History of Nigeria* (London, 1951), pp. 231-3.
64. CO 583/286/30453. Minute by Pedler, 29 Sept. 1944.
65. CO 96/775/31458/2. Burns to Secretary of State, 6 Oct. 1943. For further details of native administration and municipal government in West Africa during

the war see pp.147-54 of my 1978 Oxford D.Phil. thesis, 'The Evolution of British Colonial Policy towards Tropical Africa, 1938-48'.

66. Hailey, 'Native Administration and Political Development', p.40. Cf.the statement by Stanley, *Parl. Debates* (Commons), vol.391, col.58, 13 July 1943.
67. Shuckburgh, 'Colonial Civil History of the War,' vol.4, pp.113-14.
68. Speech at Aberdeen, 6 Sept. 1942; speech at Carmarthen, 3 Sept. 1943. Box 7. Attlee Papers, University College, Oxford.
69. *Ibid*. Speech at Greenock, 3 Sept. 1943.
70. Richards to Swinton, 15 Dec. 1945. II 6/1. Swinton Papers.
71. H. Macmillan, *The Blast of War* (Macmillan, 1967), p.166.
72. Shuckburgh, 'Colonial Civil History of the War,' vol.2, pp.531, 541.
73. *Financial News*, 12 Mar. 1942.
74. Macmillan, *The Blast of War*, p.167.
75. CO 554/139/33718/1. Note of Secretary of State's Discussion with Lord Swinton, 2 Aug. 1944.
76. CO 852/578/18706. Colonial Economic Advisory Committee: Industry Sub-Committee. 'The Development of Manufacturing Industries'. 29 Apr. 1944.
77. CO 852/586 Pt.1/19250/2. Minute by W.A. Lewis, 30 Nov. 1944.
78. Letter from Sir Sydney Caine to the author, 17 July 1976.
79. CO 554/139/33718/5. Minute by Creasy, 21 Aug. 1944.

5

Creech Jones and the Labour Government's Imperial Attitudes and Impact

> Why should the mind be burdened with opinions at all ...? Why shouldn't the mind be empty? Only when it is empty can it see clearly.
>
> – J. Krishnamurti, *The Only Revolution*

The history of the Labour Government after the Second World War was governed by a significant paradox. At a time of great radicalism and optimism, Britain's wealth had slumped to its lowest point since the Napoleonic wars.[1] From 1939 to 1945 Britain had pursued what Churchill described as an economic policy of 'reckless abandon': she had sold £1,118 million of overseas investments and other capital assets and had accumulated an uncovered external debt of £2,879 million.[2] Britain's current reserves equalled only one-sixth of her short-term foreign debts, while in the final year of war she had spent £2,000 million while earning only £800 million.[3] Britain was now dependent on American help. On 14 August, 1945, the Treasury warned that the country faced a 'financial Dunkirk' and that without American aid it would be 'virtually bankrupt'.[2] Three days later American aid was abruptly stopped.

Britain's economic straits provided the situation in which Labour Ministers planned a new course. Throughout their period in office the economy, despite renegotiated American help under the Marshall Plan, remained precariously weak. In July 1946 bread rationing was introduced, though this had not been necessary during the war itself.[4] The savage winter of '46-'47 brought the country almost to a standstill, and the Tory jibe became 'Shiver with Shinwell and Starve with Strachey'.[5] The 'dollar shortage', and later the need for increased armaments in view of the Cold War and hostilities in

Korea, bedevilled the plans of the Labour Government. Britain's economic weakness now gave a new significance to the development of African resources, while at the same time it meant that Britain could not afford possibly expensive attempts to coerce rebellious subjects in the colonies. The immersion of politicians in the problems of Britain also led many of them to forget or ignore their imperial trust.

The crushing electoral victory of Labour in 1945, with an overall majority of 146, was seen as a mandate for extensive change. Aneurin Bevan wrote in *Tribune* that 'The significance of the election is that the British people have voted deliberately and consciously for a new world, both at home and abroad'.[6] The leaders of the Government were now infected with enthusiasm and euphoria for the tasks and opportunities ahead. Hugh Dalton commented that the first sensation among the victorious party was

> of a new society to be built; and we had the power to build it. There was exhilaration among us, joy and hope, determination and confidence. We felt exalted, dedicated, walking on air, walking with destiny.[7]

These emotions, as we shall see, rarely extended to the empire. The imperial hopes and plans of that section of the Labour movement which was concerned with such matters were now focused on Creech Jones. Yet it was only very narrowly that he secured a place in the new Government.

The appointment of George Hall as Secretary of State for the Colonies in 1945 seems surprising, and can be compared with that of J.H. Thomas in 1924 and Sidney Webb in 1929. It was, however, a mere formality for Attlee, who had a high opinion of trade unionist Hall and believed he had done very well as Under-Secretary of State at the Colonial Office from May 1940 until February 1942.[8] He made Creech Jones the junior minister, but only with patent reluctance. He was taking a risk. When in the following year, on 4 October, Hall for health reasons left the Colonial Office and the Cabinet to become First Lord of the Admiralty, Attlee decided to promote the second in command. 'Creech Jones succeeded Hall as S of S Colonies', wrote Attlee, 'but perhaps is hardly strong enough for the position.'[9] Creech Jones's subsequent period as Secretary of State served only to confirm Attlee's suspicions of his competence, or lack of it:

> Creecg [sic] Jones despite much hard work & devotion had not
> appeared to have a real grip of administration in the Colonial
> Office. He was bad in the House and contributed nothing to
> Cabinet ...[10]

He was not altogether sorry when Creech Jones lost his seat in the
General Election of 1950 and could be replaced by James Griffiths,
'a first rate administrator'. The ex-Minister was not found another
seat in the Commons and neither was he given a peerage, though he
made known that he was willing to accept one.[11]

There was obviously a mutual antipathy between Attlee and
Creech Jones, and it would therefore be unwise to accept the Prime
Minister's judgment as being objective. Indeed his opinions throw
light on himself as well as their object. Attlee was pre-eminently a
Little-Englander and could not understand Creech Jones's interest
and concern for the colonies.

Attlee's involvement with Indian affairs is unquestioned. In 1927
he was made a member of the Simon Commission on Indian constitutional reform – 'on the grounds, I think, that I had a virgin mind
on the subject'.[12] Thereafter he maintained his knowledge of the
Indian situation until, after the war, he handled the crisis of the
transfer of power skilfully and showed no desire to cling to the
shadow of power. 'There has been no weakness and no betrayal', he
wrote to Conservative critic Lord Salisbury, formerly 'Bobbety'
Cranborne, 'nor will there be, but there are limitations to our
powers.'[13]

As Leader of the Labour Party from 1935 onwards, Attlee also
took note of wider imperial issues. In 1937 he argued that some of
the colonies were ripe for greater measures of self-government and
that the Labour Party would always 'prefer to err in being too soon
rather than too late in the grant of self-government'.[14] He was also
quite clear that the possibilities of advance being brought about
by alien administrators were limited.[15] Yet his concern with the
empire showed little sign of genuine interest or originality, and after
the war he took a negative attitude towards the colonies. This is best
illustrated by his reaction to the possibility that Britain might have to
take some responsibility for the former Italian colonies. He could
see no strategic advantages to be gained, since the British
Commonwealth and Empire was not a unit that could defend itself;
and, if the security of the United Nations proved illusory, then the
emphasis should be put on the defence of England. Apart from this

consideration,

> I can see no possible advantage to us in assuming responsibility
> for these areas. They involve us in immediate loss. There is no
> prospect of their paying for themselves. The more we do for them
> the quicker we shall be faced with premature claims for self-
> government. We have quite enough of these awkward problems
> already. .... Cyrenaica will saddle us with an expense that we can
> ill afford. Why should we have to bear it? Why should it be
> assumed that only a few great Powers can be entrusted with
> backward peoples? Why should not one or other of the Scan-
> dinavian countries have a try? They are quite as fitted to bear rule
> as ourselves. Why not the United States?
>
> British Somaliland has always been a dead loss and a nuisance to
> us. We only occupied it as part of the scramble for Africa. If we
> now add Ogaden and Italian Somaliland we shall have a trouble-
> some ward with an unpleasant neighbour in Ethiopia. The French
> are on the spot in French Somaliland. Why not let them have it if
> they like? ... There would, of course, be the sentimental objec-
> tion of giving up a piece of the Empire, but otherwise it would be
> to our advantage to get rid of this incubus.[16]

Imperial sentiment and pride were not factors that influenced
Attlee. They are also conspicuously absent from other Labour
politicians of the time.

The attitude of Hugh Dalton is significant as an illustration of
much of the thinking of the post-war Government, while the position he held, that of Chancellor until November 1947, controller of
the colonial purse-strings, emphasizes this significance. He welcomed the independence of India and Burma:

> It is quite clear that we can't go on holding people down against
> their will, however incompetent they are to govern themselves ...
> and it would be a waste both of British men and money to try to
> hold down any of this crowd against their will. They must be
> allowed to find their own way, even through blood and corruption
> and incompetence of all kinds, to what they regard as 'freedom'.[17]

Dalton's attitude was based not on ideals of sacred trusts but on the
recognition of the reality of power. 'It [sic] you are in a place where
you are not wanted and where you have not got the force to squash
those who don't want you, the only thing to do is to come out.'[18] He
also realised that the empire was not a vital issue for the electorate,
not one person in a hundred thousand caring 'tuppence' about India,

so long as British people were not being 'mauled about'.

Yet his viewpoint is best seen from his reaction when, in February 1950, Attlee asked him to become Secretary of State for the Colonies. It was one of those moments when time seems to stand still.

> I had a horrible vision of pullulating, poverty stricken, diseased nigger community, for whom one can do nothing in the short run, & who, the more one tries to help them, are querulous and ungrateful; of Malaya & a futile military campaign; of white settlers, reactionary & as troublesome, in their own way, as the niggers; of ineffective action at a distance, through telegrams to & from Governors whom one has never seen; of all the silliness and emotion about the black man who married a white typist, & Dr.Malan, & the demand for the Protectorates; of friction over Trusteeship at UN; of initiating personal relationships with Ernie [Bevin], and Phil [Noel-Baker], and Shi[n]well; of continuing difficulties over groundnuts; of Parliamentary questions by pro-native cranks & anti-native capitalists – all this in a rush of a few seconds ...[19]

With men like Attlee and Dalton leading the Government it is not remarkable that the revival of 'imperialism' after the war was kept within bounds and that, once the danger signals of nationalist unrest had been given, important steps on the road to self-government were conceded. Nor is it surprising that Creech Jones and the Colonial Office were left to work much as they pleased.

Among the other members of the Government, Herbert Morrison was dissatisfied with colonial affairs, believing that the Colonial Office needed 'shaking up'.[20] He was undoubtedly on the 'right' in his imperial thinking. 'We are friends of the jolly old empire', he said, 'and we are going to stick to it.'[21] Yet his influence on these matters was negligible since his responsibility was for home affairs. The man with the general supervisory responsibility for the whole of external policy, including colonial affairs, was the Foreign Secretary, Ernest Bevin. He and Creech Jones were close friends. Jones had been an official in Bevin's Transport and General Workers' Union and had also been his Parliamentary Private Secretary at the Ministry of Labour and National Service during the war. Bevin had a vastly higher opinion of Creech Jones than had Attlee. In 1950 he looked back over the previous five years:

> You are rather undemonstrative. I sometimes think you hide your light under a bushel but ... I have been very encouraged by

the indefatigable way you have applied yourself to your task in this Labour Government.

Looking back over the history of Colonial development I do not think anyone has a greater record – the Constitutional changes you have carried through, the development of education, the promotion of Universities, the constant attention you have given to economic development, the way you have applied your mind to the problems of soil erosion and transport. If only it had been done long ago. What a different world it would have been! There would have been no dollar gap.[22]

In contrast to most of his colleagues, Bevin had a genuine enthusiasm for the empire. He had never been a man afraid to Think Big. The trade union he formed in 1921, the Transport and General Workers' Union, was the largest in the world. In 1938 he attended the Commonwealth Relations Conference in Sydney and was greatly impressed by Lionel Curtis: this was a turning-point in Bevin's interests and he soon began to talk to friends about proper imperial policies. He urged a Select Committee of the House of Commons to review the administration of the whole colonial empire. 'Our crime isn't exploitation. It's neglect.' He thought it shocking that no real attempt was being made to help the colonies to become self-governing and economically secure.[23]

As Foreign Secretary Bevin, while supporting Creech Jones and approving of constitutional reform, took an imperialist line. This is not to say that he did not have a genuine concern for the well-being of the colonial peoples. According to Bullock, Bevin's concern for ordinary men and women ran like a scarlet thread through all he touched.[24] But he believed that only with economic and social development promoted by Britain could the colonies advance. He also judged, in sharp contrast to Attlee, that the security of the route through the Mediterranean and the Middle East was vital to British interests and that Britain would have to take an interest in the ex-Italian colonies, perhaps accepting 'direct responsibility and the consequent financial burden'.[25] At the back of his mind was the fear that the Soviet Union wanted a base in Africa for the production of uranium, a contingency which he was determined to prevent.[26] Bevin was also aware of the other resources of Africa:

If only we pushed on & developed Africa, we could have U.S. dependent on us, & eating out of our hand in four or five years.

The great mountains of manganese are in Sierra Leone, etc. U.S. is very barren of essential minerals, & in Africa we have them all.[27]

The Labour Party had, traditionally, nurtured anti-imperialists of the doctrinaire type. Yet, although their influence was not entirely negligible,[28] the majority of the Party was happy with the reformist policies of the Government. John Strachey, at one time a Communist, was now moving to the right and, as Minister of Food from 1946 to 1950, was charged with the ill-fated groundnuts scheme. Aneurin Bevan, having founded the National Health Service, was anxious to move to the Colonial Office but was strictly excluded. He was not to be trusted '(a) not to waste money, (b) not to be carried away by his colour prejudice, pro-black & anti-white'.[29]

In his earlier days, Stafford Cripps had been a trenchant critic of empire and had forcibly advocated its liquidation in 1925.[30] Theoretically, he had seen imperialism as 'a necessary economic incident within capitalism' and a potent cause of war.[31] Personal experience in Jamaica in the 1930s had confirmed these ideas and given fuel to his judgment that Britain was wholly unfit to govern other peoples. Yet in 1942, with his Mission to India, came an important modification in his position. Forced to face the reality of a complex situation, Cripps realized that immediate British withdrawal from India would constitute an open invitation to Japan. The policy Gandhi was pursuing was therefore 'wholly impraticable'.[32]

As Chancellor of the Exchequer after the war, Cripps forgot his earlier notions and concentrated instead on the economic importance of African development to the British economy.

We have for a long time talked about the development of Africa, but I do not think we have realised how from the point of view of world economy that development is absolutely vital. ... We should increase out of all recognition the tempo of African economic development. We must be prepared to change our outlook and our habits of colonial development and force the pace so that within the next 2–5 years we can get a really marked increase of production in coal, minerals, timber, raw materials of all kinds and foodstuffs and anything else that will save dollars or will sell in a dollar market ... the whole future of the sterling group and its ability to survive depends in my view upon a quick and extensive development of its African resources. ... It is because the future prosperity of the Colonies themselves

depends upon the future strength and stability of the Commonwealth and Empire that I am convinced that their future and the
happiness of their peoples can only be made secure along the
lines that I have mentioned.[33]

It is scarcely surprising that the cry of exploitation came during these
years not as hitherto from the Labour benches but from the Conservatives.[34]

It can thus be seen that, with colleagues viewing the empire with
indifference, horror, or as an essentially economic concern, Creech
Jones with his emphasis on political development and eventual
self-government was a crucial figure.

CREECH JONES – CRITIC

Arthur Creech Jones was born of working-class origins in Bristol in
1891. He gained political experience in trade unionism and local
party politics. From 1913 to 1922 he was Secretary of the Borough
of Camberwell Trade and Labour Council. He was National Secretary of the Transport and General Workers' Union from 1919 to
1929, while from 1921 to 1928 he served as an Executive Member
of the London Labour Party. An important interruption in these
duties came with the First World War, when Creech was a conscien-
tious objector. Though applying to join the Friends' Ambulance
Unit, he was court-martialled in 1916 and imprisoned until April
1919. He was obviously a man of courage and principle, and his
socialism stemmed from Christianity rather than economic theory
intellectually conceived.[35] Later in life Creech Jones had certain
doubts, thus technically disqualifying him from being a 'Christian',[36]
but the religious *motif* is vital for an understanding of the man. The
ideal of service found expression in him not as a vague or pious
expression of goodwill but as a total, dedicated commitment.

Creech Jones first attempted to enter Parliament in 1929 when he
contested the Heywood and Radcliffe Division; but, despite a reputation in some quarters for being a young trade union leader with
industrial knowledge, he was defeated and had to wait until 1935
before entering the Commons as Member for Shipley. He made
his Maiden Speech in March 1936, introducing the debate on the
second reading of the Offices Regulation Bill;[37] but in the next few
years he made his reputation as Labour's most knowledgeable and
dedicated colonial spokesman. His interest in the colonies had in

fact begun much earlier. As a boy he had been stirred by the atrocities committed in the Congo and by the work of Morel and Casement. He had grown up with a liberal international faith that prejudiced him against economic and political domination.

> Consequently, when in 1925 a distinguished teacher asked me to give a helping hand to a struggling black trade union, I eagerly responded. ... I felt that the struggle of the African workers in South Africa could be helped by a type of organisation which had contributed so much to the making of British democracy ...[38]

Creech Jones soon became known as the 'unofficial member of the Kikuyu at Westminster'. The extent of his efforts is remarkable. It has been calculated that in the first four sessions of his membership he asked 46, 55, 153, and 123 Parliamentary Questions respectively. This is easily the greatest number asked on colonial affairs during that time. (His nearest rival, W. Paling, asked only 48, 35, 53, and 74.) Jones also joined the Labour Party Advisory Committee on Imperial Questions and was diligent in his attendance.[39] From 1944 to 1945 he was Chairman of this body.[40] More and more the work of the Advisory Committee began to be taken over by the Fabian Colonial Bureau, founded in 1940, but this did not lessen the work load of Creech Jones, who was the Bureau's founding Chairman. As if this were not enough, he also served on the executive of the Anti-Slavery Society from 1938 to 1954 and as a member of several other similar groups. In 1939 Creech Jones wrote that he was 'an overwhelmingly busy person';[41] and in 1941 he noted that he was 'overwhelmed with work now'.[42] One can only imagine that this state intensified as the years passed.

Creech Jones was a hard-working, earnest, and sincere man. He was undemonstrative and never sought the limelight. In committee he refused to talk on subjects he was not competent to discuss 'or to say the obvious or to repeat ideas that have already been put'.[41] He was essentially serious-minded: his speeches and writings rarely, if ever, reveal a sense of humour. In many ways he was a shy man. Unconcerned with superficialities, he was always concerned to be of use. Many critics of empire preferred to work from the sidelines, so to speak, not having to compromise their principles or dirty their hands. They had an emotional disposition to avoid responsibility. But Creech Jones from the first seems to have aimed at having a practical effect. He realised that it was only through the official machine that reforms could be made. In 1936 he joined the Colonial Office advisory committee on education, becoming its Chairman during the Second World War.[43] In 1943 he was a member of the Elliott Commission on higher education in West Africa. His role of well-informed, practical critic of colonial affairs bred respect in the minds of many Government ministers, especially Malcolm Mac-Donald:

> ... when I was Secretary of State for the Colonies, you were one of my most valuable allies by being one of my chief critics. ... As I have often told you, I learnt more from your criticism and Questions than from all the praise of my colleagues on this side of the House.[44]

Other reactions, as we shall see, were not so complimentary.

Creech Jones as critic of empire escaped the left-wing identification of imperialism and capitalist exploitation. This is not to say that he did not think that exploitation occurred. He complained that the price paid for primary products was far too low, that indirect taxation was driving many Africans from agriculture to industry, where conditions were deplorable and wages were scandalously low. Most important of all, in his opinion, was the fact that certain private companies in West Africa had a stranglehold over the economic life of those communities.[45] Yet he saw the vast majority of the economic problems in dependent territories as the result simply of harsh natural conditions. There seemed to be a positive conspiracy of nature against all human life in the colonies. His trip to West Africa in 1944 profoundly shocked him: he had not hitherto imagined that life was possible at such low levels. 'This is not a problem of exploitation, but one created by nature herself.'[46]

Creech Jones did not therefore dogmatically condemn imperialism *per se*, though he did voice doubts about the 'basic rightness' of the British presence in certain areas, particularly Kenya.[47] Many of the criticisms he made in Parliament were simply attempts to encourage Britain to live up to her 'laudable declarations of principle' made in the past, to make trusteeship real, for without being put into effect these ideals constituted 'the cant of empire'.[48] He believed it was Britain's duty to tackle the backwardness and deficiencies of the colonies. So long as imperial control was designed to help the native peoples to lead a fuller life, then Creech Jones would have no quarrel with it: such a policy was not imperialism but 'good neighbourliness'.[49] It would only make matters worse for Britain to walk out of her dependencies, a course of action he openly repudiated.[50]

Yet Creech Jones did not merely advocate a more efficient or more humane empire. He quite definitely called for the end of the British empire. He wrote during the war that 'Colonial territories, as such, need, to use an ugly American expression, to be liquidated as rapidly as circumstances permit'.[51] He voiced the same opinion in 1945 when discussing the new Colonial Development and Welfare Bill:

> It is a commonplace of American criticism in respect of British Imperialism ... to demand of us the liquidation of Colonial status. It is significant that the very purpose of this Bill is to achieve these very purposes. I doubt if any Imperial Power has ever before embarked upon a policy of deliberately disintegrating its Empire. That is the effect of this Bill in the long run.[52]

The proper task of colonial administration was therefore, in his opinion, that of 'nation-building'.[53]

Creech Jones was never explicit on the subject of how long the development of self-government would take. Above all, he deprecated time-schedules as 'very unrealistic' and as traps to be avoided.[54] Experience in West Africa confirmed his suspicion that an early withdrawal from the African colonies was not practicable.[55] He wished to see the maximum amount of social and economic development possible before self-government were granted; and in the meantime Britain would be able to exercise 'the privilege of service',[56] though her efforts themselves could not solve Africa's problems. He clearly recognized that the co-operation and collaboration of the colonial peoples were vital. This recognition runs through almost all his speeches. In 1938 he stressed it was important that 'the views of the people themselves should be heard', and that the workers in the empire were fellow citizens.[57] In 1940 he expressed the hope that when schemes under the Colonial Development and Welfare Act were under discussion there would be full consultation with the people who would be affected.[58] In 1943 he was arguing that

> We may help from the top but, unless there is a response from the masses and deliberate efforts to build up the standards of conduct and to develop an appreciation of responsibility, things cannot go far.[59]

As Secretary of State he was to be fully aware of the importance of generating enthusiasm and participation among the subjects of the empire. Only they themselves could determine the pace of economic growth and of advance generally.

Since self-government was not an immediate prospect, Creech Jones continued his efforts to ensure that colonial government was humanized and campaigned for reforms that would facilitate the eventual transfer of power. During the war he was a constant critic of the Colonial Office. He resented the imposition of forced labour[60] and generally championed the rights of Africans. His outspoken criticisms are best illustrated by his complaints at the suppression of three African Associations in Kenya – the Kikuyu Central, the Ukamba, and the Teita Hills Associations – and the internment of nineteen of their members.

> Some of these men are my friends. I have for years had much correspondence from them & with them. ... To my mind, this is an outrage. I cannot remain quiet about it on the facts as I know them. ... Our Kenya policy has been wicked enough without adding more indefensible acts to it. I beg you ... that you do all you can to get these Africans back their liberty without more injustice being done to them.[61]

When the Secretary of State replied that, in the Governor's opinion, the detention of these men was necessary for security reasons,[62] the critic remained critical.

> I am not satisfied with the position indicated. ... Surely all this is specious pleading in justification for a line of action that ought never to have been taken & the invention of excuses to find justification? ... it seems to me that the dangerous situation has been made by this long detention of men who in all their dealings with me have revealed consistency and sincerity of purpose, high integrity & accuracy of statement and absolutely no disloyalty. I cannot let this matter stay where it is. I urge that the whole matter be reconsidered & the men released.[63]

Creech Jones was proving more than an annoyance to the Office, and it was debated whether to send him a curt reply or none at all. This particular matter was ended when George Hall showed his Labour colleague the secret information forwarded from Kenya by the Governor.[64] But Creech continued to represent African interests to the Colonial Office, often to the despair of officials:

There runs through so much of the criticism of Mr. Creech Jones' letter the notion that the Secretary of State can impose what policy he likes on East and Central Africa. That notion pays no regard to realities.[65]

If he did suffer from this delusion, it was soon to be exploded by personal experience.

Creech Jones certainly called for more boldness in Colonial Office policy. As he argued in 1942:

We cannot much longer palm Africans off with talk about parallelism and wink at segregation and land apportionment. We must formulate a positive policy in place of a weak negative one. There must be recognition of Africans' rights and status. There must be a big drive in social services, in education and in economic development. We must also associate the Africans in the administration of local government. We should nationalise the mineral resources of these areas. We should redistribute the land and there should be planned development of smaller industries. If we do not do these things the future will be black ...[66]

He believed that Africa was, on the whole, a disintegrating society and that it would inevitably be pulled into the modern world. Yet there was a danger that, unless a degree of control were exercised, certain areas would revert to chaos. Hence there was a need for Britain to do some hard thinking and 'to find a positive and constructive line of advance – to put the progress and experience of centuries into a generation'.[67] Further study was necessary on certain vital issues, but specific reforms were undoubtedly crystallizing in his mind.

He believed that the increased representation of Africans in the central Councils was of fundamental importance. He was particularly insistent that educated Africans should figure more prominently. At the 1939 Labour Party Conference he had urged that Britain should not allow herself to be 'hoodwinked by anthropologists and those who believe in indirect rule and who would ask us to work through the chiefs'.[68] To other audiences he was more moderate in his attitude to indirect rule. To the National Peace Council in 1944 he put the point that, from the historical point of view, no suitable alternative to indirect rule could have been devised. It was the 'framework in evolution of local government'.[69] To the Royal Empire and Royal African Societies in 1945 he called for greater flexibility in indirect rule – for the integration in the colonial life of the young and educated classes and the granting of greater opportunities for administration and the practice of responsibility in local and municipal government ...'[70]

Most important of all, he wrote to the Colonial Office in 1945 that there should be

an increasing place for the educated and able men and women in government and administration and an adaptability which eliminates the feudal character of indirect rule and finds representative people (by democratic machinery) instead of hand picked chiefs and others who conform to 'official' needs.[71]

This stress on the educated elite stemmed partly from Creech Jones's colonial contacts. He had formed a complex and extensive network of correspondents in all parts of the empire. These were not confined to the intelligentsia, and several chiefs were represented. Yet there was a preponderance of trade union officials, newspaper editors, and nationalists.[72] He found it easier to co-operate with and understand the point of view of the moderate, westernized, nationalist leaders. He corresponded with Nnandi Azikiwe and I. T. A. Wallace-Johnson and was especially friendly with J. B. Danquah, who was later to invite Creech Jones to his wedding in Accra.[73] These contacts impressed the importance of the educated elite on the mind of Creech Jones. His membership of the Commission on higher education served a similar purpose: the backwardness of the majority could not be expected to hold back the minority, for the progress of the many depended on the few.

Towards the end of the war Creech Jones had come to the conclusion that the fundamental problem in African government was the widening rift between the Government officials and the African intelligentsia. This problem was crucial and it could not be solved merely by giving the Africans a few seats on the Executive Council or by appointing one or two African Administrative Officers. As an overall strategy he recommended a conception of policy nearer to that advocated by Governor Burns than to Hailey's ideas.

Every time Government is manoevred [sic] into the position in which a reform is merely given as a result of pressure and agitation, it only confirms to politically-minded Africans, that if they attack the Government hard enough it can be induced to give way to any demand. Their thinking is becoming more and more bitter.

... This tendency is not just a natural process but is being deliberately fomented by certain forces out for their own ends. The counter to it is so close an understanding and contact with the disinterested forces within the country that Government can foresee and prepare any constructive and needed reforms long before there is an agitation for them.[74]

Despite his regard for the educated elite, he well knew that 'irresponsible nationalism' was taking shape in some areas,[75] and this was a force that could ruin the best laid schemes of Colonial Governments. Hence it was necessary to conciliate the moderate, 'disinterested' members of the intelligentsia by a bold extension of their powers in both central and local government. Only thus could Britain ensure the loyalty and co-operation of the bulk of educated Africans. If there were an identity of purpose between Government officials and the leaders of local opinion, then a true partnership would be achieved, and the ending of duality would be the beginning of progress.

From the above description of the ideas and actions of Creech Jones during the war, it will be seen that the future Secretary of State had his arguments with the Colonial Office. Yet by 1945 there was far more common ground between the officials and the critic. The transformation that took place in official policy – with the recognition of the goal of self-government, the advances in the central councils, and the acknowledgment of the need to democratize native administration and of the new importance of the educated elite – meant that the Colonial Office conception of advance equated more nearly with that of its future political head. Creech Jones exhibited the greater impatience and a more willing readiness to experiment. He was more 'advanced' than the leading officials but intended to travel in a not dissimilar direction. It was because of the transformation that had taken place in the Colonial Office during the war that the impact of Labour did not produce the immediate revolution that many wished to see.

There seems, in retrospect, little justification for the belief that the Socialists after 1945 would produce radical and swift changes in the colonies. Labour's policies had been set out with clarity in a series of pamphlets.[76] The most important of these were *The Empire in Africa: Labour's Policy* (1921), *The Colonial Empire* (1933), and *The Colonies* (1943). Each of these bears the stamp of its author, Leonard Woolf, though others contributed as well. Woolf is sometimes seen as the archetypal anti-imperialist. His experiences from 1904 to 1911 in the Ceylon Civil Service were essential for the development of his ideas. It was there, he later commented, that he learned 'the absurdity of one civilisation and mode of life trying to impose its rule upon a people of an entirely different civilisation and mode of life'.[77] In fact, he found the life of an official in Ceylon entirely uncongenial and vastly depressing. In January 1905 he commented that the ' "society" of this place is absolutely incredible ... the women are all whores or hags or missionaries or all three'. A few months later he was complaining that 'It is absolutely incredible how futile life can be: and if one doesn't become engrossed in its futility, I don't see how there is anything to stop one going mad'. In February 1908 he attempted suicide.[78] Later his researches into the acquisition of the British colonial empire in Africa led him to the conclusion that 'The motive power ... behind modern imperialism is economic'.[79] This agreement with the views of Hobson and Lenin confirmed his belief in the evils of empire and led him to devote tireless energy thereafter in an attempt to 'forestall events' by encouraging Britain to leave her colonies before inevitable nationalist risings. He served as Secretary of the Labour Party Imperial Advisory Committee from its inception as a separate body in 1924 until 1945.

Labour thinking on the colonial empire differed from that on India because it was necessary to deal with 'backward peoples or peoples of primitive culture'.[80] Hence there could be no immediate self-determination. Nevertheless in popular Labour mythology there was a great bond between 'the black-faced men in the pit and the black-faced men in the Colonies'.[81] Both were the supposed victims of capitalist exploitation. Hence socialism, though very much Europe's response to the industrial revolution, was thought relevant to the agricultural and undeveloped tracts of Africa. Labour's policy was basically a combination of socialism and ultimate self-government, thus exhibiting a certain duality. It was argued that the two policies were complementary; and yet the granting of self-government and the fostering of economic and 'socialist' advances are not synonymous. Indeed the need to improve the life of the African occasionally seemed to conflict with the ultimate aim of self-government. Labour's dualistic policy bred an ambivalent reaction from Africans.

Labour's commitments in African policy were made clearly in the three pamphlets. There is a striking similarity between the statements and, since the recognition of eventual self-government was made in the first of them, there is nothing which parallels the striking change of heart that came over official policy during the Second World War. In 1921 it was argued that:

> In Africa the policy of Labour must ... aim at substituting a system based on the common economic interests of the inhabitants for the existing system based on the economic exploitation of the native by the white man. At the same time Labour must aim at substituting a political system of responsible and representative government for the existing autocracy. In a word Labour's policy ... must be the abolition of economic exploitation and the education of the native so that he may take his place as a free man both in the economic and political system imposed upon Africa.

The 1933 statement succinctly stated that Labour's aim was to 'develop the Empire into a Commonwealth of self-governing Socialist units within the League of Nations'. Finally, in 1943 the dual policy was reiterated:

> (1) The territories should be administered by colonial powers as a trust for the native inhabitants, the principal object of the administration being the well-being, education and development of those inhabitants.

> (2) A primary object of the administration should always be to train the native inhabitants in every possible way so that they may be able in the shortest possible time to govern themselves.[82]

Self-government, which even in 1943 could not be expected for a 'considerable time to come', was to be developed through changes in the Legislative Council. There was no flirtation, as there was in official thinking, with the possibility of novel political institutions more suitable to indigenous conditions and traditions. In 1921 it was stated that Britain's aim should be the genuine representation of Africans on the Legislative Councils and the gradual transfer to those Councils, after education had spread and representation become established, of responsibility. A training for central executive power was to be given in the localities with the supervision of sanitation, irrigation, roads, and possibly education. Where the institutions of local self-government had been retained,

> they should be encouraged and developed, care being taken that
> the development is in the direction of popular rather than auto-
> cratic control. Where as in parts of East Africa they have been
> destroyed, the administration must develop new institutions of
> native local self-government in accordance with the needs and
> desires of the population.[83]

By 1943 these proposals had become more explicit. Africans
should either be nominated or, where education had reached suitable levels, elected to the Legislative Council. The development of
this system would facilitate the transition from paternal to responsible government. Woolf enumerated the stages in the transfer of
power quite clearly. He believed that the Legislative and Executive
Councils had been deliberately designed as the embryos of a parliamentary system of government. The first stage was a council consisting entirely of official and nominated members; the second was one
consisting of official, nominated, and elected members, the elected
being in a minority; in the third the council would comprise official,
nominated, and elected, with the elected members being in a majority, but with certain subjects reserved. In the fourth and final stage
there would be a council consisting of elected members to whom
Ministers forming a Cabinet would be responsible for the whole
administration. The Governor would be reduced to a figurehead,
and the civil service would be responsible to the Ministers.[84]

Woolf urged that training for self-government should begin at
once. Risks would have to be taken, but 'the only way to learn to do a
thing is to do it'.[85] It did not behove Europeans, who had produced
world wars and a calendar of crimes, to insist on perfection. As for
local and municipal government, this should be

> energetically developed, and it should be used by the administra-
> tion as the most effective method of training Africans for self-
> government and democracy. Where there are local organs of
> government, tribal or otherwise they should be democratised;
> where they do not exist they should be created ... indirect rule
> should not be used as an excuse for maintaining autocratic tribal
> rulers and for preventing the education and development of
> Africans so that they can stand by themselves in the political and
> economic world which Europe is imposing on them.[86]

Labour's policy in opposition was well in line with that adumbrated in the 1947 Local Government Despatch. The ending of indirect rule had been prefigured. Indeed some of the greatest critics of this form of administration were in Labour ranks. Josiah Wedgwood defined it as 'the bolstering up of landlords and aristocratic domination',[87] while Norman Leys believed that indirect rule as prescribed by the anthropologists was an open failure: tribal institutions were as unfit to provide what a modern society needed as King Arthur's Court would be to perform the functions of the London County Council.[88] Another powerful critic, Leonard Barnes, had long argued that indirect rule was not a 'road to the democratic control of Africa by Africans, but a substitute for it'.[89]

The other side of the policy of the Labour Party was economic and social. It was argued in 1921 that the land in Africa should be treated as the property of the native community, definite alienations being prohibited and each family being provided with sufficient land for its support. In East Africa land that had already been alienated would be returned to the black population.[90] Labour reforms were also recommended: compulsory labour should be largely prohibited, while labour contracts should no longer fall within the sanction of criminal law. Above all, the development of effective trade unions should be encouraged.[91] Educational reform was also seen as vital: elementary education should be made accessible for all children, while secondary and higher education should be expanded.[92] Finally, Labour called for immediate economic planning to increase the production of wealth and to ensure its equitable distribution. More money was needed from the Colonial Development and Welfare Fund to break the vicious circle of colonial poverty, and large-scale loans would have to be negotiated. To ensure that wealth remained in Africa, all mining would have to be controlled entirely by the state.[93]

Labour's policy did have its critics. Norman Leys had wanted in 1939 to draw up a programme, including an announcement that the privileges of minorities would be ended by an electoral law which would not allow discrimination on grounds of race or colour, to be put into practice by the next Labour Colonial Secretary.[94] Leys believed that patience was at breaking-point in East Africa. Hopes there would be raised by the presence of a Labour Government, and if these proved unfounded Britain would have to use repression or give way to a particularly brutal and uncontrolled violence.[95] At the 1942 Party Conference Dr Haden Guest was also dissatisfied with

Labour's policy and called for 'A Charter of Freedom for Colonial Peoples'.[96]

Yet Labour had very few external critics. The *Manchester Guardian* called the 1943 pamphlet an 'excellent statement', while Margery Perham found it moderate and well-informed.[97] The Colonial Office had few criticisms – certainly no more than a Liberal or Conservative version would have elicited.[98] It was thought that the Labour Party had moderated their position, now having a firmer grip on realities.[99] Yet it would be truer to say that it was the official position which had changed. This is revealed by the voice from the past within the Office itself: Sir Alison Russell commented with gusto and dissatisfaction on the 1943 pronouncement:

> It is sad and somewhat pathetic to observe the eagerness with which persons who have spent their lives for the benefit of the labouring man in England are prepared to hand over the labouring man in Africa to the Administration of men of his own race. The only hope for the labouring African is the British administration and British justice.

Russell argued that it was ridiculous to talk about self-government 'at the earliest possible date' for the Africans of Kenya, while the idea of making tribal institutions in Tanganyika 'democratic and efficient' was a contradiction in terms.[100]

The new dispensation at the Colonial Office was able to find far more of value in Labour's aims and was also able to co-operate with the other organ of socialist opinion on the colonies, the Fabian Colonial Bureau. This body, set up in 1940 with Rita Hinden as Secretary and Creech Jones as Chairman, was essentially an ameliorationist organization. Hinden has given a very adequate description of its work:

> the Bureau did not begin with any general declaration of policy. It did not set out to tackle 'imperialism' as a world force. Its work was, implicitly, to fight the abuse it knew of in the British Empire, to urge on economic change, and to hasten the day when self-government, or – if desired – independence, could be achieved. ... It had no illusions that any of its aims could be secured by a wave of the hand. To be effective one had to arm oneself with facts, to plunge into statistics and reports, to know exactly what was happening everywhere, to build up contacts with the struggling democratic movements in the Colonies, to research into problems and to fight every issue as it arose.[101]

Hence the Fabian Colonial Bureau often dealt with the *minutiae* of colonial affairs, drafting Parliamentary Questions for willing MPs to represent to the Minister. Though the ultimate aim was self-government, this was not an immediate prospect, and meanwhile the British connection could serve the cause of progress. Hinden recognized that imperial control was not the worst of evils. Would not the native population of South Africa, she asked, have been infinitely better off if Britain had not granted self-government to the settlers after the Boer War?[102] The Bureau's work was essentially a 'struggle for the securing of social justice', of which political freedom was only a part.[103] There can be no doubt about the sincerity of Hinden and the other Labour workers: they were even conscious of a sense of guilt for Britain's misdeeds in the empire. Yet their outlook was fundamentally different from that of the Africans they were trying to help.

The Bureau favoured educated Africans. Where is leadership to come from in the colonies? asked Dr Arthur Lewis in 1946. His answer was unequivocal. 'The only people who can form the colonies into anything worthwhile are the educated Natives, the intelligentsia.'[104] However, despite the fact that there were Africans like J.B. Danquah who considered themselves 'black Fabians',[105] Hinden recognized the difference of aim and approach between British and African. British socialists did not understand what it was like to be dominated by a foreign power. When Fabians said the worker should be free, they meant he should be free from the disabilities from which workers had traditionally suffered. 'When Colonials say they want to be "free", they mean that Britain should clear out.'[106] When Fabians recommended the nationalization of valuable mineral deposits, this simply meant, to the Africans, that the wealth of their country would be owned by an alien government. Perhaps, mused Hinden, Britishers had an inevitably patronising and superior attitude.[107]

The clash between the two outlooks is best illustrated from the dissension in 1946 between Hinden and Kwame Nkrumah. The nationalist called for 'absolute independence', but he failed to impress the Secretary of the FCB:

> It seems to me that colonial peoples today want self-government and independence. British socialists are not so concerned with ideals like independence and self-government, but with the ideal of social justice. When British socialists look at the Eastern

Europe of today, they ask themselves whether independence in itself is a worthwhile aim. We think of the colonies from two points of view – independence and social justice. ... There is a difference of focus and historial approach ...[108]

Nor did Hinden's attempts to construct a specifically 'socialist' policy towards imperialism – which basically concluded with her wish that British socialists should promote socialism within the colonies, while the colonials played their part in the struggle against capitalism[109] – seem particularly relevant to African nationalists.

The response of Africans to the work of the Bureau reveals their different outlook. As time went on, social and economic amelioration was sometimes seen as an attempt to fob them off with trifling concessions to delay the day of freedom. Insofar as the Bureau 'attempted to suggest social or economic policies, or even political policies that did not go the whole way towards immediate, one hundred per cent, self-government, it incurred suspicion and hostility'.[110] A similar response was elicited by Colonial Office initiatives after the war.

The policies of the FCB were voiced explicitly in 1942 with a Colonial Charter. Though the Bureau believed that the essential task was to reform the 'enormous, slow-moving, creaking' machine of colonial administration,[111] it did recommend extensive changes in political organisation and in social and economic development. In a thirteen-point plan for West Africa, the Legislative Council of each of the territories was to be reconstituted, giving full representation to all areas, while a majority of elected members was to be granted. These members were to be trained in executive power. Their election was to be by block vote if necessary, but universal adult suffrage was to be granted after twenty years, at which time the constitution was to be further revised. There were to be African mayors and majorities on all municipal councils. Free and compulsory elementary education was to be introduced within ten years of the ending of the war. Health services were to be built up, mines nationalized, stable prices guaranteed for export crops, agricultural and industrial development promoted. A grant of £100 million was to be given for public works and services, covering the twenty years after the war.[112]

The thirteen-point plan for East and Central Africa contained many identical proposals. On the Legislative Councils, however, African representation, by block vote if necessary, was to equal half the elected Council immediately and to be in a majority in twenty years' time. European immigration for permanent settlement was to cease.[113]

The Bureau decided that the main aim of colonial policy should be the 'well-being of colonial peoples under their own responsible governments'. Wherever possible, responsible self-government should be granted within a fixed period after the end of the war.[114] Asked by the Bureau to express the object of British policy in more concrete terms, Arthur Lewis defined it as the attempt

> to raise the cultural and economic standards of colonial peoples in the least possible time, so that, even those now most backward, may within at most two generations be governing themselves and taking an equal part with other peoples in world affairs.

The Fabian Colonial Bureau may not have pleased all Africans with their constitutional proposals but there is little doubt that, at this time, their ideas were in advance of those held by the Colonial Office. The Bureau wished to see responsible self-government within a generation in West Africa and within two generations in Central and East Africa. These were progressive notions which did not become official policy until after the war. There was, however, nothing easier than to postulate measures like the introduction of free and compulsory education in the African colonies: the important question was whether they could actually be achieved.

After the war the Chairman of the Bureau, Arthur Creech Jones, became a responsible minister. He had occasion to criticize Rita Hinden for having 'no sense of responsibility', in that though she knew what was desirable she did not always appreciate what was practicable.[115] Nevertheless there was after the war an important merging of 'Labour' and 'official' ideas. Between the Bureau and its former Chairman occurred 'one of the most remarkable instances of sustained and creative interchange between a minister and a pressure group which recent British political history is able to provide'.[116]

THE IMPACT OF LABOUR

The years following Labour's victory in 1945 proved to be of crucial value for the colonial empire in Africa. By the time Labour was out of office colonial policy had moved irrevocably towards rapid decolonization. There was now an essentially different situation from the inter-war years. The rationalization of government was now as a progressive welfare agency, and Colonial Governments drew up ten-year development schemes. The attempt to develop the colonies was presented as a humane and moral policy which would also benefit Britain and the world.[117] At the same time there was a definite commitment to self-government, which would have to be underpinned by economic and social change. Hence the development of Africa was necessary for three reasons: to help the British economy, to justify the British presence, and as a preparation for the end of that presence.

External opinion gave most weight to the last requirement; and indeed another major difference from earlier days was the degree of international publicity which the colonies now attracted. Only the old Mandates actually became Trusteeship Territories, but the United Nations Organisation ensured that the progress made in all colonies received wide publicity and scrutiny. In October 1947 the General Assembly adopted a resolution expressing the hope that all colonies would be put under Trusteeship. Sir Alan Burns, who became U.K. representative on the Trusteeship Council in 1947, found the conceptions of its members far too political and ideological for his liking.[118] Creech Jones judged that the new system had 'little new except its defects. ... The atmosphere was one of hostility. To possess Colonies was to acquire opprobrium'.[119] When India became independent in 1947 a new 'champion' of the colonies had reached the international scene – this was one of the reasons the Colonial Office advised against pressing India to join the Commonwealth. It would be easier to withstand the criticisms and demands of India as a foreign state.[120] Hence after the war, as *The Observer* commented, 'the whole Colonial Empire is on trial'.[121]

This was a period in which the moral value of 'imperialism' was non-existent: any recourse to repressive measures against nationalists would have heaped vituperation on Britain's head, while her own weakness militated against the desire to become embroiled in any such entanglement. Yet at the same time this very weakness gave to empire an added value and attraction in some minds. One Conservative spokesman urged that

> We are either a great Imperial Power or we are nothing. Unless we can rely on our overseas countries to help us and to stand by us, we are just a friendless island in the North Sea.[122]

Paradoxically, it was just at the time of an upsurge of imperialist feeling that the empire in Africa began to be dismantled.

The other main change after the war was the presence of the first majority Labour Government. The work of this Government helped to ensure that the increasing value of Africa to Britain in economic terms did not detract from its constitutional development. The majority of the Labour Party was not concerned with the empire; and of those who were interested, most watched the Indian situation with concern, regarding their leaders' actions on this issue as the 'acid test' of their good faith.[123] The Parliamentary Labour Party simply wished the Government to have a progressive policy towards the colonies, and one that was distinct from that pursued hitherto by the Conservatives. Yet apparently, in the years following the war, Labour and Conservative were in substantial agreement. In 1949 *Tribune* published a cartoon depicting Labour catching the Tories bathing and stealing their clothes, entitled 'Empire Policy'.[124]

This seeming identity of approach is explained by several factors: Creech Jones and Oliver Stanley were both moderate men who respected each other; Stanley, who contrived to look like a conservative while acting like a liberal, tempered the excesses of his own right-wing colleagues; and Labour's left-wing was not at this time particularly concerned with the colonies. A lack of concrete divisive issues also allowed the harmony to remain substantially undisturbed.[125] There was, however, some disagreement over the emphasis that should be given to private as opposed to public investment in the colonies.[126] Also of importance was the Conservative claim that, after the constitutional changes of the war-time period, there should be a lull in political development and a concerted effort to foster social and economic progress. As Stanley urged in 1948:

> I believe we are reaching the position today when the greatest danger is the danger of going too fast, when, in fact, we have extended constitutional development considerably beyond the economic and social development on which any sound constitutional advance has to be based.[127]

His Tory colleague Dodds-Parker averred that further fragmentation of the empire had to be ruled out. 'We have seen enough of this breaking-up.'[128] The Government's policy of promoting further political and constitutional changes was therefore against the advice of the Opposition.

There was a good deal of bi-partisan feeling in the House of Commons, especially amongst the leading figures, on the colonial issue. Yet each side did manifest some party feeling, criticizing a stereotyped conception of the opposing Party. In Conservative eyes, Labour supporters 'nurse a few prejudices and call these policy, but they regard the responsibilities of the Colonial Empire as a tiresome hindrance to other things'.[129] At the same time Labour were accused of imagining that 'universal suffrage, elections and self-government with a few trades unions and co-operative wholesale societies thrown in spell immediate peace, prosperity and happiness'.[130] On the other hand Labour professed to believe that the Tories thought of all colonials as 'wogs': indeed some of them believed that 'wogs' started at Calais.[131] The Conservatives, it seemed, considered themselves as superior beings, had no sympathy with the aspirations of the colonies, and were determined to hold on to the empire for Britain's economic gain.

The other main voice from the Opposition in these years, and one that conformed to type, was that of Winston Churchill. His essential complaint was against the changes that were proceeding on the Indian sub-continent. He found appalling the indecent haste with which independence was being conceded. 'Scuttle' was the only word that could be applied to the process.[132] Many, he argued, had defended Britain against her foes, but none could defend her against herself.[133] Though there was no overt reference to the colonies here, it may well be that Churchill's jibes helped create the sense that Britain would soon be pulling out of the empire altogether.

There can be no doubt that the loss of a large part of the empire (in India, Pakistan, and Burma) did affect the remainder, weakening imperial morale and making the loss of the other areas seem much more possible. India had long been regarded as the corner-stone of the whole empire, and in many ways had been the reason for the acquisition of some of the African colonies in the first place. Churchill had argued from about 1930 that 'the loss of India would be final and fatal to us. It could not fail to be part of a process that would reduce us to the scale of a minor power'. Labour politicians certainly drew the moral from the Indian experience that instead of giving 'too little too late' it was better to err on the side of generosity. Having made the fundamental decision in India, no great question of principle was involved in the extension of this policy to West Africa. Yet this is not to say that the Labour Government had any intention of immediate withdrawal from Africa. The conviction in the colonies that Britain's days were numbered may well have been inculcated partly by the criticisms of Churchill.

There can be no doubt that there was a sense of British impermanence in the colonies. Once self-government had been officially conceded as the aim of British rule, it was inevitable that British power and prestige would begin to ebb and that African leaders would become impatient for the day of fulfilment. High hopes had been raised, especially among the African intelligentsia, by Labour's victory in 1945. Azikiwe wrote from Nigeria to congratulate Creech Jones.

> We are looking forward to necessary dash and vigour in the formulation of colonial policy so that worthwhile risks may be taken in order to bring happiness and contentment to the masses. This is a great opportunity for service and we are anxiously hoping that you who are entrusted with this sacred task will carry it out unmindful of the difficulties that lie ahead.[134]

From all part of the empire letters flooded into the offices of the Fabian Colonial Bureau expressing confidence that at last the problems and grievances of the colonies would be dealt with. The Bureau, through its magazine *Empire*, commented that these hopes were exaggerated and that almost inevitably many of them would be unfulfilled.[135]

The elevation of Creech Jones to the office of Secretary of State in October 1946 also led to the anticipation of immediate and revolutionary change. *Empire* sang his praises loudly: there was no other person in British politics who had devoted so much time and energy to colonial problems. As Chairman of the Fabian Colonial Bureau he had shown 'his enthusiasm, his infinite capacity for taking pains, and the quite incredible attention he gave to every facet of the work'.[136] Yet in a world of duality and relativity, the very presence of hope presupposes that of its opposite, despair, of hopes that have proved abortive. Soon the expectations associated with the Labour Government and Creech Jones in particular had evaporated in the minds of many of those who had previously been most confident. Amongst others, Wallace-Johnson had rejoiced at the news that Creech had been appointed to responsible office: yet he judged that once in power the Labour Minister had fallen victim to Colonial Office Bureaucracy, to Colonial Red-tapism, and Colonial Stringpullism. Creech was a convert who had accepted uncompromisingly the creed of Colonial Officialdom.[137]

The career of Creech Jones at the Colonial Office certainly failed to please the more strident voices from the colonies. It was equally regarded as a failure by Clement Attlee. Alternatively, his successor as Secretary of State, James Griffiths, regarded him as 'one of the outstanding Colonial Secretaries of the twentieth century'.[138] His period in office was largely unspectacular and he never hit the headlines. Though his speeches today read well, and are incisive and logical, he had a poor delivery and was never really at home in the House of Commons.[139] When defending the Cabinet's decision to exclude Gerald Brooke from Sarawak, he broke down under questioning. One member of the Opposition remarked that Creech had 'got himself completely tied in knots'.[140] When it was commented that he had turned from poacher to gamekeeper, he reacted with characteristic self-righteousness when satire or pleasantry would have served his cause better:

> I ... want to repudiate the malicious and libellous insinuation ...
> that I have been guilty of making trouble in the Colonies, and that
> in this case I am poacher turned gamekeeper. It is a wicked
> insinuation. I have consistently and for many years fought for
> justice in Colonial administration. ... At least the hon. Gentle-
> man might have the decency to withdraw his lying insinuation.[141]

Order was called in the House and Creech Jones was forced to withdraw the word 'lying', though not its content.

Nevertheless high opinions of Creech were current towards the end of the Government's period in office. There was praise from the Opposition: an embarrassed Creech Jones was told that he had done magnificently and urged to carry on the good work.[142] Nor were congratulations any less profuse from Labour ranks. John Dugdale argued that he had 'accomplished what was little short of a revolution during his tenure of office'.[143] Indeed so high was the standing of Creech Jones among Labour M.P.s towards the end of the 1940s, when Labour Members were congratulating themselves and no doubt hoping to boost their stock for the election, that the Conservative Mr Gammans felt constrained to comment that

> soon they will begin to re-write the history of the Colonial
> Empire, and we shall have the story of how General Creech-
> Wolfe stormed the heights of Abraham, and how Sir Creech-

Raffles founded Singapore, and how Dr. Creech-Livingstone explored darkest Africa.[144]

His reputation was equally high in the Colonial Service. When news of his defeat at Shipley reached Sir Alan Burns, he wrote to say that if 'people in the colonies, and ex-officials like myself, had been able to vote ... you would have been returned by an over-whelming majority'.[145] The Governor of Kenya, Sir Philip Mitchell, a man with whom Creech Jones had difficulties and disagreements over the previous years, wrote before the election to wish him luck:

> Ex Officio, Governors have no politics, but I can assure you with all sincerity that I ask for nothing better than your continuance in office as our Secretary of State. I believe that to be the generally held view, certainly among the Colonial Service but also very largely among the public of all races. The British here are largely conservative by class. ... But that makes it all the more remarkable that there should be among them so widespread a recognition of your great value to the Colonies as Secretary of State ...[146]

A similarly high opinion existed in the Colonial Office. After the 1950 election T.I.K. Lloyd expressed his disappointment at the result. There could be no consolation for the defeat, but, he wrote to Creech Jones, 'you would ... have been sensible of the real regret there is in the Office if you could have heard ... the quite general and genuine sorrow that this should have happened to you'. Reviewing the previous years, Lloyd judged that they had been a time of considerable achievement largely because of

> the deep personal interest which you have taken in the work of every Department in the Office; there can never have been a Secretary of State with a greater capacity to stimulate and encourage his staff by his personal knowledge and interest.[147]

It was this close relationship between the politician and the permanent officials – this union between Labour thinking and that of the most progressive section of officialdom – that produced sweeping changes in African policy.

Creech Jones had at first harboured some suspicions about the colonial bureaucracy. He was especially suspicious of the 'public school prefect' mentality of the Colonial Service and of their innocence of the 'real world'.[148] In particular he was critical of Sir Ralph Furse, who had been Director of Recruitment since 1931, believing him to be prejudiced in favour of the products of public schools.

Creech Jones even went to the lengths of insisting that the final decision on each Colonial Service appointment be reserved to himself. His desk was consequently soon piled high with files and letters to candidates requiring his signature. Furse was also alienated from the other members of the Colonial Office; and Sir George Gater, the Permanent Under-Secretary, with the approval of Creech Jones, attempted to force an assistant upon him in order to diminish his control. Frederick Pedler, a grammar school boy, was appointed as Furse's assistant to redress the balance in recruitment (but soon felt frustrated and resigned).[149] In order to destroy complacency in the Service the Secretary of State also appointed a technical officer as Governor in the Seychelles, Dr Selwyn-Clarke, and appointed Governors from outside the Service: Lord Baldwin to the Leeward Islands and F.C.R. Douglas to Malta in 1948.[150]

Significant changes were also made in the Colonial Office itself. With the retirement of Gater in 1947, Creech Jones appointed not the Deputy Under-Secretary of State, Sir Arthur Dawe, but the more liberal Thomas Lloyd. In the following year Hilton Poynton was promoted to the position of Deputy Under-Secretary of State, advancing over colleagues whose seniority would usually have guaranteed their succession. But perhaps the most significant promotion was that of Andrew Cohen, who was elevated from Assistant Secretary, a position he had held since 1943, first to Superintending Assistant Secretary and then to Assistant Under-Secretary of State in April 1947. In this position he was head of the Africa Division in the Colonial Office.

There was an especially close relationship between Cohen and Creech Jones, as the surviving letters between them illustrate. When the politician became Secretary of State in October 1946, Cohen lost no time in sending his congratulations, making known the 'enormous encouragement' that would be derived from it in the Colonial Office and in Africa.[151] When Creech lost his seat in 1950, Cohen sent condolences and reviewed their years together. He greatly appreciated the kindness and understanding the Minister had shown him:

> I have never enjoyed working for any Minister so much before and the last five years have been happy ones for me in the Office for that reason. They have been years also when one has felt that constructive ideas would be encouraged and I believe that, through your inspiration, a really important change has been

brought about in the general approach to Colonial peoples, away from paternalism to giving them the responsibility and passing the initiative onto them.[152]

The Secretary of State was in turn complimentary about his permanent officials. He had been aware of the danger that the civil servants could dominate their Minister; but most of his officials, though of a different political persuasion, were 'loyal & enthusiastic men & women & extremely fertile in ideas and lines of action. I am much in their debt ...'[153] The hard-working Creech Jones took an interest in all that the Colonial Office did, but it was a practical necessity for him to rely to a large extent on his most trusted civil servants. On becoming Secretary of State he was forced to spend more than half of his time each day on the problem of Palestine,[154] on which issue Creech Jones, and all those who favoured the partition of the state, came up against the opposition of Bevin. Only in May 1948 was the British mandate ended and the state of Israel proclaimed. After the British withdrawal, and after self-government had been granted to Ceylon in 1948, Creech Jones had hoped that there would be more time for him to take stock of the colonial empire. But instead the volume of work, of visitors, troubles, and demands, actually increased.

> One's tables and floor are flooded with files and telegrams and the Secretary of State's rooms are submerged with papers from diligent officials the world over and obstinate officials in Whitehall.[155]

Small wonder, then, that he looked to his civil servants for ideas and initiatives as well as straightforward competence of administration. Yet there can be no doubt that the proposals stemming from the officials accorded well with the ideas that Creech Jones had already espoused as a Labour critic and Chairman of the Fabian Colonial Bureau. The view that, since initiatives came from the civil service and since officials drew up the details, the resulting proposals were the brain-child solely of the Colonial Office permanent officials, is not tenable. The civil service must certainly take some of the responsibility; but it was the Government that was constitutionally responsible for its policy to Parliament. Civil servants flowed with the political tide and put forward suggestions that were likely to appeal to ministers, in this case Creech Jones. And it was only the Secretary of State who could translate proposals into policy.

The immediate impact of Labour on the Colonial Office was not great. George Hall was the first Secretary of State, but ill health and absorption with Palestine meant that Creech Jones had an almost free hand with the colonies. Hall admitted privately that he was 'right out of his depth' and that Palestine was 'a crushing burden'.[156] But Creech Jones was dealing with problems that were familiar to him. His minutes in the Colonial Office files show that the new broom intended to sweep clean. He was adamant against any form of closer political union in East Africa:

> I am not unduly alarmed at the danger of precipitating a major political crisis. It is the European settlers' method in Kenya of asserting their claims to a degree of political dominance and of showing resentment. Whatever privilege they may have had in the past cannot be perpetuated much longer.[157]

He personally specified likely individuals for Colonial Advisory Committees, putting forward Dr Harold Moody and Dr Hastings Banda for the Social Welfare Advisory Committee, though the candidature of the latter was withdrawn when he was judged in the Office to have been guilty of fraud in accepting advances from the Government of Nyasaland and the Church of Scotland to work for both at the same time.[158]

During the war Creech Jones had complained about forced labour in the colonies, and as a responsible minister he tried to end the system of compulsory labour as soon as possible.[159] The special war-time use of forced labour was to be liquidated not later than the end of September 1946; but the African Governors insisted that, in order to combat sleeping sickness, locusts and the like, the use of forced labour could not be completely abolished. Nor did the Governors believe that penal sanctions for breaches of contract could be more than progressively phased out.[160] It was quite obvious that there were no short-cuts to reform in the colonies. Racial discrimination and the colour-bar would not disappear overnight because the new Secretary of State disapproved of them. Creech Jones realized that he could only proceed slowly and with caution. In January 1947 he circulated a memorandum to all colonies on the extent to which legislation in colonial territories discriminated between Europeans and non-Europeans, but not with the hope that all discriminatory legislation could be immediately swept away.[161] The wheels of the colonial empire could not but grind slowly, and there seemed little guarantee that they would grind small.

Labour's performance in office was soon attracting criticism. The FCB journal *Empire* drew attention to this fact:

> The Labour Government has been in power for less than a year, but already the Jeremiahs are lamenting its performance in the colonial field; already we are being told that Labour is a disappointment. These elements come mainly from the colonial peoples, though also from some of the ranks of the Party at home.[162]

The Bureau believed that the sense of disappointment stemmed from over-facile hopes: there was no magic button for the man at the top to press and transform the situation. Nevertheless the Government had so far done nothing that captured the imagination. 'There has been a crying need for some warm, courageous statement of purpose from the Secretary of State ...'

A suitable opportunity for such a declaration came in June 1946 with the annual Estimates Debate. In fact, Hall's speech served only to intensify criticism of the Government – to such a point that a new course in African policy had to be charted. The Secretary of State's definition of policy seemed to show no real advance on that of the Coalition Government:

> I can say without hesitation that it is our policy to develop the Colonies and all their resources so as to enable their peoples speedily and substantially to improve their economic and social conditions, and, as soon as may be practicable, to attain responsible self-government. ... To us the Colonies are a great trust, and their progress to self-government is a goal towards which His Majesty's Government will assist them with all means in their power. They shall go as fast as they show themselves capable of going.[163]

Hall had reiterated that responsible self-government was the goal of colonial policy; but this had become platitudinous by 1946, and meanwhile political development was to be governed by social and economic progress. The Conservatives were in substantial agreement with these views but could not resist making political capital out of the lack of innovation. Sir Peter MacDonald called it a 'sound, Tory Colonial policy' and gave it his blessing 'however embarrassing it may be to the right. hon. Gentleman'.[164] Stanley also noted the similarity with previous declarations of policy, as did Squadron-

Leader Donner.[165] Labour supporters were consequently greatly discouraged. Dr Morgan, among others, 'could not possibly see any hope that the Labour Party was making anything new with regard to Colonial affairs and Colonial development'.[166]

The press was equally certain that it made very little difference to the colonial empire whether the Government of the day was Labour or Conservative. According to the *New Statesman*, Hall's declaration meant that there was 'no real change, and no nearer prospect of any change'.[167] The *News Chronicle* argued that 'There was not much new in Mr. Hall's speech, and there was nothing revolutionary in policy'.[168] To the *Sunday Times* and the *Daily Telegraph* this was cause for rejoicing rather than dismay, since it showed that ministers were above the bigotry of the party zealots in an area where broad continuity of national policy was vital.[169] But when *Empire* reported the fact that Hall's speech, more calculated to induce sleep than enthusiasm, might well have been made by any Conservative Secretary of State, it was with a sense of considerable dissatisfaction and frustration.[170]

In part these criticisms of the Government's declaration stemmed from misunderstanding. It was not widely appreciated how great had been the changes in official policy during the war. Stanley's statement of 1943, that Britain was pledged to guide the colonial peoples along the road to self-government within the framework of the empire, had been presented not as the important innovation that it really was but as traditional policy. In 1946 Hall at least made the definition less ambiguous by adding the word 'responsible' to Stanley's 'self-government'. Creech Jones also added that there were important differences between the two parties 'in tempo and in emphasis, in economic conceptions, and in our attitude to racial relations'.[171]

The fact is, however, that Labour's policy pleased no one, and certainly not Creech Jones. There had been two strands in earlier Labour thinking: the liquidationist and the ameliorationist. In 1946 there was no thought of immediate liquidation, and yet the alternative idea of amelioration – of colonial development and welfare leading to self-government in a vague and unspecified future – seemed insufficient also. Rita Hinden believed the Party had reached an impasse.

> Although we may push ahead with our reforms more zealously than the Tories, and be more consistent in putting native interests

paramount; although this work of amelioration is absolutely essential and we cannot stray from the tasks to which we have set our hand; yet we feel in our bones – and the colonials tell us – that it is not enough. ... Labour will not be successful in its colonial work, or convince anyone that it differs from its predecessors, until it has enunciated its long-run policy towards the Empire in terms which are clear beyond doubt.[172]

Labour's 1946 policy was not in itself inadequate, but it was insufficient in view of the hopes and expectations that had been aroused by the war and the electoral victory of 1945. It had no emotional appeal, though it did cause an emotional backlash.

Fenner Brockway, for long one of the most vocal champions of Indian nationalism, was becoming increasingly concerned with the colonies. In a letter to the *Manchester Guardian* he gave further evidence of the effects of the 1946 Estimates Debate.

During the last few days I have met many representatives of the colonial peoples and I find that their attitude towards the Government and Britain has undergone a radical change. Since the general election the tendency among them has been to give the Labour Government a chance to inaugurate a new relationship. Now the hope of this has gone. It was not merely the small attendance ... it was the policy announced by the Government which has brought about the shock. Mr. Hall ... emphasised the continuity of his policy with that of his Tory predecessor, and even Mr. Creech Jones ... stressed the altruism of Britain towards the colonies rather than the right of the colonies to govern themselves. ... I draw attention to this urgency because we do not want to repeat in the colonies the long, tragic story of India. The colonial peoples do not desire Britain to be good to them. They desire freedom to decide their own good.[173]

Brockway's advice was contained implicitly in the last two sentences of this letter: the initiative should be passed to the colonies, and the transfer of political power should not be dependent upon social and economic advance.

Further advice was forthcoming which at the time seemed more realistic. In the Estimates Debate two Labour M.P.s voiced constructive criticism. Mr Skinnard noted that he could not discern a pattern in constitutional development and called for 'a main plan ... a set of general principles shaped for the guidance of those who have to draw up these constitutions'. He also wished for the whole process and procedure of achieving responsible self-government to be speeded up.[174] David Rees-Williams was another who could not see the pattern of development: he wanted the construction of 'a schedule for the stages on the road to self-government'. Would it be necessary to go from Crown Colony government, through dyarchy, to representative government, or was there a short-cut?[175]

The Fabian Colonial Bureau was also ready with comments and suggestions. First, it has always to be kept in mind that the overall aim was to convert the 'discontented, slum-ridden old Empire ... into a *voluntary* association of free nations'. The problem was how to achieve this before the colonies flared up in angry rebellion. One recommendation to which Hinden gave the utmost importance was that the Colonial Office should give adequate publicity to its actions and should counter the many misrepresentations then current. If possible there should be specific acts to show the abhorrence with which Britain viewed racial discrimination: anti-colour bar legislation, even if of no great legal significance, would be of psychological value, as would the appointment of a black governor. The FCB also urged the Office that

> a large Colonial Conference be called in London at the earliest possible date. Almost all Colonies now have Legislative Councils, and the colonial representatives of this conference might be elected from among the elected members of these Councils. They might be invited to London to discuss problems common to the Colonies as a whole.

The Bureau also put forward economic proposals at the same time: large-scale co-operative methods were recommended to improve African agricultural productivity, while export markets and prices should be guaranteed. New industries ought to be assisted, and mineral companies and other powerful private enterprises should be either nationalized or at least controlled.[176]

The Labour Government reacted positively to the criticisms voiced in mid-1946. Parliamentary Under-Secretary of State Ivor Thomas discussed Rita Hinden's proposals with the civil service and decided there should indeed by a Colonial Conference, though limited geographically to the African territories.[177] He realised the need for 'a new approach to policy in Africa. ... The aim of any conference which is held should therefore be to decide on new principles of policy'. A preliminary conference would be held with

Governors and senior officials before the major meeting, and an official committee was instituted to prepare policy statements in advance. The Labour Government had thus shown itself sensitive to Labour criticism; but the state of international opinion and the internal situation in the colonies were also given as reasons for the new course. Ever since the Second World War began the Colonial Office had had to be responsive to international pressure; and now, with the United Nations, and the Trusteeship Council, and with the championship of the African cause by men like Nehru,[178] British policy had to keep on the right side of progressive opinion and had to be seen to be aiming directly at self-government.

The situation in the colonies – or rather, not the objective situation itself, but the subjective view of it taken by the British – had already led to proposals for local government reform in the Colonial Office; and this sphere had for several years been linked with, and seen as a preparation for, reform of the Legislative Council. The need for a superstructure of central reform was thus simply made more urgent by party and other considerations. The result was a new boldness in African planning. Paradoxically, though the strategy was of undoubted significance for the future of the colonial empire, opposition to the constitutional proposals meant that they were not publicly avowed, and so political capital could not be derived from them. Thus Labour could never express a distinctive policy towards the colonies.

In later years Creech Jones was able to claim that Labour's work was not simply a series of *ad hoc* decisions: 'Labour did not wait on events and stumble and fumble with no over-all conception of principle or purpose or of where it was going.'[179] He may well have been alluding here to the plans drawn up in 1947. Certainly the new policy informed his speech in the 1947 Estimates Debate.

> ... we must adjust ourselves to a much quicker tempo of constitutional development than would have seemed practicable a few years ago. We have to experiment boldly ... and to recognise that while the transfer of power to people not fully trained or with adequate experiences or traditions to exercise it will lead to mistakes being made, it is only through actual experience in the exercise of responsibility that people can acquire a sense of duty and of service. The process may be a painful one, but the alternative of increasing bitterness and tension in the relationship of the people to the Government would be disastrous ...[180]

Yet the Conservative Lennox-Boyd was able to argue that the reason for the paucity of party controversy in the debate was clear: 'It is that the present Government was largely carrying out the Colonial policy of the Coalition Government, which was itself the logical development ... of the Conservative Colonial policy of the past.'[181] In fact, not only had the Coalition Government made important changes in colonial policy, but the 1947 policy of the Labour Government, as we shall see, introduced far-reaching and extensive innovations. It is by no means certain that these developments would have occurred under a Conservative administration: indeed, since even the forward-looking Oliver Stanley was calling for a halt to constitutional advance, it is extremely improbable that they would have done so. Yet this cleavage between the parties was never widely recognized, and Creech Jones was able to derive no political credit for it.

The policy formulated in 1947 was the distinctive contribution of the Colonial Office, officials and ministers, to the transfer of power in Africa. As we shall see, orders could not simply be promulgated for its implementation: instead there had to be concerted attempts to persuade Colonial Governments of its virtue. In part, the significance of the policy lies in its illustration of the views of the British side of the colonial equation. Events in Africa, not under the control of the Colonial Office, were also of great importance. Yet, as always, events and situations have to be interpreted, and the growth of African nationalism was seen in relation to the 1947 policy. Nationalism simply persuaded Britain to implement the proposals at a swifter pace than had been anticipated. Indeed if nationalism affected colonial planning, it can also be argued with justification that nationalism was affected, and boosted, by British reactions to it.

NOTES

1. A. Bullock, *The Life and Times of Ernest Bevin* (London, 1967), vol.2, p.391.
2. A.J.P. Taylor, *English History* (Oxford, 1965), p 599.
3. C.J. Bartlett, *The Long Retreat* (London, 1972), p.9.
4. H. Thomas, *John Strachey* (London, 1973), pp.235-6.
5. *Ibid*. p.238.
6. M. Foot, *Aneurin Bevan* (London, 1973), vol.2, p.18.
7. H. Dalton, *High Tide and After* (London, 1962), p.3.
8. Attlee Papers, Churchill College. Draft Manuscript. 1/17. p.3.
9. *Ibid*. 1/17. p.8.
10. *Ibid*. 1/17. p.15-6.

11. ACJ 7/2 3. Creech Jones to S.N. Evans, 19 Apr. 1954.
12. Attlee, *Empire into Commonwealth* (1961), p.33.
13. Attlee Papers, University College, Oxford. Box 7. Attlee to Salisbury, 21 Dec. 1946.
14. Attlee, *The Labour Party in Perspective* (London, 1937), pp.240-1.
15. Attlee, *Empire into Commonwealth*, p.34.
16. CAB 129/1. CP(45) 144. 'The Future of the Italian Colonies'. 1 Sept. 1945.
17. Unpublished Diaries of Hugh Dalton, 20 Dec. 1946. British Library of Political and Economic Science.
18. *Ibid*. 24 Feb. 1947.
19. *Ibid*. 28 Feb. 1950.
20. *Ibid*. 28 Feb. 1950.
21. *Daily Telegraph*, 12 Jan. 1946. Quoted in Donoghue and Jones, *Morrison* (London, 1973), p.378.
22. ACJ 7/1 43-4. Bevin to Creech Jones, 10 Feb. 1950.
23. F. Williams, *Bevin* (London, 1952), p.209. See also Bullock, *Bevin*, vol.1, p.628.
24. Bullock, *Bevin*, vol.2, p.193.
25. CAB 129/2. CP(45) 162. 'Disposal of the Italian Colonies'. 10 Sept. 1945.
26. Dalton diaries, 5 Oct. 1945.
27. *Ibid*. 15 Oct. 1948.
28. See D.N. Pritt, *The Labour Government* (London, 1963), p.178.
29. Dalton diaries, 30 Oct. 1950. There had been hints in the colonial press (e.g. *Daily Service*, Lagos, 22 June 1949) that Bevan was to replace Creech Jones.
30. Goldsworthy, *Colonial Issues in British Politics*, p.114.
31. C. Cooke, *Cripps* (London, 1957), p.181.
32. Article for the *New York Times*, 23 Aug. 1942. Cripps Papers. Nuffield Coll.
33. Speech to the African Governors' Conference, 12 Nov. 1947. Cripps Papers.
34. E.g. *Parl. Debates* (Commons), vol.443, col.2081. 6 Nov. 1947.
35. For his early Christian involvements see ACJ 2/1 Item 2.
36. I am indebted to Mrs P. Pugh, the present biographer of Creech Jones, for this information.
37. ACJ 2/4 12-16.
38. ACJ 9/5. 'Calling the West Indies'. Broadcast talk. c.1941.
39. P.S. Gupta, *Imperialism and the British Labour Movement* (London, 1975), p.230. Tables 3 and 4.
40. Leonard Woolf Papers, Sussex University Library, D 2 a. Creech Jones to Woolf, 22 Dec. 1943.
41. CO 859/1/1201/8. Creech Jones to MacDonald, 4 Jan. 1939.
42. Woolf Papers, G7. Creech Jones to Woolf, 5 Oct. 1941.
43. J. Huxley, *Memoirs*, p.165.
44. ACJ 7/3 8. MacDonald to Creech Jones, 9 Mar. 1950.
45. *Parl. Debates* (Commons), vol.400, cols.1256-8. 6 June 1944.
46. ACJ 12/2. Text of speech on 'Impressions of West Africa', delivered on 19 July 1944.
47. ACJ 7/3 51. Creech Jones to P. Mitchell, 17 Oct. 1946.
48. *Parl. Debates* (Commons), vol.337, col.151, 14 June 1938; vol.342, col.1257, 7 Dec. 1938; vol.337, col.152, 14 June 1938.
49. ACJ 9/5 59. Article for the 'International Socialist Forum' in 1943.
50. *Parl. Debates* (Commons), vol.400, col.1250, 6 June 1944.
51. ACJ 15/1 221. 'Colonies in the Modern World'. n.d.
52. *Parl. Debates* (Commons), vol.408, cols.541-2. 16 Feb. 1945.
53. *Ibid*. vol.387, col.1091. 16 Mar. 1943.

54. ACJ 12/1 5. Speech to Institute of Pacific Relations, Canada, 1942. Gupta, *Imperialism and the British Labour Movement*, p.335.
55. Swinton Papers. II 5/6. Stanley to Swinton, 24 Apr. 1944.
56. *Parl. Debates* (Commons), vol.391, col.81. 13 July 1943.
57. *Ibid.* vol.332, col.797. 28 Feb. 1938.
58. *Ibid.* vol.361, col.1212. 11 June 1940.
59. *Ibid.* vol.387, col.1091. 16 Mar. 1943.
60. *Ibid.* vol.380, col.2044. 24 June 1942.
61. CO 533/529/38481. Creech Jones to Moyne, 11 Aug. 1941.
62. *Ibid.* Moyne to Creech Jones, 24 Sept. 1941.
63. *Ibid.* Creech Jones to Moyne, 26 Sept. 1941.
64. *Ibid.* Minute by Hall, 30 Oct. 1941.
65. CO 533/524/38032/A. Minute by Dawe, 23 May 1942.
66. *Parl. Debates* (Commons), vol.380, col.2046. 24 June 1942.
67. FCB 18/2 2-4. Creech Jones to Hinden, 18 Dept. 1943.
68. Gupta, *Imperialism and the British Labour Movement*, p.264.
69. ACJ 12/2 74. Text of speech given on 12 June 1944.
70. ACJ 9/3 Item 4. Speech given 25 April 1945.
71. CO 583/286/30453. Creech Jones to Stanley, 17 Apr. 1945.
72. This generalisation is based on study of the letters in ACJ Boxes 7, 8, and 18.
73. ACJ 5/6 Item 1. Wedding invitation for 15 July 1950 at 3.00 p.m.
74. ACJ 34/1 15. Summary of conversation with Creech Jones by H. P. Elliott, June 1944.
75. ACJ 7/3. Creech Jones to P. Mitchell, 17 Oct. 1946.
76. For Labour's colonial policy, see Gupta, *Imperialism and the British Labour Movement* and Goldsworthy, *Colonial Issues in British Politics*, pp.113-22.
77. *Encounter*, July 1958.
78. Monk's House Papers, Sussex Univ. Woolf to G. F. Strachey, 23 Jan. 1905, 4 June 1905, 26 Feb. 1908.
79. Quoted in D.K. Fieldhouse, *The Theory of Capitalist Imperialism* (London, 1967), p.167.
80. *The Colonies*, 1943, p.2, but used in previous publications also.
81. *Parl. Debates* (Commons), vol.380, col.2059. 24 June 1942. Maxton.
82. *Empire in Africa: Labour's Policy*, pp.2-3. *The Colonial Empire*, p.2. *The Colonies*, p.2.
83. *Empire in Africa: Labour's Policy*, p 9.
84. *Fabian Colonial Essays*, 1945. 'The Political Advance of Backward Peoples', p.87.
85. *Ibid.* p.96.
86. *The Colonies*, p.3.
87. *Parl. Debates* (Commons), vol.348, col.527. 7 June 1939.
88. Labour Party Advisory Cttee. No.189, Nov. 1937. 'Politics in the Gold Coast'. Leys.
89. Barnes, *Empire or Democracy?*, p.275.
90. *Empire in Africa: Labour's Policy*, pp.3-8.
91. *The Colonies*, pp.11-12.
92. *Ibid.* pp.12-14.
93. *Ibid.* pp.16-17.
94. Imp. Adv. Cttee. Nos.205, 205A, 205B. June 1938. 'Labour's Colonial Policy'.
95. *Ibid.* No.209. 'Conditions in East Africa'.
96. See Goldsworthy, *Colonial Issues in British Politics*, p.122.
97. *Manchester Guardian*, 3 Apr. 1943. Perham, *Colonial Sequence*, vol.1, p.260.
98. CO 323/1858 Pt.1, 9050/3. Minute by Eastwood, 20 July 1943.

99. *Ibid*. Minute by J.B. Williams, n.d.
100. CO 533/530/38561. Report by Russell, 17 June 1943.
101. Hinden, *Socialists and the Empire* (Fabian Pamphlet, 1946), p.11.
102. *New Fabian Colonial Essays*. 'Socialism and the Colonial World', p.16.
103. *Socialists and the Empire*, p.18.
104. *Domination or Co-operation?*, Oct. 1946, p.6.
105. FCB 81/1 1-2. Danquah to Hinden, 20 May 1941.
106. *Domination or Co-operation?*, p.17.
107. Hinden, *Empire and After* (London, 1949), p.174.
108. FCB 19/3 183. Speech at FCB Conference at Clacton, 12-14 Apr. 1946.
109. FCB 43/1 29-33. 'Socialists and the Colonies', n.d.
110. *Socialists and the Empire*, p.15.
111. *Ibid*. p.23.
112. ACJ 15/1 224-5. Charter for the Colonies. June 1942.
113. ACJ 15/1 225-6.
114. ACJ 15/1. 'A Colonial Charter'. Supplementary Document, June 1942.
115. Interview with Aiden Crawley, (P.P.S. to Creech Jones), 26 July 1977.
116. Goldsworthy, *Colonial Issues in British Politics*, p.144.
117. *Fabian Colonial Essays*. Introduction by Creech Jones, pp.10-11.
118. Alan Burns, *In Defence of Colonies* (London, 1957), p.8.
119. ACJ 15/4 176, 186. 'Colonial or Dependent Territories and the U.N.' n.d.
120. CO 537/1442/25078. Gater to Sir David Monteath. 6 Dec. 1946.
121. *The Observer*, 14 July 1946.
122. *Parl. Debates* (Commons), vol.420, col.145. 4 Mar. 1946. Mr Gammans.
123. K. Martin, *Harold Laski* (London, 1953), p.152.
124. *Daily Worker*, 1 Mar. 1949. Palme Dutt drew attention to the *Tribune* cartoon.
125. Goldsworthy, *Colonial Issues in British Politics*, pp.377-81.
126. *Parl. Debates* (Commons), vol.427, col.394. 23 Oct. 1946.
127. *Ibid*. vol.543, col.691. 8 July 1948.
128. *Ibid*. vol.544, col.598. 22 July 1948.
129. Alport at Conservative 1950 Conference. Quoted in Goldsworthy, *Colonial Issues*, p.168.
130. *Memoirs of Lord Chandos* (London, 1962), p.346.
131. *Parl. Debates* (Commons), vol.469, col.2845. George Wigg.
132. *Ibid*. vol.431, col.2350. 20 Dec. 1946.
133. Pelling, *Winston Churchill* (London, 1974), p.570.
134. ACJ 7/1 28. Azikiwe to Creech Jones, 5 Nov. 1945.
135. *Empire*, vol.8, no.2, Sept.-Oct. 1945.
136. *Ibid*. vol.9, no.6, Nov. 1946.
137. ACJ 2/2 Item 5. 'Exit Creech Jones' by Wallace-Johnson (c.1950).
138. Goldsworthy, *Colonial Issues*, p.22.
139. *Obituaries from The Times*, 1961-70 (1975), p.419.
140. *Parl. Debates* (Commons), vol.431, col.2361. 20 Dec. 1946.
141. *Ibid*. cols.2379-80.
142. *Ibid*. vol.467, cols.1476-9.
143. *Ibid*. vol.477, col.1484. 12 July 1950.
144. *Ibid*. vol.465, col.1654. 27 May 1949.
145. ACJ 18/4 41. Burns to Creech Jones, 26 Feb. 1950.
146. ACJ 8/4 60. Mitchell to Creech Jones, 19 Feb. 1950.
147. ACJ 8/4 56. Lloyd to Creech Jones, 24 Feb. 1950. ACJ 8/4 57. Lloyd to Creech Jones, 2 Mar. 1950.
148. J.M. Lee, *Colonial Development and Good Government*, pp.40, 52.
149. Interview with Sir Frederick Pedler, 25 Apr. 1977.

150. Lee, *Colonial Development and Good Government*, pp.57, 127.
151. ACJ 8/1 1. Cohen to Creech Jones, 7 Oct. 1946.
152. ACJ 8/4 32-3. Cohen to Creech Jones, 12 Mar. 1950.
153. ACJ 4/4 75-6. Creech Jones to unknown historian, n. d.
154. ACJ 8/5 56. Dr Belfield Clark to Mrs Creech Jones, 25 Oct. 1964.
155. ACJ 48/3 23. Speech at Corona Club, 30 June 1948.
156. Interview with Ivor Bulmer-Thomas, 9 Oct. 1976. The Diaries of Sir Philip Mitchell, 9 Aug. 1946. Rhodes House.
157. CO 822/114/46523/2. Minute by Creech Jones, 20 Sept. 1946.
158. CO 859/113/12530. Minute by Creech Jones, 18 Nov. 1946. Minute by Watson, 20 Nov. 1946. Philip Short, *Banda* (London, 1974), p.38n, writes that these allegations 'appear to be untrue'.
159. CO 822/117/46748. Minute by Creech Jones (probably 9 Oct. 1945).
160. CO 859/91/12252. 'Memorandum prepared in the Colonial Office on the subject of (a) Forced Labour, (b) Penal Sanctions, and (c) Minimum Wage Legislation'. 7 May 1946. C. A. Grossmith.
161. CO 323/1879/95051. Creech Jones to Governors, 8 Jan. 1947.
162. *Empire*, vol.9, no.1. May-June 1946.
163. *Parl. Debates* (Commons), vol.425, col.238.
164. *Ibid.* col.298.
165. *Ibid.* cols.266, 334.
166. *Ibid.* col.287.
167. Goldsworthy, *Colonial Issues*, p.15.
168. *News Chronicle*, 10 July 1946.
169. *The Sunday Times*, 14 July 1946. *Daily Telegraph*, 10 July 1946.
170. *Empire*, vol.9, no.3. August 1946.
171. *Parl. Debates* (Commons), vol.425, col.343. 9 July 1946.
172. FCB 43/1 198-204. 'Labour in Difficulties'. Article for the *New Statesman*.
173. *Manchester Guardian*, 20 July 1946.
174. *Parl. Debates* (Commons), vol.425, col.299.
175. *Ibid.* col.325.
176. ACJ 25/1 242-62. Hinden to Creech Jones, 21 Oct. 1946. See also FCB 48/1 3-5: 'Colonial Policy from the Public Relations Point of View'. Memo by FCB, n. d.
177. CO 847/36/47238. Minute by Ivor Thomas, 18 Jan. 1947.
178. See D. Norman (ed.), *Nehru, the first sixty years* (London, 1965), vol.II, p.208. Nehru saw Nkrumah as 'the hope for the salvation of Africa'. (B.M. Pandey, *Nehru*, London, 1976, p.408.)
179. *New Fabian Colonial Essays*, p.37.
180. *Parl. Debates* (Commons), vol.441, cols.266-7. 29 July 1947.
181. *Ibid.* cols.359-60.

6

The Making of African Policy in the Colonial Office, 1945-48: The End of Indirect Rule and the Planning of Local Government

> The rain could turn to gold
> And still your thirst would not be slaked.
>
> *– The Dhammapada*

A crucial feature of the African policy enunciated after the Second World War was the new emphasis given to educated Africans. British power had been conserved by alliance with the chiefs, but so inevitably had traditional African customs. In order to accelerate the pace of change, it was necessary to secure the support and co-operation of the intelligentsia, whose collaboration could only be bought by introducing the kind of political changes they wanted to see. In order to westernize Africa, western political power would have to be relinquished. Thus, while the war had seen the attempt to prevent the divergence of the chiefs and intelligentsia, the years after the war saw the emphasis of British policy shifting clearly to the educated Africans, with the chiefs having the main function simply of preventing the premature transfer of power to an elite whose own progress meant they might be divorced from the needs of their society. This goal was formulated in the Colonial Office in 1947.

The war had seen great changes in the African 'world-view' which help explain the novel importance the educated African assumed for British policy. The effects of the war on the African consciousness were certainly profound and have been compared with those of World War I on India.[1] It has been argued that the war had an essentially liberating effect on the African in that, by exposing him to new experiences and a paradoxical situation, he was able to explode the imperial myth. This is well voiced by Sithole:

> During the war the African came into contact with practically all the peoples of the earth. ... He saw the so-called civilized and peaceful and orderly white people mercilessly butchering one another just as his so-called savage ancestors had done in tribal wars. He saw no difference between so-called primitive and so-called civilized man. In short, he saw through European pretensions that Africans were savages. This discovery ... had a revolutionizing psychological impact on the African. But more than this, World War II taught the African most powerful ideas. During the war the Allied Powers taught their subject peoples ... that it was not right for Germany to dominate other nations. They taught the subject peoples to fight and die for freedom. ... After World War II, the Africans began to direct their British-aroused anti-domination spirit against the Allied Powers who had extensive colonial empires in Africa.[2]

The moral and ideological climate, which was doing so much to weaken the British imperial morale, was boosting the confidence of African nationalists. Indeed the balance between British defensiveness and African assertions seemed to be a quantitative one, at any rate after the war, with a rise on one side leading to a corresponding decline on the other.

There can be no doubt that the Second World War saw a vast escalation of African criticisms and demands. It has been argued that in these years we see the emergence of true as opposed to proto-nationalism.[3] Acceptance of this development is conditioned by our definition of the word 'nationalism', but what is certain is that during the war individuals emerged who wanted not merely a greater part in the government of their lands, and fairer shares for Africans, but actually demanded the right to form the government for themselves. They began to call for the end of British rule. If their lack of truly mass support leads us to avoid the word 'nationalism', this changed after the war.

In the inter-war years African demands were moderate and fell within the colonial frame of reference. For instance, when the National Congress of British West Africa was set up in 1920, meeting first in Accra, the delegates asked that half of the seats in the Legislative Councils be reserved for Africans, who would be elected by the people.[4] In 1925 the President of the Congress, Casely

Hayford, argued that it was the delegates' duty merely to study the constitutions of West Africa, decide how far they fell short of the Congress proposals, and make representations accordingly.[5] Most African organizations at this time were attempting to reform the colonial regimes from within.

During the war, however, African demands escalated and indeed changed in kind when the British were asked to withdraw altogether. The West African Students' Union in London provides a good illustration of this process; and since their demands were well known to the Colonial Office we can clearly see the British reaction. In 1940 WASU called for the adoption of full Dominion Status as the ultimate objective of the West African States. Adult suffrage should be introduced into the Colony areas of the territories, with an extension to the Protectorates in due course; there should be African majorities on the Legislative Councils, and Africans on the Executive Councils; foreign economic combines should be regulated, and compulsory elementary education introduced.[6] In 1941 WASU resolved also that Municipal Councils should have African majorities and an African President. It was also specified that Executive Councils should each contain six Africans. WASU urged that tribal loyalty be gradually submerged by Nigerian national loyalty and that democratic rather than traditional considerations should prevail in the system of native administration. The Union advised

> That every Native Authority be established, remodelled, and developed on the principle of a constitutional monarchy, the effect of which shall be that no Chief ... shall have right or power to decide any 'national' matter except with the express advice and consent of the people over whom he rules ... in future and by gradual process, character, education, ability, and high merits rather than mere customary titles should be the criteria or qualifications for admission to every Native Administration Council ...[7]

In 1942, spurred on by the loss of Malaya and Burma, WASU called for 'INTERNAL SELF-GOVERNMENT NOW, with a DEFINITE GUARANTEE OF COMPLETE SELF-GOVERNMENT WITHIN FIVE YEARS AFTER THE WAR'.[8]

There were, of course, still demands for piecemeal reform within the colonial system, for Africans simply to take a greater share in government. But increasingly the call was for the end of colonial government altogether. In 1942 Wallace-Johnson of Sierra Leone demanded election by universal adult suffrage to the Legislative and Municipal Councils: the latter should have African majorities, while the Legislative should have proportional representation of races, creeds, and colours. He believed that all nominated membership to the Legislative Council should be abolished, since the chiefs were 'space-fillers to dance always to the tune of the Governor'.[9] In 1943 the Sierra Leone branch of the West African Youth League, of which Wallace-Johnson was the organizer, resolved that the time had come when Sierra Leone should have complete self-government.[10]

In Nigeria it was Nnamdi Azikiwe who called for the end of colonial rule. He was determined that the war should see a fundamental shift in British policy. In 1943 he produced a 'Political Blueprint for Nigeria', attacking indirect rule and calling for political autonomy. Azikiwe argued that Britain should have responsibility only for foreign affairs, defence, and currency management. After ten years Nigerians, with British help, should have mastered these functions, and after another five years Nigerians should be completely self-governing.[11] Later in 1943 the Nigerian Youth Movement petitioned the Secretary of State, demanding that African Ministers be appointed from among the members of the Legislative Council as heads of certain departments. In August 1944 the National Council of Nigeria and the Cameroons was formed, with Azikiwe as Secretary, and the real battle against British colonial rule in Nigeria can be said to have started.[12]

We have seen that recognition of African aspirations in West Africa led to reforms under Burns and Bourdillon. The Governor of Nigeria recognized that though the views of educated Africans were crude, ill-informed, and not always disinterested, these were inevitable faults and ones clearly discernible in the columns of Hansard. Bourdillon believed that the educated Africans did have a 'great potential capacity for good', and that whenever possible they should be conciliated.[13] In sharp contrast to his successor, Bourdillon won the respect and even affection of 'Zik'.[14] But on the whole the ambitions of educated Africans were, during the war, treated with great suspicion by the colonial establishment.

It was acknowledged in the Colonial Office that certain aspirations of the educated elite were reasonable. Unlike the chiefs, the intelligentsia favoured economic and social development. In 1941 F.J. Pedler minuted that WASU's resolutions were interesting and sound: 'The part on indirect rule in particular contains a lot of good stuff.'[15] Yet the official attitude was to see WASU, and indeed the educated elite as a whole, as a small unrepresentative minority out of touch with the lives of the bulk of the African population (an argument which would have applied even more forcibly to the British themselves). WASU, it was decided, could not be taken as representing the views of Africans as a whole, nor indeed of educated West Africans, since the Union primarily represented Nigerians, and of these mainly Yoruba interests. Education, it was thought, had not entirely westernized the elite but had simply cut them off from Africa as it existed outside the towns. The calibre of men elected to the Legislative Council was widely believed to be of a low order.[16] Moreover the educated Africans were seen as being selfish and irresponsible: their aim was 'to oust Europeans from as many well-paid jobs as possible'.[17] In 1943 Williams passed the verdict on WASU that it was the focus for 'a good deal of half-baked political activity, some of it mildly mischievous and some of it merely silly, but with a certain amount of shrewdness and good sense intermingled with it'.[18]

The aims of educated Africans were on the whole thought to be wildly exaggerated and were not taken completely seriously. In 1945 the Pan-African Congress, which had first met in 1900, was called in Manchester. The Congress affirmed 'the right of all Colonial peoples to control their own destiny. All Colonies must be free from foreign imperialist control, whether political or economic'. Though the African people were peaceful, the use of violence to achieve their ends was not ruled out.

> We are determined to be free. ... We are unwilling to starve any longer while doing the world's drudgery, in order to support by our poverty and ignorance a false aristocracy and a discredited Imperialism.

The all-star list of later nationalist leaders who attended the Congress is impressive: Nkrumah and Kenyatta were co-secretaries; Banda, Awolowo, H.O. Davies, and Wallace-Johnson were all present. Yet we have Creech Jones's word for it that the Manchester Congress was scarcely noticed in the Colonial Office.[19]

During the war, when the need for security was pre-eminent, paranoia was at a premium in the Colonial Office. The official view was that a harsh line should be taken with all those educated Africans whose views smacked of disloyalty. When Danquah, later to be regarded as a most desirable collaborator, applied in 1941 for the post of Secretary for Native Affairs in the Gold Coast, he was firmly rejected by the Governor, Sir Arnold Hodson. Details of Danquah's police dossier were sent to the Colonial Office: he had fathered an illegitimate child, accumulated bad debts, and was 'pronouncedly anti-white and anti-Government'.[20] In October 1944 he was arrested on suspicion of trying to prevent witnesses giving evidence in a murder trial, but in December he was acquitted.

The more radical Wallace-Johnson had far harsher treatment. In November 1939 he was sentenced to a year's imprisonment for criminal libel. The Colonial Office believed him to be 'an unscrupulous and dangerous agitator'[21] and wished to acquiesce in the Governor's plan of putting him in detention after his release from prison. Despite friction with Labour M.P.s – including Creech Jones, Stafford Cripps, Sorenson, and Adams[22] – Wallace-Johnson was detained again; and, after his second release in March 1942, he was placed under an Order restricting his movements until October 1944.

A tough line was certainly taken with educated Africans who agitated for reform during the war. But after hostilities had ceased, the situation was changed. Economic advance required the active collaboration of the educated elite: their ideas on social and economic advance had already been judged sound, while it was no longer possible to dismiss their constitutional claims as completely unrealistic. Indeed it was soon to be recognized that only rapid political concessions could secure their support. In the post-war period there was also a greater recognition afforded to the rights of Africans: any infringement of these rights would be given wide publicity. And yet there was no immediate deviation in the treatment of educated Africans in all the British colonies, as the example of Azikiwe illustrates.

Sir Arthur Richards was certainly not pursuing a policy of attempting to conciliate the educated elite as collaborators in Nigeria. At the end of 1945 he was writing that the time had come 'to go for Zik'.[23] On June 22 of that year a general strike had started in Nigeria, lasting forty-four days and temporarily paralysing the economic life of the nation. Two of Azikiwe's newspapers, the *West African Pilot* and the *Daily Comet*, had been suppressed during the strike, and Zik complained in Britain that the whole of his group of papers was being victimized and that the freedom of the press was at stake.[24] He even accused the Nigerian Government of planning his assassination.[25] Extensive pressure was put on the Colonial Office to intervene in this matter. Enquiries were made by the Institute of Journalists, the League of Coloured Peoples, and the West African Secretariat, with Wallace-Johnson and Nkrumah threatening to take the issue to the United Nations. Sorenson wrote to Creech Jones asking for the facts to be produced, and so did Harold Laski. Both the British Centre Against Imperialism and the Council on African Affairs voiced the dissatisfaction with 'such petty victimisation'.[26]

In the Colonial Office, Creasy was very much against a policy of appeasement[27] and the Governor was supported, though Creech Jones did point out that the screw should not be turned further on Zik, who would then have a legitimate grievance.[28] On the whole Creech Jones thought that the Governor had been justified in his action;[29] but the Colonial Office had certainly been made aware of pro-African lobbying strength and of the deadlock that could occur when a Colonial Government and African nationalists were locked in confrontation.

Richards took an intransigent attitude towards the nationalists and prepared a memorandum on the National Council of Nigeria and the Cameroons in order to show the selfish aims of that body.[30] Azikiwe was depicted as a quiet and unassuming man to meet, but whose character was coloured by

> what appears to be a bitter hatred of the white man and a conviction that the only aim of the European in Africa has been to exploit the African. He has consistently pursued an editorial policy which is bitterly opposed to Government and has not scrupled to use lies and misrepresentations to further his propaganda campaign.[31]

Richards believed that anti-Government literature was having 'a noted effect' on the clerical and semi-educated classes in Lagos but that the bulk of the country, and particularly the Northern Provinces, was completely unaffected.[32]

The situation in Nigeria was clearly unsatisfactory. The Governor made certain the situation did not get out of hand and was wisely refusing to exaggerate the danger, but much disruption was being caused. The case was similar in Freetown, where Africans refused to register as voters under a new Municipal Ordinance which left control over the Estimates with the Governor.[33] Governor Stevenson decided to avoid all compromise, and by the end of 1946 the Ordinance was still in abeyance. The clash between Africans and the Government had not proved constructive.

Yet despite these examples there was in the years following the end of the war a more willing acceptance in Britain of the importance of working with the educated Africans and winning their confidence. It was recognized that nationalism had grown in Africa: not only had organizations mushroomed in West Africa but in 1944 the Nyasaland Congress had been formed. This body operated within the colonial framework and eschewed subversion, but in 1946 Hastings Banda was arguing that the Congress rather than the Provincial Councils truly represented the African people. Typically he used democratic ideas derived from Britain to appeal to the Colonial Office and the Labour Government. The chiefs, he wrote, 'do not express the feelings, desires and aspirations of the Africans of Nyasaland any more than dukes, earls and barons ... express the feelings, desires and aspirations of the British people in Britain'.[34]

It was soon recognized in Whitehall that only the educated Africans and the enthusiasm aroused by nationalism could lead Africa into the modern world. The task was not to repress nationalism but to direct its energies into constructive channels. The necessity for British policy was to work with the educated elite. 'Colour prejudice in the Colonial civil service', wrote Sir Charles Jeffries in 1945, 'is the one unforgivable sin.'

> We have now to deal with the educated leaders of Colonial communities, whom our policy has produced, and must continue to produce in increasing numbers. The European whose prejudices will not allow him to accept them as colleagues, as social equals, as opposite numbers in negotiations, and even as official superiors may be an admirable person, but should seek another vocation.[35]

The Governor of Uganda, Hathorn Hall, made a similar point. He noted that while officers readily gained the confidence and respect of the peasants, they showed artificiality, constraint, or condescension with educated Africans. The Governor thought it vital that this attitude be changed: 'if we do not win over to our side the educated youth of Uganda and direct their energies and interests into constructive channels Uganda will inevitably follow the dreary political pattern of India'. He felt there was still just enough time to avert this catastrophe.[36]

It was not the case that African nationalism could force concessions from the British. Most of the future African leaders, like Nkrumah, Kenyatta, and Banda, had not yet returned to the continent, and no effective political parties with mass support existed at that time. It was rather that Britain was determined that wholesale repression should not be necessary. Men like Creech Jones believed that colonial rule was justified only insofar as it was dynamic and productive of political, social, and economic change; and therefore it was necessary to work with the educated Africans wherever possible. The chiefs were believed to be wedded to the old dispensation and consequently to be of little use in developing Africa. The Colonial Office after the war placed increasing hope on the educated elite, but at first there were few favourable responses.

We have seen how the Fabian Colonial Bureau's support of development schemes attracted the suspicion of educated Africans. The Colonial Office elicited a similar response. Perhaps notions of capitalist imperialism had become so popular that all economic development was seen as exploitation. Hugh Elliott, seconded to the Colonial Office from Nigeria, summed up:

> At present we are trying to do more for our Colonial peoples than we ever did, but, with isolated exceptions, we are getting less co-operation from them than ever before. We are working ourselves silly on schemes for their benefit, but instead of having the bulk of all the educated colonials pulling with us in teamwork, they are largely pulling against us. The best economy in manpower and the only way to get lasting results is to put all our present efforts into reversing this process.[37]

Creech Jones himself was acutely aware of the need to secure the collaboration and goodwill of the colonial people, and he was also aware that changes in Africa were being resisted by the people who would most benefit from them.

> The immediate problem is how to win their understanding, their co-operation, and their goodwill in regard to the things which are being done. ... We have therefore a big problem here – how to retain goodwill and prevent embitterment. We have also to see to it that we adjust our machinery so that the people can play a more effective part in their own affairs and that at least some of the suspicion and distrust of our motives is removed.[38]

In a period of impatience, when extensive goals were being hampered by economic conditions, such as a lack of consumer goods and a consequent inability to spend all the Colonial Development and Welfare money available, it was imperative to try to secure the co-operation and support of Africans themselves.

THE POLICY OF LOCAL GOVERNMENT

The first response of the Colonial Office to this situation was an attempt to transform African Native Administration into English-style Local Government. By the end of the war it had become official policy that the NAs should be democratized, in the sense that educated Africans should whenever possible be brought onto the Native Authority Councils. Participation by the educated Africans in local administration would provide training in the art of government and would form the basis, by the use of Regional Councils, for an extension of African representation in the Legislative Council. It would also help to generate the efficiency needed for economic advance. Yet, despite the fact that some progress had been made in many areas, the growth of representative councils had not gone far enough to effect any major alteration in the Native Authority system. A more forceful stimulus was thought necessary by some in the Colonial Office; and this accorded well with the ideas expressed during the war by Creech Jones and the Labour Party.

Colonial Office consideration of this issue began in early 1946 with a memorandum by G. B. Cartland. From 1935 to 1945 Cartland had served in the Gold Coast, first as a Cadet and than as a District Commissioner. His experiences there, though with well-organised tribal units, showed him that the NAs 'were not really capable of doing much more than deal with the most primitive administrative problems'. In 1945 he was seconded to the Colonial Office and was encouraged by Cohen to comment on native administration policy.[39] In his 1946 memorandum Cartland argued that indirect rule had been criticized by responsible officers and by educated Africans even before the war, but that now, with the need to pursue economic development actively and with the critical demands of returning African troops, an authoritative statement of policy was needed. No longer would it be sufficient for a Native Authority to be 'a mere expedient to provide the Central Government with cheap local agents to carry out the details of its day to day administration'.

Cartland did not specify the details which a statement of policy should contain, but he did advise that the system of native administration be re-named 'local government' or 'African local government' in order to avoid the term 'native', to distinguish the new phase of policy, and 'to indicate the proper and intended sphere of this form of government'.[40]

With his African experience, Cartland was aware of the fact that the application of the policy would inevitably depend on the local officers. Yet many of them felt frustrated. Their energy and enthusiasm had been sapped during the war by overwork, long tours, difficult conditions, and rising costs. Nor were they being supplied with adequate leadership; and here an authoritative statement of policy could have positive effects.

> Much could be done to improve the existing position by inspiring in the district staff a feeling that there is a conscious overall policy, and that the local application of that policy is being carefully planned by enlightened Provincial Commissioners, ready to give the district staff an enthusiastic and sympathetic lead.

Cartland also called for an official journal and reiterated the plea of Lord Hailey that District Officers should be given extra assistance to enable them to cut down on the burden of routine work. He also advised the calling of regular conferences between people in the same work in order to pool experience and infuse new spirit.

Cartland's idea, that the morale of the Colonial Service could be boosted not only by material improvements but also by a greater precision in policy, was supported by several memoranda on the Service which were circulating in the Office in 1946.[41] It was argued that junior members of the Colonial Service were frustrated because they were ill-informed of the Colonial Government's aims. Instead they should be fully briefed. A parallel was drawn with Bomber Command during the war, when each crew was told how its effort fitted into the overall strategic picture.[42] The need to revive a flagging *esprit de corps* was certainly one factor in the decision to issue a statement of policy. Yet there was a considerable rift among the civil servants on the future of native administration and on the practicability of issuing a generalized statement.

Cohen was very pleased with Cartland's memorandum and showed a copy to Creech Jones.[43] He believed that local government was an issue on which the Colonial Office could take the initiative and make a useful contribution to progress in the colonies.[44] Having had little experience of Africa himself, he sought the comments of those in the Office with recent service in Africa. Opinion was very divided indeed.

Mr Footman[45] agreed on the new designation of 'local government' but argued that the central government should ultimately be composed of a federation of NAs or local governments. Mr P. Wilkins[46] thought that there should be no attempt to define the ultimate goal of policy: the defects of the NAs were due to lack of education and supervision rather than to any fault in the system itself. C. Y. Carstairs[47] believed that no simple aim could be devised for British policy: goals could not be predetermined but would change as experimentation proceeded. O. S. Wallace[48] thought it inevitable that the councils of the NAs would become more democratic but saw no need for an official statement of policy on those lines.

M. H. Varvill[49] was in broad agreement with Cartland but did not believe the Colonial Office could produce a statement likely to evoke the enthusiasm of the Service. In order to embrace the differing circumstances in Africa it would be 'pretty woolly'. 'It will be difficult enough to cover Nigeria only; it would be virtually impossible to frame a definition of practical value which would cover all Africa.' Any re-statement of aim ought therefore, in Varvill's opinion, to be decided separately by the Colonial Governments. C. Rankin[50] was also in sympathy with Cartland but thought there would be variations in policy to meet tribal differences.

Wholeheartedly in support of Cartland's views was A. H. Dutton.[50] He had served in Nigeria before the war and came back to England in 1939 'with the feeling that NAs, formed as they were, created a definite barrier to progress and an incitement to discontent among educated Africans'. He wished the Authorities to be reformed so as to represent all classes of Africans. J. B. Williams[52] also agreed that the NAs had to be transformed from 'an interesting historical relic' into proper organs of local government. Lastly, Frederick Pedler[53] threw his weight in favour of a declaration. He wished to see not piecemeal but radical changes. 'Lugard's ideas ... have played themselves out. Decades have gone by, and the present age demands something more up to date.' A re-definition of policy should certainly proceed. He called for the breaking-up of units that were too big and the amalgamation of NAs that were too small.

They should have local government functions and should be made as democratic as possible.

A similar variety of viewpoints is discernible from other sources. It was reported in Nyasaland that the chief and his council had 'failed to inspire the people to interest, let alone effort'. Young men returning from the war would want to make their voices heard, but there was no provision for this in the traditional system.[54] An Officer in Tanganyika reported on the illiteracy, superstition, and generally primitive state of the majority of chiefs there and suggested they be replaced by literate Africans.[55] On the other hand, Hugh Thomas, the Secretary for Native Affairs in the Gold Coast, saw no irreconcilable rift between chiefs and educated Africans. He argued that the chief was still in touch with his people and felt the pulse of local opinion, while the educated men were increasingly fitting themselves into the Native Authorities. Time alone, according to Thomas, would show whether the Africans would prefer the educated men or the old type of chief: at present they seemed to have a preference for the educated chief.[56]

The views of the Fabian Colonial Bureau on the future of indirect rule were being clarified at this time. A paper on the subject was prepared by the Bureau at the end of 1946 and presented to the Colonial Sub-Group of the Parliamentary Labour Party. It was first written by George Houston, who pointed out that though the middle classes had slightly modified the tribal authorities, the principle of indirect rule was still intact. Yet in his opinion any political system based on tribal relationships was doomed: instead, local elected councils should perform the duties of local government in rural areas. He wished to see Regional Councils elected on the widest possible franchise, but he did not think that these bodies should elect African members of the Legislative Council. Instead these representatives at the centre should also be elected on as wide a franchise as possible.[57] Houston's views were in fact rejected by the Bureau as being too extreme and a paper written by Rita Hinden was presented to the Labour M.P.s. Hinden was concerned that no dogmatic views should be reached on the subject since the Group wished to decide policy itself, and she made only tentative recommendations. She argued that 'wherever possible, the Native Councils must include educated Africans'. But her main concern was with the pyramid of councils, tapering off at the Legislative Council. There were doubts whether the NAs would be effective electoral colleges, while the educated Africans tended to dislike this 'hybrid development', but Hinden professed to see no practical alternative.[58]

The recommendations of the Bureau were lacking in novelty and precision, while the Fabians' major work on the subject was not published until 1950. It was argued in this later work that the chief would become

> increasingly a figurehead, an ex-officio member of councils, or an ex-officio magistrate. We have not far to go to find a parallel in the Custos Rotulorum in Jamaica, or our own Lord Lieutenant.[59]

Yet these views were not in advance of official policy, and we can clearly see that the initiative for the local government policy enunciated in 1947 came from the Colonial Office. Whitehall was no longer lagging behind the progressives on the Left.

Throughout the formulation of the new policy, the Colonial Office was anxious to obtain the opinions of the Colonial Service. Cohen not only obtained the views of those in the Office with recent African experience but also consulted officers on leave in London.[60] There can be no doubt that the Office genuinely desired the valuable advice that the Service had to offer. Yet this was not the only reason for the association of Colonial Governments with the new policy. Indeed, it seems clear that, on the whole, Cohen and other officials, in concert with Creech Jones and the Labour Party, were already certain of the broad changes they wished to introduce. Nevertheless, they could not simply announce their policy and expect it to be loyally executed in Africa. Instead they had to convince the Colonial Service of the desirability of change.

The relationship between Whitehall and the colonies was a complex one. The constitutional theory of the matter was that the Secretary of State was responsible for all that happened in the empire and had the power to dismiss any member of the bureaucracy. But in practice officers overseas enjoyed a good deal of independence. We have seen how Hodson in the Gold Coast was able to defy promptings from Whitehall on the issue of indirect rule, while the first order of Sir Arthur Richards, on becoming Governor of Jamaica in 1938, was that there should be no communication with Whitehall except that necessitated by law.[61] The traditional rivalry and suspicion between the Colonial Office and the Colonial Service exacerbated these divergent tendencies. One officer from Nigeria has written that there was a deep-rooted prejudice against the Colonial Office and all its works in the minds of the majority of officers serving overseas, particularly those serving in the provinces: too much paper and not enough realism, and too many instances of officers home on leave being patronized by men many years younger than themselves who had never been near the countries with whose affairs they dealt.[62]

Official policy had therefore to be made to appeal to the men who were to carry it out. This issue was complicated further after the war by the increasing association of Africans with the Legislative Councils of the African colonies, which in some cases amounted to unofficial majorities. As the Under-Secretary of State told the Commons in 1948:

We have to recognise the fact that the Colonial Office are very often not in a position to insist upon many things. We can suggest to many of the Colonial Governments, advise them and help them, but in many instances they have the final word and if they do not take our help and advice, there is very little further that we can do. Once it is realised, that it is not really possible to have a tight, Whitehall control and, at the same time, have an ever-increasing devolution in the Colonies, then we can see exactly where we stand.[63]

Hence the Colonial Office acted with extreme circumspection in the negotiations leading to the Local Government Despatch. Cohen put forward the view that post-war conditions called for a reconsideration of native administration; but he hastened to assure the Colonial Governments that they themselves would provide the answers.

I hope that you will not think that I am asking you to take part in the production of a blue-print of native administration, or that we are trying to put ourselves in a position to bring to birth a declaration of policy composed of platitudes. The objective which we have in mind is much less ambitious and I hope a good deal more practical. We believe that there are a number of problems to be tackled, all affecting native administration and all closely related with each other, and we are inclined to think that it would help us and Colonial Governments, and above all officers in the field, if a statement of these problems could be produced with some indication of the general method of approach in dealing with them ...[64]

This studied moderation was designed to calm the fears and secure the support of the Colonial Governments. Yet the response from the colonies was not wholly favourable. Burns doubted whether anything other than 'vague and ill-defined platitudes' could be produced.[65] The statement that did emerge early the following year pleased few of the African Governors.

The Local Government Despatch of 25 February, 1947, marks the abandonment by the Colonial Office of the view that Britain could rule with effectiveness in Africa through the traditional tribal institutions. Indirect rule was repudiated, and in its place was to be a form of government comparable to the English model. The first draft of the Despatch expressed this clearly, though in a palatable form:

> Hitherto African Administration has commonly been described by the term 'Indirect Rule', a phrase which has frequently been misunderstood and has, in any case, served its purpose, since it is now axiomatic that the administration of Africa should be carried out through their own institutions. I suggest that the term African local government would be more appropriate to the modern conception of policy, and I propose in future to make use of that term.

These remarks, penned by Cohen, were left out of the final version of the Despatch: they themselves, by their broad definition of indirect rule and by their lack of reference to the importance of the traditional chiefs in the system, had veiled the significance of the new emphasis in British policy, and this purpose was also served by the absence of the above passage. Nevertheless a change in nomenclature did take place. 'Local government' was consistently preferred to both 'indirect rule' and 'native administration'. This was indicative of the change in policy that the Office wished to be effected in Africa.

Whitehall policy-makers had to walk a tightrope, mindful of their own wishes and what were believed to be the susceptibilities of the Colonial Governments. Hence any new initiative on policy had to be made to appear traditional, while there could be no appearance of any desire to dictate to the men on the spot. The Local Government Despatch may well be seen as a brilliant example of the 'politics of administration', of the presentation of what were considered by many to be unwelcome and unwarranted reforms in the guise of moderate and yet essential proposals. Throughout the Despatch the

Secretary of State was careful to insist that he was not introducing any new conceptions into African administration but merely clarifying traditional ones. He was at pains to point out that he had no intention of 'centralising the machinery for the formation of policy in each Territory': indeed there was to be the maximum degree of decentralization for all forms of African government. Yet, Creech Jones insisted, decentralization could only exist within a 'framework of known and accepted general policy', which would be applied differently in different areas.[66]

Andrew Cohen regarded local government as 'so near being the key to all future developments in our African territories', and he added, in a letter to Rita Hinden, that it was to him 'the most fascinating of all the subjects with which we have to deal'.[67] The vital importance of this form of administration was stated clearly in the Despatch from Creech Jones to the African Governors:

> I believe that the key to success lies in the development of an efficient and democratic system of local government. I wish to emphasise the words efficient, democratic and local. I do so ... because they seem to me to contain the kernel of the whole matter; local because the system of government must be close to the common people and their problems, efficient because it must be capable of managing the local services in a way which will help to raise the standard of living, and democratic because it must not only find a place for the growing class of educated men, but at the same time command the respect and support of the mass of the people.

These broad aims were to be the same for all the African colonies. They were principles to which lip-service had been paid for a number of years, and hence Creech Jones could claim that there was nothing new in the policy he was putting forward. Yet the idea that NAs should be confined to the sphere of local government, that their efficiency should if possible be increased and that educated Africans should be associated with them, had scarcely received universal assent and had not comprised a practicable policy. In fact the Colonial Office was suggesting more than a new emphasis and was beginning an attempt to translate ideals into realities. Yet this was not fully revealed in the Despatch: only the broad aims were discussed, and only in outline. The means were not enunciated but would be discussed with administrative officers at a forthcoming Summer School in Cambridge. The policy was revealed in stages in order not to alienate the African Governors but rather to win them over.

Reasons were, however, given in the Despatch to support the notion of the evolution of a democratic and efficient form of local government. The success of development and welfare schemes would depend on the co-operation that could be elicited from the people by the leadership of the local authorities. Local government also had an important part to play in the political development of each territory. Africans were everywhere playing an increasingly important part in the central organs of government, and their political progress would inevitably be rapid in some areas. Since almost all of these Africans at the centre would have to be drawn from the educated minority, there was the danger that they would become absorbed in politics and out of touch with the people themselves. Hence the development of local government was necessary to train the people in the arts of popular control and safeguard against the premature transfer of power to a small unrepresentative group. The pyramid of councils, from local to Regional and then to Legislative, which was endorsed in the Despatch, would also serve this purpose. The new policy, presented in this way, could appeal to some colonial officials as a conservative measure designed to slow down the rate of political advance. *In toto*:

> Local government must at once provide the people with their political education and the channel for the expression of their opinions. An efficient and democratic system of local government is in fact essential to the healthy political development of the African Territories; it is the foundation on which their political progress must be built.

No details of proposed constitutional changes were given in this Despatch, but we shall see more clearly in the next chapter of this book the complementary nature of local government reform and political evolution at the centre. Cohen wrote to the Fabian Colonial Bureau that local government reform was being concerted 'with a conscious and deliberate policy aimed at self-government as rapidly as possible'.[68]

Having dealt with these major principles, and tried to placate possible opposition, Creech Jones went on in the Despatch to enumerate reforms which would facilitate the introduction of local government in Africa and appeal to the political officers. He wished to see systematic arrangements for the compilation and exchange of . information, including special studies of particular branches of local government. The valuable experience gained in certain areas should be recorded and transmitted, perhaps by a journal. To monitor the progress of local government and to encourage the flow of information, the Secretary of State called for an African Affairs branch to be established in each territory, while in the Colonial Office a reorganization of the Africa Division would be necessary. Creech Jones was particularly concerned that the District Staff in Africa should be made fully aware of Government policy and should be relieved of the mass of routine work that diverted them from their true task of local government supervision. Every district office was to be provided wherever possible with a competent office manager and the requisite mechanical aids. The District Staff would then have scope to show energy and initiative within the general framework of policy. The importance the Colonial Office gave to these officers – and indeed to the local government policy – is shown by the fact that the Despatch was to be made available, confidentially, to all the administrative officers.

The process of transforming native administration into local government had begun. Generalizations, perhaps even platitudes, had been ventilated; but that was only the beginning. The Colonial Office was determined that detailed proposals should be worked out and that the district officers should be left in no doubt about the tasks they should be pursuing. The next stage in the formulation of policy came with the Summer School held at Queens' College, Cambridge, in August 1947.[69] This was attended mainly by administrative officers, with an average of six from each British African colony, of varying degress of seniority. An opportunity was thus provided for a pooling of experience and for officers to meet each other; but the main aim of the Summer School was to clarify the local government policy, under the close supervision of the Colonial Office and without the authoritative voice of the Governors. Only one Governor, Sir Philip Mitchell, attended: he was to be an outspoken critic of much of the Office's new strategy, but he supported the local government policy because, as we have seen, it could be interpreted as a check on political advance:

> ... democracy is not a patent medicine. Democratic institutions improperly understood and badly handled may become perverted. Time is needed to inculcate a sense of the responsibility

and obligations involved, and for this purpose the devices of local government offer the best approach.[70]

Other guest speakers also praised the idea of developing local government in Africa. Carol Johnson, Secretary of the Parliamentary Labour Party and an Alderman of the Lambeth Borough Council, as well as a close friend of Creech Jones, argued that the principles of English local government were clearly applicable to colonial conditions. Labour opinion had long given much emphasis to the utility of local government as a training-ground in political responsibility: after all, a substantial proportion of the House of Commons, including fifty-six per cent of Labour M.P.s, had graduated from local authorities.[71] All the speakers at the Summer School were in fact carefully chosen. Of the administrative officers who spoke, one was from the Eastern Region of Nigeria, where indirect rule had, in Crowder's words, been a 'disastrous failure'[72]; another was from Uganda, where he had experience of the hierarchy of democratically elected councils in the Eastern Province; and a third spoke of the Provincial Councils in the Gold Coast. The School was being carefully stage-managed by its Chairman, Andrew Cohen.

The officers at Queens' were divided into six groups, each of which attempted to elaborate one aspect of local government policy. The groups were concerned with the functions and finance of local government bodies, with land usage, urban government, district staffs, and race relations. But the most important discussion was that chaired by Cohen on the political aspects of local government. Cohen wrote the preparatory paper which this group considered and supervised the production of the Report which they finally issued.

In his paper, Cohen expanded the ideas contained in the Local Government Despatch, drawing out their logical implications but at the same time attempting to assuage fears of sudden innovation.[73] He noted that the development of local government machinery in rural Africa would inevitably affect the position of the chief, the bulwark of the old dispensation. Cohen saw a clear dichotomy in the role of the tribal chief: his traditional function could only be modified by the Africans themselves, and in this the Government could hardly interfere; but his political role in relation to the Government, for which there were no inherent rights, was another matter. Cohen argued that in the short term the chief would maintain his political duties:

> Taking a longer view, however, a time may come when ... chiefs
> will no longer be in a position to make an effective contribution to
> the development of local government. It is suggested that the
> evolution of native administration must be conceived in the light
> of this possibility.

Though expressing it in these moderate terms, Cohen was indicating
that the star of the chiefs was on the wane and that the councils
should be gradually developed by the increasing introduction of
educated Africans. Ultimately, he argued, the council should
become the directing authority, the chiefs by implication fulfilling
merely their traditional magico-religious role.

The proper representation of the educated classes could be facili-
tated in the first instance by nomination by the District Officer, the
chiefs, or the various interests concerned, but later some form of
election would have to be used. Cohen reiterated the value of
indirect election to the Legislative Council through a pyramid of
councils, with the local authorities forming the base. The direct
election of educated Africans was already established in some areas,
and so election by indirect means would be needed as a counterbalance. But only if the selection of representatives at the lowest
level were democratic would the superstructure likewise be democratic. Cohen therefore urged that the gradual introduction of election into local government should be the aim of policy.

Having foreshadowed the substitution of educated Africans for
chiefs as collaborators, Cohen also advised that where no tribal
authorities existed, councils on the Kenya model would have to be
introduced and that committees be set up, either within or outside
the authorities themselves, to deal with particular subjects, such as
finance, education, and health. He also called for the size of the
areas controlled by local authorities to be made more convenient,
and for increased training facilities to be made available for members of local government bodies and their staff.

The final Report that emerged from Cohen's group endorsed
most of his proposals. It was agreed that local bodies should be made
representative of all the genuine residents of an area, rather than
merely of the principal tribe. Yet it was stressed that in all areas the
traditional elements still had an important part to play. Ultimately
the appointment of representatives would be through election,
though this did not necessarily mean the ballot-box. Assent was also

given to the notion of indirect election to all but the lowest grades of councils. It was concluded that:

> We regard it as urgent that African local Authorities should be stimulated to introduce as great a measure as possible of democratic representation into their system, while retaining their good traditional elements. We recommend that Governments should consider issuing a directive instructing all officers concerned that this objective is to be maintained in the forefront of policy.[74]

Cohen could be well pleased with the Summer School. One of its results was a legacy of goodwill; and one of the officers attending at Cambridge later commented that the School

> was to mark the beginning of a new era. From now on the relationships between us and our opposite numbers in the Colonial Office were to undergo an almost complete transformation. Their visits to us would soon become more frequent and more welcome, for now they would often come as personal friends.[75]

Cohen could also rest assured that his ideas had been substantially accepted. One hurdle had been very successfully negotiated. Most important of all, the new local government policy had been clearly stated. It was given its most unambiguous expression in the summary of the Summer School conclusions written by Cohen for the African Governors' Conference in November 1947. The aim of the new policy was stated as being

> to build up institutions of local government fully representative of all the people of the area through the development of the council system, and by the increasing introduction of the more progressive elements in the population, the ultimate aim being that the council should become the directing local authority and the organ through which the people make their wishes felt.

The representatives on the council were to be chosen by the people, with some form of election being used wherever possible, and were to be accountable to the people 'in the sense that they are removable by them'. The general model for the new policy was to be the English local authority: African local government was to 'incorporate the essence if not the precise forms of English Local Government'. These changes were to be actively 'stimulated' by the Colonial Governments.[76]

The post-war policy of African local government had now

received its most concise and clear exposition, and a new chapter in the history of Britain's policy towards her African dependencies had been reached. But how novel were these local government ideas? It was part of the Colonial Office's propaganda to emphasize their traditional links, since only in this way could a conservative cadre of colonial officials be induced to embrace them. Creech Jones argued that the new policy had not

> just been 'discovered'; it has developed over a period of years as the need for development in all fields and the growth of African aspirations has been studied and appreciated. It is the result of a natural organic growth which has quickened in pace as it developed and it owes much to the many far-sighted administrators who guided it through the various stages of native administration to present conceptions.[77]

A convincing case was made out that the 1947 proposals introduced no 'revolutionary break with the past'.[78] Local government was 'both logically and historically' simply another step forward from the doctrine of indirect rule. Lugard's relatively static conception of indirect rule, with its emphasis on the preservation of indigenous institutions, and particularly on the Emirs and chiefs, had been reorientated by Cameron and his progressive principles of indirect administration. Cameron had been less interested in preservation and more in the development of democratic forms, less in upholding law and order than in economic and social welfare; he had given less emphasis to the chiefs and more to their councils, stressing that acceptability and traditional right were both important in assessing the composition of a Native Authority. Local government was presented as the 'third stage' in this progression. Both indirect rule and indirect administration had been working towards forms and standards of 'civilized government': and local government was doing exactly this, though now the content of this laudable aim was more precisely defined. Continuity with past policy was accentuated.

There is undoubted force in these arguments. The local government policy built on the foundations it inherited and thereby constructed a logical concatenation, of which previous policies formed an integral part. The past could well be seen in the light of later developments:[79] but the very effort of the Colonial Office to emphasize the roots of its policy is indicative of its novelty. Only proposals that contained radical recommendations would have to be presented in so conservative a light. The Office was protesting too much. The propaganda was true insofar as it went, but it told only one side of the story: previous ideas did lead to the 1947 policy, but they could well have taken a different direction.

The work of Lugard and Cameron did provide the framework or skeleton on which local government was to be grafted. Their work served to integrate indigenous traditional authorities into the central state machinery as local government agencies, though they were not called by this name and for a time many thought these agencies would eventually federate to form a central government. Vestiges of 'inherent right' were effectively eradicated from the authorities, while Cameron did begin the process of democratizing the NA councils. Yet there was still a very long way to go before the emergence of African local government modelled on English lines. An essential figure in this development was, as we have seen, Lord Hailey, whose report of 1940-42 forms a bridge between the pre-war and post-war policies. Hailey effectively destroyed indirect rule as a system.

The new local government policy obviously owed a great deal to Hailey, and yet it differed in important ways from his recommendations. Hailey's idea of a pyramid of councils to secure the indirect election of African representatives certainly found an important place in the new policy; but he had proposed this system because of his uncertainty that the Westminster model would ever be suitable for Africa and to enable an alternative to the use of the Legislative Councils to evolve. But the new policy implied that the British model would be adopted: at some future date there was to be direct election to the intermediate councils and eventually to the central legislature. Hailey had also called for Government to associate the educated elite with the NA councils, but he had not advocated that the chief be superseded by his council as the controlling authority. Nor did he formally advocate the election of councillors or their accountability, as the new policy proposed. Hailey in fact had not totally abandoned the idea that natural, organic growth would bring about the desired changes in native administration, whereas in 1947 the idea of spontaneous evolution was jettisoned completely, changes having to be actively 'stimulated'. The new local government ideas foretold the decline of chiefly power: there would have to be a transition period in which the chiefs and the educated Africans devised some sort of *modus vivendi*, but the future was thought to lie with the latter. Hailey had been far from definite on this point. His whole attitude had been cautious and pragmatic and he made no attempt to forecast the future accurately.

It may be argued that the Colonial Office was simply making emphatic and authoritative what Hailey had only implied. There is some justification for this idea, though at the same time we must recognize the importance of the new emphasis that emerged. For Hailey had been so 'judgematic' that his report could have been used to support a very different set of proposals. The fact is that the local government policy, though building on some of Hailey's recommendations, went against the whole ethos of his work. Hailey had been aware of the 'infinite variety of forms' that native administration took in Africa and of the impossibility of imposing any uniform system upon them. He believed that there would have to be a considerable diversity in African administration and that the really crucial requirement of local authorities was not that they conformed to any theoretical pattern but that they did their work effectively. Hailey implied that there should be no attempt to impose any uniform system of local administration on Africa, and certainly not the British model. The future would, in his opinion, be decided by Africans themselves and Britain should therefore be flexible in her policies and not attempt the impossible by trying to force African local government into a preconceived mould.

It is not surprising, therefore, that Hailey refused to give his support to the new local government policy, despite Colonial Office prompting for him to do so. He was troubled that 'local government' could become a slogan, like indirect rule, which would merely serve to conceal the reality of the African situation. Far more important than the theory and method adopted was whether native administration satisfied the needs of the African for the present and foreseeable future.[80] He also doubted that local government could be effective in very backward areas, unless it was in reality carried out by the District Commissioner.[81]

By his original *African Survey* and his later report, Hailey had done much to encourage a pan-African approach to the administration of the continent, but he had no wish for a uniform pan-African policy towards the British territories. He agreed that there should be universal aims, so long as these were general enough, but wished to see a variety of methods commensurate with the diversity of African conditions. Yet the local government policy was to apply without exception to all the British colonies. Never before had a single policy been laid down for all the territories. Though the philosophy of indirect rule had permeated official attitudes to native administration, administrative policy had been prepared by each Colonial Government separately, and indirect rule had existed side by side with the East African conciliar system. Now the two systems were fused and a uniform policy emerged for the first time. This pan-African approach heralded a new technique for the formation of policy. The Colonial Office, wishing to escape from the impotence that had characterized its role in the inter-war years, was now taking the initiative more often. A series of conferences took the place of discussion by despatch with the Governors. This new method had the result of emphasizing the common ground between the African territories and of minimizing the differences, since the policy of each Government was assimilated to that of the rest. Such conferences could usually be effectively 'managed' by skilful civil servants, while disputes and disagreements could be glossed over in the official reports that were subsequently issued.

Hailey's pragmatic and cautious approach, with its attitude that there was enough time to experiment and put off final decisions, was overruled after the war and replaced by a uniform policy – what Hailey considered another system. The Colonial Office did not believe that there would be sufficient leisure to watch events and then judiciously decide Britain's attitude. Instead, with no time to lose, it was necessary to act on *a priori* conceptions. The result was a system that exceeded Lord Lugard's in that it was to apply to the whole of British Africa, but which in many ways was an inverted mirror image of indirect rule.

Both indirect rule and local government policy provided a clear and definite theory for native administration whose practical application proved complicated and imprecise. While Lugard centred his policy on the chief as the native authority and dismissed the educated elite, Cohen and Creech Jones emphasized that it would be the council, and the educated African members, who would control the local authority, while the power of the chiefs would steadily decline. Lugard saw his policy as a necessary shield to prevent premature over-exposure of Africans to Western civilization: local government was to introduce this civilization as quickly as possible. A defensive policy gave way to a positive one. Lugard had recommended the motto 'Festina lente' to the Colonial Office and had argued that the real danger with 'native races' was that of going too fast.[82] At the 1948 Africa Conference Andrew Cohen provided a sharply contrasting viewpoint:

> I think one element of the new policy is that it is now generally recognised that one can no longer accept fully the proposition that the development of local government must take place at the pace which the people of the area are prepared to accept. ... I think that modern thought is coming to the conclusion that radical changes may have to be made, even in areas where the extreme conservatism of the majority of the people make changes extremely difficult to carry through. ... It is sometimes said that the risk lies in going too fast; whereas there may be an even greater risk in going too slowly.[83]

The new dynamic role of local government was to complement political progress at the centre of government. While the issue of responsible self-government had, not surprisingly, been absent from Lugard's calculations, it was in the forefront of Colonial Office thinking in 1947. Local government was to fulfil the function of giving political experience and inculcating responsibility to a new generation of African politicians, while at the same time, by a system of indirect election, it was to exclude a premature transfer of power to a small, unrepresentative group of 'ballot-box politicians'. It was also hoped that local politics would have the welcome effect of training Africans in the arts of popular control.

These were ambitious objectives; but they were not the only aims of the policy-makers. Local government was also to give a new inspiration to the Colonial Service and revive a flagging *esprit de corps*. It was to gain the support of the educated Africans and transform native authorities into agencies capable of effectively running social services. It was also to help the economic development of Africa. Little economic progress seemed possible under the old tribal authorities; and Creech Jones attached considerable importance to this problem. In February 1947 he called for a 'revolution in African productivity', especially in agricultural production but also in the development of secondary industries. Important social change, he argued, would arise out of this revolution and might indeed be a necessary precondition for it. There was evidence that a continuation of the present methods of land utilization would 'lead inexorably to a decline in agricultural production within a very short time', especially in East Africa. There would have to be substantial changes in land tenure, and 'very great sociological and political repercussions' would result. 'In its social repercussions', wrote the Secretary of State, 'the problem of increased productivity is closely connected with the development of an efficient system of African local government.' Native administration had to be efficient and to adapt to the needs of social and economic progress: for without the support of these bodies, and the co-operation of the people, little effective progress could be made.[84]

It has been argued that the 'tragic' aspect of the local government policy was the optimism that expected too many consequences from the same action.[85] There is much justification for this comment. In many ways the post-war policy towards the African dependencies was too brilliant and schematic an attempt to anticipate and at the same time to mould the future development of Africa; it was a policy that supplied a consistent theoretical plan whose rigour was belied both by the diversity of Africa and the unpredictable nature of events. Yet to appreciate why so many contrasting consequences were expected of local government we have to realize that the Colonial Office was not setting itself a minor task – it was attempting no less than to build 'nation-states' which would not only be self-governing but democratic and economically self-supporting. The differing expectations of local government were therefore complementary and necessary aspects of a comprehensive policy.[86] This is clearly revealed by the 1947 Report.

NOTES

1. Emerson and Kilson (eds.), *The Political Awakening of Africa* (New York, 1965), p.13.
2. N. Sithole, *African Nationalism* (Oxford, 1968), pp.48-9.
3. Crowder, *West Africa Under Colonial Rule*, p.407.
4. *Ibid.* p.427.
5. Emerson and Kilson, *Political Awakening of Africa*, p.49.
6. CO 554/125/33657. Memo by WASU, presented to Lord Lloyd, 29 Aug. 1940.
7. CO 554/130/33675. Resolutions of WASU, 29 and 30 Aug. 1941.
8. CO 554/127/33655. Resolution passed by a General Meeting of WASU, 4 Apr. 1942.
9. CO 267/682/32303. Article in *The New Leader*, 3 Oct. 1942.
10. CO 267/681/32216/2. Resolution by WAYL.
11. Emerson and Kilson, *Political Awakening of Africa*, p.58.
12. G.O. Olusanya, *The Second World War and Politics in Nigeria* (London, 1973), pp.69-74.
13. CO 583/261/30453. 'A Further Memorandum on the Future Political Development of Nigeria'. Bourdillon, Oct. 1942.

14. N. Azikiwe, *My Odyssey* (London, 1970), pp.324-5, 368, 409.
15. CO 554/130/33675. Minute by Pedler, 14 Oct. 1941.
16. CO 267/667/32010/1. Governor Jardine to Secretary of State, 14 Dec. 1939.
17. CO 583/259/30231. Minute by Williams, n.d.
18. CO 554/127/33544. Minute by Williams, 26 Oct. 1943.
19. G. Padmore, *History of the Pan-African Congress* (London, 2nd ed. 1963).
    ACJ 4/4 28. Letter by Creech Jones to unknown newspaper, n.d.
20. CO 96/771/31079. Minute by Talbot Edwards, 31 Oct. 1941.
21. CO 267/682/32303. Minute by C.A. Grossmith, 12 Feb. 1941.
22. *Ibid.* Minute by Williams, 5 Feb. 1941.
23. Swinton Papers II 6/1. Richards to Swinton, 15 Dec. 1945.
24. Letter to *Manchester Guardian*, 1 Feb. 1946.
25. Olusanya, *Politics and the Second World War in Nigeria*, pp.89-90.
26. Minutes in CO 583/276/30647/3.
27. CO 583/265/30022/422. Minute by Creasy, 27 Apr. 1946.
28. *Ibid.* Minute by Creech Jones, 1 May 1946.
29. CO 583/276/30647/3. Minute by Creech Jones, 14 Feb. 1946.
30. CO 583/277/30658. Richards to Secretary of State, 9 Aug. 1946.
31. *Ibid.* Notes by the Government of Nigeria on the NCNC.
32. *Ibid.* Richards to Gater, 17 Oct. 1946.
33. CO 267/686/32120. Speech by Governor in Legislative Council, 20 Nov. 1945.
    CO 267/688/32348. Governor Stevenson to O.G.R. Williams, 22 Aug. 1946.
34. CO 525/199/44379. Hastings Banda to Secretary of State, 14 June 1946.
35. CO 877/24/27065/2. '"Job Analysis" for the Colonial Service'. n.d. (1945).
36. CO 536/215/40329. Governor to Secretary of State, 2 Jan. 1946.
37. 'Notes on priorities in colonial administration', by H.P. Elliott, Oct. 1946. (In possession of Hugh Elliot.)
38. ACJ 9/8 Item 11. Speech to the colonial affairs study group of the Empire Parliamentary Association, 23 Mar. 1946.
39. Letter to the author from Sir George Cartland, 23 Dec. 1977.
40. CO 847/25/47234. 'Memorandum on Factors Affecting Native Administration Policy'. n.d.
41. *Ibid.* 'Morale in the Colonial Service' by A.H. Dutton, 14 May 1946; 'The Introduction of a new spirit into the Colonial Service' by R. Johnson and N. McClintock, 1 May 1946; and 'Morale and Conditions' by A.A. Hughes, 29 Apr. 1946.
42. *Ibid.* Memo by Dutton.
43. *Ibid.* Minute by Cohen, 15 Feb. 1946.
44. *Ibid.* Minute by Pedler, 11 Mar. 1946 (with marginal comment by Cohen).
45. *Ibid.* Minute, 15 Mar. 1946.
46. *Ibid.* Minute, 21 Feb. 1946.
47. *Ibid.* Minute, 5 Mar. 1946.
48. *Ibid.* Minute, 23 Feb. 1946.
49. *Ibid.* Minute, 19 Feb. 1946.
50. *Ibid.* Minute, 27 Feb. 1946.
51. *Ibid.* Minute, 9 Mar. 1946.
52. *Ibid.* Minute, 11 June 1946.
53. *Ibid.* Minute, 11 Mar. 1946.
54. 'Native Administration'. n.d. No author. ('Nyasaland' file, Rhodes House.)
55. FCB 40/2 102-3. Anonymous enclosure, M.U. Rounce to Hinden, 6 Dec. 1946.
56. FCB 80/1 20. Oral evidence by Hugh Thomas, 24 Jan. 1944.
57. FCB 49/1. 'Constitutional Advance and Indirect Rule' by G. Houston, 27 Sept. 1946.

58. FCB 49/1 Item 5. 'Constitutional Advance and Indirect Rule' by Hinden, n.d.
59. *Local Government and the Colonies*. A Report to the Fabian Colonial Bureau, edited by Rita Hinden (London, 1950), p.237.
60. CO 847/25/47234. Gater to the East African Governors. (Drafted by Cohen, 20 May 1946.)
61. Typescript of Interview with Lord Milverton, 22 Feb. 1969. Rhodes House.
62. Sir B. Sharwood Smith, *But Always as Friends* (London, 1969), p.169.
63. *Parl. Debates* (Commons), vol.454, col.616. 22 July 1948. Rees-Williams.
64. CO 847/25/47234. Gater to the Governors of Kenya, Uganda, Tanganyika, and Nyasaland, 22 May 1946. Drafted by Cohen.
65. *Ibid.* Creasy to Lloyd, 11 July 1946.
66. Creech Jones to the African Governors, 25 Feb. 1947. The bulk of the Despatch is reprinted in Kirk-Greene (ed.), *The Principles of Native Administration in Nigeria*, pp.238-45.
67. FCB 49/1 14. Cohen to Hinden, 7 Apr. 1947.
68. *Ibid.*
69. 'African No.1173. Confidential: Colonial Office Summer School on African Administration'. 18-28 Aug. 1947.
70. *Ibid.* p.9.
71. ACJ 48/2 32-7. 'Local Government as a Training-Ground for Parliamentary Government'. n.d.
72. Crowder, *West Africa under Colonial Rule,* p.227.
73. For Cohen's paper, see African No.1173, pp.19-22; for the Report of the group, pp.24-5.
74. *Ibid.* pp.34-5.
75. Sharwood Smith, *But Always as Friends*, pp.171-2.
76. CO 847/36/47238/14 Pt.1. African Governors' Conference, paper no.12.
77. *Journal of African Administration*, vol.1, no.1. June 1949.
78. *Ibid.* vol.II, no.3. 1950. 'Why "Indirect Rule" has been replaced by "Local Government" in the nomenclature of British Native Administration'. R.E. Robinson.
79. As Sartre argues, 'the meaning of the past is strictly dependent on my present project'. Human history 'would have to be *finished* before a particular event ... could receive a definite meaning'. (*Being and Nothingness*, London, 1969, pp.498, 501.)
80. Lord Hailey, *Native Administration in the British African Territories* (4 parts, H.M.S.O., 1951), part 4, p.36.
81. Mitchell diaries, 29 Oct. 1947.
82. Lugard, *Dual Mandate*, p.198.
83. African No.1176. 'Minutes of the Africa Conference', 1948, Minute 6. (ACJ 23 Item 4.)
84. Secretary of State to the Governor of Nyasaland, 22 Feb. 1947. Also sent to the other Governors. ('Nyasaland' file, Rhodes House.)
85. Lee, *Colonial Development and Good Government*, p.182.
86. Hence it is unreal to judge which of the strands of the local government policy was considered to be the most important. U. Hicks, *Development from Below* (Oxford, 1961), pp.5-6, argued that the desire for economic efficiency was pre-eminent.

7

Planning the Transfer of Power

You praise the firm restraint with which they write —
I'm with you there, of course:
They use the snaffle and the bit all right,
But where's the bloody horse?

  — Roy Campbell, 'On Some South African Novelists'

The committee set up in early 1947 to chart a 'new approach' to African policy did precisely that when it reported on 22 May, 1947. The Report it produced embodied a radical reorientation of British aims and conceptions: it has even been called the 'Durham Report of the African Empire'.[1] It gave a clear and comprehensive picture of post-war Colonial Office strategy and is thus of essential importance for an understanding of British actions and reactions in Africa. The notion that 'planning' was a practicable proposition for the African territories had started with the 1940 Colonial Development and Welfare Act and now reached its zenith. Initiatives from African nationalists were soon to become of vital importance, but in 1947 it still seemed possible for British officials to anticipate and mould the future; all the speaking parts in the drama of Africa's development were taken by the whites, though leading roles were now being reserved for the Africans. In the Report local government policy, already revealed in outline in Creech Jones's Despatch of February, was complemented by a full-fledged and consistent policy for the development and demise of the African empire. No more than the broad outline of this plan was in fact revealed to the Colonial Service, but the political strategy it defined and the attitude it embodied were undoubtedly of major significance in the years that followed.

  This is a suitable opportunity to say something of one of the most important members of the committee and the author of its constitutional proposals, as well as of its local government and education recommendations, Andrew Cohen. It was Cohen who, with the political support of Creech Jones, dominated Colonial Office thinking in 1947. At the Cambridge Summer School in August he had been particularly successful. One of the officers who attended it later remarked that

> the dominant impression that most of us were to carry away was that of the tall, fair-haired figure of Andrew Cohen striding restlessly up and down, deep in conversation, or sprawling untidily, a half-demolished pencil between his lips, behind the chairman's table.[2]

Given to long periods of deep, impenetrable silence, Cohen would suddenly explode with a veritable tumble of ideas.[3]

He was an extremely complex man – moody, sensitive, and romantic, with tremendous energy and enthusiasm. A classical scholar from Cambridge, he developed a pervading intellectuality but was determined to express it in practical and effective action. He saw himself in the heroic mould. When asked to describe his goal in life, he replied – with what is no doubt revealing irony – that it was one of 'rolling back the frontiers of darkness'.[4] As head of the Africa Division of the Colonial Office he was able to give expression to both his intellect and his desire to be practical. The 1947 Report reveals great powers of constructive ability, bringing together diverse strands into a policy that was remorselessly logical and consistent and was designed to bring the maximum benefit to both Africa and Britain. Cohen's genius is shown by his ability to appeal to both radicals and conservatives at the same time and to present what he considered desirable as what was expedient and necessary. He was determined to cut across red-tape and to achieve something positive.

Cohen had entered the Colonial Office in 1933, but on his first trip to Africa – to Northern Rhodesia in 1937 – he had become disillusioned with colonial rule: trusteeship seemed to be doing little for the colonial wards. Returning from Malta, where he had been lieutenant governor from 1940 to 1943, he became an Assistant Secretary until his promotion by Creech Jones. Of all the officials in the Office it was Cohen who most attracted the loyalty of the Secretary of State. The two men were very different in character and background, and yet they had a similar vision of the future of Africa. The civil servant shared with his political master a conviction that imperial control was only morally justified if it served the promotion of African interests: and this meant that ultimately self-government would have to be conferred, since the possibilities of development by an alien government were by their very nature limited. He also shared a socialistic conception of the duties of government as an ameliorationist welfare agency. The welfare state utopianism of the post-1945 period was inevitably projected from Whitehall to the African continent.

The committee had been given very wide terms of reference. It was to prepare papers for the 1948 Conference of Unofficials which the Fabian Colonial Bureau had urged the Secretary of State to call. It was this Conference which was to decide 'new principles of policy'; but first the Colonial Office proposals were to be discussed by the Governors and Governors-designate of the African territories.[5] The committee was to cover all areas of African policy but was directed particularly to five topics: the closer association of unofficial members of the Legislative Council with the executive work of government; the economic development of the territories; the development of social services, especially educational and medical; the development of African local government; and the improvement of the machinery of government with a view to a greater degree of devolution of responsibility to Colonial Governments and Legislative Councils.[6] The committee was chaired by Sydney Caine and included senior members of the Colonial Office as well as a Treasury representative. It produced seven memoranda, which were included in the Report as appendices. Important papers were written on the general political development of colonial territories, constitutional development in Africa, local government, the Colonial Service, agricultural production, marketing policy, and education policy. Papers were already available on mining, manufacturing industries, and co-operation, while it was intended that papers would be prepared later on international organizations, public relations, Colonial Development Corporations, fisheries, medicine and health, and the 1948 Africa Conference. All the essential parts of the Colonial Office's policy were available in May 1947.

The Report was intended as a basis for discussion not as a finished product. The committee made it plain that their suggestions were

> by no means intended as a fixed blue print of future policy but merely as suggestions for future lines of policy on which the views of the Conference will be obtained.[7]

The Colonial Office wished above all to avoid the impression that it was dictating policy to the Colonial Governments. Inviting the Governors to the Conference of November 1947, Creech Jones stressed that he was anxious not to reach any conclusions until after the meeting.[8] The Report was assuredly not the final word on African policy; but its proposals were the considered opinions of the Colonial Office and they did win the enthusiastic support of the responsible ministers. Under-Secretary of State Ivor Thomas thought the committee had done 'a fine job of work in a relatively short time' and judged that the ensuing Conference might well 'mark a turning point in colonial thought'.[9] Creech Jones described the Report as 'an excellent piece of work'.[10] In fact the Colonial Office deliberately minimized the significance of the committee's Report in order that the Governors should not feel presented with a *fait accompli*. There seems little doubt that though minor criticisms would be gratefully accepted at the two conferences, the Colonial Office simply wanted to secure acceptance for the broad strategy that had already been worked out and to convince the Colonial Service of the virtue and necessity of this policy.

The committee was concerned to put forward radical suggestions for reform, since only far-reaching proposals could satisfy 'the large body of opinion in this country, in Africa and internationally which holds that more rapid political, economic and social development is required in the African Territories'.[11] Of crucial significance for the whole of African policy was the necessity for a political transfer of power. Political issues affected the whole range of recommendations that were being put forward: education policy, for instance, was seen in the light of changes in government.

> Political development will go forward with an increasing strong impetus irrespective of Government action, and if educational development can not keep pace with it, the results may well be disastrous.[12]

It was argued that while no level of education should be neglected Britain's main effort ought to be concentrated on higher education: this would provide the men and women to fill the upper posts both inside and outside government; it would produce independent and realistic citizens qualified to lead the people; and it would supply the technical and professional men needed to develop the natural resources of the territories. It would also provide the teachers needed in the lower levels of education, while colleges and schools in the British tradition would provide a lasting link between Britain and Africa. It was suggested that Colonial Development and Welfare monies should be used to help finance higher education and that primary education should be funded from local revenue.

In the same way political expectations provided the framework for the recommendations on the Colonial Service.[13] It was regarded as vital that increased opportunities should be given for local people to serve in the higher posts, that the optimum use be made of those officers of ability, and that responsibility for the Service be devolved as far as possible to the Colonial Governments. Africanization was essential if the Colonial Service was to become in time the civil service of new self-governing states. Increased efficiency was desirable in itself and was particularly needed at a time of rapid development in many areas. Devolution of authority was a pre-condition for the gradual emergence of such states. Politics dictated policy towards the Colonial Service. The committee, taking its lead from Sir Charles Jeffries, proposed that certain posts should continue to be filled at the discretion of the Secretary of State but that the remainder should be put at the disposal of the local Governments. Public Service Commissions were to be established in each territory to deal with appointments, promotions from grade to grade, discipline and petitions.

The economic side of the Report was also to an extent influenced by political considerations in that the proposed self-governing states would have to be economically self-supporting. The main premise of the committee's recommendations was simply the desirability of the fullest possible expansion of African production and services. There was an urgent need to increase the productive capacity of the colonies. To this end, means had to be found of reorganizing existing industries and establishing new ones.[14] Proposed Colonial Development Corporations would facilitate these aims and also aid agriculture. Indeed it was agriculture which held the pivotal position in the African economy and would do so for some time to come. Radical changes were required, moving away from the system based on the family towards operations 'on a larger scale, with increased use of mechanical assistance and with the object of increased productivity'.[15] There was to be an extended application of scientific knowledge. The possibilities were broached of larger holdings for individual farmers, of co-operation amongst small-holders, and of large collective farms. Above all, there was a need for 'widespread and bold experimentation'. A paper on marketing recommended that, alongside international action to stabilize prices, Britain should attempt to equalize prices over a number of years and to encourage capital investment in primary production. Statutory marketing boards, run by the industry concerned and encouraged by the government, were to promote these aims.[16]

The political section of the 1947 Report stressed the inevitability of some form of self-government for the African territories. Because of Britain's own public declarations and because of international pressure, coupled with the example of other colonial states, the movement towards self-government involved 'aspirations of virtually irresistible force'. The Chairman of the committee, Sydney Caine, judged that Britain

> must assume that perhaps within a generation many of the principal territories of the Colonial Empire will have attained or be within sight of the goal of full responsibility for local affairs.[17]

The larger colonies were expected to achieve full Dominion Status, while the smaller and poorer ones would probably achieve some analagous position. Since the Colonies would in future become self-governing, it was necessary to redistribute power from His Majesty's Government to the Colonial Governments and to devise 'links of consultation for the present links of control', and to transform a relationship of 'benevolent domination' to one of 'friendly association'. It was obviously necessary to associate Africans more closely with the legislatures, but Caine refrained from making detailed suggestions and left these to the constitutional expert, Andrew Cohen.

Cohen was equally certain that self-government for the African territories was inevitable. Nationalist feeling would automatically grow.

> Broadly speaking there is little demand yet for self-government among the mass of the rural African population either in West or East Africa, but in West Africa the educated minority and large numbers of people influenced by them through the press and otherwise are asking for more rapid progress towards self-government and this demand will become more insistent as time goes on.[18]

He regarded it as idle to speculate on how long the achievement of self-government would take, though in the Gold Coast it was unlikely to be achieved in much less than a generation and elsewhere it would probably take longer. Cohen argued that the foundations upon which self-government would be built already existed: these were the Legislative Council, the Executive Council, the Colonial Service, and the pyramid of representative councils. It was clear that these Colonial Governments had to be built up as entities on their own and authority devolved on them from Whitehall, powers of control not being retained unless they were required in practice. Significant in this respect was the concession of an unofficial majority on the Legislative Council, which Cohen recognized as 'an important step forward on the road leading ultimately to self-government'.[19] After this had been granted, there were to be four stages of political change culminating in responsible self-government.

It should not be imagined that Cohen and the Colonial Office were trying to establish an inflexible blue-print of constitutional development. On the contrary, Cohen was aware that the British programme would, almost inevitably, have to be revised in the future since 'internal political pressure may radically affect both the pace and the manner of political advance'. It was vitally necessary therefore that long-term planning be flexible. All Cohen was trying to do was to

> establish a broad framework within which the political development of the African territories can take place with the minimum of friction, the maximum of goodwill for this country and the greatest possible degree of efficiency.[20]

In the first stage, government was to be divided into groups of departments, with a Member of the Executive Council responsible for each group. This would be the embryo of a full Cabinet system, though for the time being each Member would be directly responsible to the Governor. The Executive Council was to be treated more as the Government of the territory and less as a purely advisory body.

In the second stage, unofficial members of the Executive Council were to become Members, responsible to the Governor, in charge of departments. Their numbers were to increase progressively during this period, while the Executive Council itself was to become increasingly responsible to the Legislature. Africanization of the upper levels of the Colonial Service was to proceed rapidly during these first two stages, as was the development of local government.

In the next stage, some of the Members would become Ministers under a system of Cabinet responsibility, the Governor gradually subsiding into merely the King's formal representative. His final responsibility would only cease when the Ministers became fully responsible to the Legislative Council, and this could only happen when the Legislature was democratically elected (and thus responsible to the people) by direct or – more practically – by indirect means. Hence the third stage was thought by Cohen to be a considerable way in the future, since it required the existence of popular election through the development of the local government system of councils.

In the fourth and final stage, which would follow rapidly on the heels of the previous one, all governmental departments would come under the control of Ministers and internal self-government would thereby be achieved. The control of the Secretary of State would then, presumably, be limited to external affairs; but little was said in the Report about the period following self-government. Since authority would then be devolved from Whitehall, and since the new Governments would derive their powers from the African citizens, there was little that usefully could be said. The 1947 Report would have achieved its aim of the end of empire, while at the same time Britain's willingness to transfer power would have ensured that the new states continued to trade and have close relations with Britain.

Such, in outline, was the 1947 Report on British African policy. Several features of this crucial document are worthy of comment and analysis. The major premise behind the 1947 proposals was a recognition of the inevitability of self-government at some time in the future. Above all, there was an expectation of the rise of African nationalism. On this point, we may well accuse the Colonial Office of prejudice: the issue had been pre-judged. Officials were well aware that in 1947 powerful nationalist movements did not exist, but there were certainly indications that African organizations were growing in strength as well as in disloyalty to Britain. The precedent of Indian and other nationalisms seemed to guarantee that eventually Africa would tread the same path, while the political and moral climate in Britain and at the United Nations Organisation seemed to preclude the possibility of the British use of lengthy repressive measures. Cohen argued at a Fabian Conference in May 1947 that the existence of a nationalist movement would determine whether or not a country achieved self-government. But he added that territorial unity, democratic representation, and an efficient system of local government were also desirable qualities.[21] The empire would be laid to rest when African nationalists could insist that power be transferred to them, but the Colonial Office was determined that the end was to be the best possible beginning for the successor states. Empire had to be ended constructively.

It was thus thought necessary to transfer power, and to do so to the educated elite of Africans as they became able to take over the reins of government. Hence it was necessary for the Colonial Office to delineate the steps by which constitutional change would proceed; and Cohen did precisely this. There would be no repression and no attempt to cling to power: in this sense self-government would be conceded at the earliest possible date. Yet at the same time there would be every attempt to secure the maximum amount of development before colonial rule ended, in order to provide the basic requirements of the new states. For this purpose the collaboration of the educated elite had to be secured, and constitutional development was the best means of achieving this. Yet there was always the danger that their concentrating on political power, together with their very Westernization, would estrange the members of the educated elite from the needs of their country. Therefore the 1947 plan was designed to secure the collaboration of the nationalists and at the same time to slow their political progress by making representation at the centre dependent on the support of the rural, illiterate majority. The use of Provincial Councils as electoral colleges would tend to exclude the 'ballot-box' politicians. Political concessions would only be granted when the nationalists had achieved the unity and popular support required to insist on them, that is at the latest possible date.

The British strategy can therefore be viewed as either radical or conservative, as an attempt to hasten the end of empire or to stave it off for as long as possible. While on the surface this seems illogical and ambiguous, it was in fact sound, practical politics. Cohen and Creech Jones were certain that the empire in Africa would and should be wound up, but they were determined to bequeath the best possible inheritance. It was senseless to hand over power to a small unrepresentative oligarchy of educated Africans; it was also meaningless to become involved in repression and to retain power for its own sake. Self-government was to be granted at the earliest and at the latest possible date. This paradoxical policy was sensible politics – not least in that it could be presented so as to appeal to progressive and 'die-hard' alike, both in the Colonial Service and in the British Government.

There was much that was radical, and indeed revolutionary, in the 1947 Report. Never before had there been a clear, comprehensive policy to end the empire in Africa. Plans had been drawn up during the war; but in 1943 the proposals drafted by Williams, which were confined to West Africa, were to cover several generations and did not attempt to foreshadow the final stages of self-government. Cohen's proposals applied to the whole of British Africa. He was, of course, aware of the profound differences between West, Central, and East Africa and commented on the 'extreme difficulty' of talking about the different situations at the same time;[22] but the new strategy was designed to apply to all areas, though the time-scale would obviously vary. Cohen stressed that in East and Central Africa progress at the centre would not be made until the Africans were playing their full part and that this fact made all the more vital the development of effective and representative organs of local government.[23] Nevertheless the notion that responsible self-government would be conceded 'possibly within a generation', if only in the major West African territories, marks a substantial shift in official ideas since the war, and is even more startling if compared with the pre-war idea that self-government would only be achieved, if at all, in the next century. In 1947 the lazy, hazy doctrine of 'indefinite time ahead' was finally swept aside. Cohen and Creech Jones were consciously racing against time, attempting to be of the maximum practical use in the short period that was left.

The model for constitutional advance put forward in the Report provided a clear scheme for the transfer of power. No longer was there any diffidence about determining the precise form of self-government in the African colonies. Hailey's 'judgematic' approach found no support. Nor was there any hesitation about using essentially British forms for both central and local African government. There was to be no formal system of dyarchy, by which certain subjects were to be reserved for imperial control, but a straightforward transfer of power in stages. Cohen's recommendation that African councillors be made into responsible ministers was now accepted. In effect, the Member System was to be grafted onto Colonial government.

Before the war the Chief Secretary's office had been the central institution of colonial administration. The Chief Secretary was the principal executive officer of the Governor and the administrative head of the civil service. During the war the increased pressure of work meant that his multifarious activities were shared among the senior secretariat officials. In Northern Rhodesia unofficial members of the Legislative Council were appointed to key posts, as Director of Supplies and Director of Manpower. After the war some territories restored supreme power to the Chief Secretary; but in Kenya, Tanganyika, and Northern Rhodesia the Member System, as it became known, was introduced. Executive Councillors were placed in charge of a group of related departments: they were directly responsible to the Governor but answered for their policy to the Legislative Council.[24] In 1947 Cohen called for the development and extension of this system, with black as well as white Members and the eventual introduction of Cabinet responsibility. Part of Cohen's genius lay in his adoption of the techniques of East Africa, in ways not originally intended, for the territories of West Africa. The first stage of his constitutional programme had already come about in Kenya and Northern Rhodesia and was, to his mind, urgently required in Nigeria and the Gold Coast. The second stage, which was designed to follow quickly from the first, was in existence in Kenya. Techniques for the constitutional development of Africans were being derived, ironically, from settler-dominated communities.

One of the main features of the 1947 Report was the crucial part assigned to the educated Africans. They would have important roles in political and economic development. Creech Jones was well aware that Colonial Governments, even with grants from the 1945 CD & W Fund, could only achieve very limited social and economic advances. 'Development from above can only ever make limited progress. It must come in addition from below.'[25] He believed that Britain's primary task in Africa was to stimulate the initiative of the local people, to encourage them to want change 'and to equip them with the power themselves to create change'. He was also alive to the distrust with which intelligent and educated Africans viewed alien rule:

The emotional fervour attached to nationalism infects and

spreads. Unless a serious effort is made to channel it, it may become disruptive and destructive. Our task is to channel this emotion and concept towards constructive courses ...

An effort was therefore to be made to associate the educated Africans with efforts at social and economic progress. If the British welfare ideal was to become a reality in Africa, the full support of the Africans would have to be secured. This could best be achieved by the transfer of political power: the African had to feel that the Government was 'his' Government if he was to give it his full support.

Educated Africans were to play a major part in advance at the centre and in the localities. Constitutional progress complemented progress in local government – they were part of the same policy. The strategy proposed by Cohen in 1947 built òn the infra-structure of local government. The NAs were to be transformed into agencies of local government on the British model, with educated members elected by the people and responsible to them. These authorities were to send representatives to Provincial Councils which, along with some municipal authorities, were either to select the African representatives for the central Legislature or were to form an African Council to perform this function. No longer was imperial power to be conserved by alliance with loyal but unprogressive chiefs. It is true that indirect election was to form the major basis for representation at the centre, and that this method had been used for the Burns and Richards constitutions in West Africa; but since local government was to be democratized, and the Provincial Councils thereby made representative, this form of election would not so much preclude or obstruct the election of educated Africans as slow down the process, making sure that the elite could not become divorced from the needs and wishes of the masses. Experience in local government would not only benefit the local councillors but would also create 'an intelligent and responsible public opinion which will act as the sheet anchor of genuine democratic control'.[26]

The key to the whole strategy was therefore in the localities. If the base of the electoral pyramid was truly representative of the forces in African society, then the higher levels would be as well; but if the local councils fell prey to sectional interests, the superstructure could have no chance of being satisfactorily democratic. Cohen was pleased in 1947 that the indirect election of Africans to the Legislative Council had successfully 'married' the traditional policy of indirect rule with the parliamentary system at the centre. In the future a more effective means of securing democratic election would perhaps be found; but in 1947 the indirect method, allied with direct election from the large municipalities which already enjoyed the privilege, seemed the best solution. Cohen was well pleased with the progress that Provincial Councils were making: he noted that those in Northern Rhodesia were 'democratic in the proper sense' in that the members were selected by the people themselves, though the District Commissioners no doubt gave friendly assistance in a number of cases. He observed 'a good mixture of Chiefs, Native Authority Councillors and educated Africans on these Provincial Councils'.[27] Creech Jones was also encouraged by them.[28] The first session of the Northern Rhodesian African Representative Council met in November 1946.

British colonial policy towards the empire in tropical Africa had obviously been formulated more clearly than ever before with the 1947 Report. Instead of the pre-war static and defensive attitude, Britain's ideas were now dynamic and positive. Policy had truly been revolutionized: the strait-jacket of indirect rule was to be sloughed off, and Britain was now prepared to concede responsible self-government within a generation. The debate between the notion that the colonies were 'decolonized' by an enlightened Britain and the alternative that they were 'liberated' by African freedom-fighters can now be seen to be unreal. Britain would transfer power to the nationalists when they had power to force concessions. Britain's strategy was that the empire in Africa would be decolonized and liberated – the two concepts were not contradictory but mutually compatible. Britain had worked out the stages on the road to self-government and was prepared for rapid progress, but nationalists would have to demand and secure the actual transfer of power. Meanwhile Britain would use the time at her disposal to foster, in alliance with the educated elite, those social and economic developments desirable for the healthy birth of a nation.

The Colonial Office had therefore, to some extent, to conceal its willingness to grant substantial reforms and be content to await developments in Africa. Even if the Office had wished to do otherwise, there was no practicable alternative. Britain had the theoretical power to dictate to Colonial Governments, but in practice she could only advise and urge a particular course of action. And now Britain had decided to divest herself of even her theoretical authority, devolving power to the Colonial Governments as separate entities. Here we see a significant paradox of the 1947 policy: the Secretary of State's control of the African colonies was to be substantially reduced while at the same time he wished to foster a definite scheme for political and constitutional advance, as well as important economic and social reforms. His authority would only be devolved to the Colonial Governments as they became responsible to African legislatures; but there was still a very difficult task ahead for the Colonial Office, one not of dictation but of persuasion.

The 1947 Report was therefore remarkably ambitious. The task of nation-building was onerous and formidable.

> The modern conception of African Government, in its economic and political aspects, may well be regarded, if it succeeds, as one of the most remarkable feats of constructive statesmanship in modern times. It will do this if it enables Colonial Governments to lead a variety of separate and undeveloped tribal communities to a practical understanding of and a firm belief in the institutions and processes of democratic government on a national scale. We cannot, of course, be sure that we shall succeed.[29]

Yet the Colonial Office could not, in 1947, fully reveal its policy. Its role was passive in that it had to await African initiatives. Hence British policy seemed to be conservative and traditional and its revolutionary character has never achieved proper recognition. The Tory jibe, that Labour's policy was merely a continuation of that of its Coalition and Conservative predecessors, was never entirely dispelled. Whereas the 1947 Report had implied that political and economic progress might well not proceed *pari passu* (the one being inevitable and the other merely desirable), Creech Jones, anxious to secure the maximum degree of development in the time available, stressed in the Commons that rapid political progress had to wait for an expansion in the social services and for the creation of the conditions of good living.[30] He reassured M.P.s that he could not, in 1949, foresee a point, 'for a long time ahead anyway', when the work of the Colonial Service would come to an end because of the achievement of self-government.[31] There was no point in saying anything else – except to the Colonial Service, and Creech Jones bravely did so, informing officers in the Gold Coast that their jobs would have to be given up in favour of the Africans.[32]

Because of the necessary secrecy that surrounded the 1947 proposals the Labour Government did not gain the credit for a new and dynamic policy. It had originally been intended to reveal the plan to the conference of African Unofficials which was to meet in London the following year, but criticisms of some of the proposals led to the abandonment not of the strategy itself but of its disclosure. The 1947 Report, therefore, though implicit in offical statements, appeared only in diluted form:

> The central purpose of British Colonial policy is simple. It is to guide the colonial territories to responsible self-government within the Commonwealth in conditions that ensure to the people concerned both a fair standard of living and freedom of oppression from any quarter. ... The broad aim of policy is to transform the Legislative Council from a body, in its most elementary form, comprising principally officials or members nominated by the Governor, to a body on which the members are wholly elected by the people and to which falls responsibility for appointing and controlling the executive council.[33]

In 1948 it was noted that

> at all levels of government, from the central machine to the rural and urban local authorities, a single deliberate policy of broadening popular representation and enlarging responsible public control of local affairs is being implemented in each of the African territories.[34]

In 1949 Lord Listowel, Minister of State at the Colonial Office, referred to 'a single coherent and comprehensive plan for an evolutionary and balanced political advance of the whole population of the British African territories'.[35]

Opposition to the new strategy had driven it underground. The resistance did not come from within British politics: as we have seen, the Labour Government was unimpressed with colonial issues and lacked imperial will. Attlee was informed of the plan, and copies were also sent to the Foreign Office and the Dominions Office, but it was not presented to the Cabinet as a whole.[36] Instead resistance came from the Colonial Service. Statements about the Service may obviously be too generalized. A 'Jamaican' believed in 1947 that there was a

> lag of more than a hundred years between the enlightened philosophy on which the present colonial policy, though imperfect, is based and the 'keep the natives in their place' attitude of far too many colonial officials.[37]

In fact, there were considerable divergences of opinion amongst British officers in Africa: in the Gold Coast there was a very definite 'generation gap' between younger and older officers.[38] Yet it is clear that a substantial section of the Colonial Service was not at ease with the new principles which the Office was attempting to usher in from 1947 onwards.

A good example of an officer wedded to the older conceptions is the Chief Commissioner of the Gold Coast Colony, T. R. O. Mangin. When he became Assistant District Commissioner in 1920 he had been advised to 'think black'; and that, he believed, was good advice.

> So many of our troubles are caused by trying to force on the African a European outlook simply because of a non-realisation of the fact that their standards and principles are on a completely different plane to ours.[39]

Mangin believed, with C.L. Temple before him, that the native races should be allowed to evolve naturally. He strongly favoured indirect rule and deprecated all talk of 'democratising' the native institutions – 'for how can one democratise a system which in itself is a very fair example of "democracy"?' Hence Mangin was completely out of sympathy with the new local government policy, and he made it known that he, and officers of like mind, strongly disapproved of being told what to do by Whitehall.

> I should like it to be borne in mind that apart from men who have retired after long service in Colonial Administration no-one in England knows anything at all about native administration in West Africa though unfortunately there are some who have no compunction in using Africa for the purpose of exploiting their crackpot views.

These outspoken comments are indicative of the tension, and difference of outlook, between officers in Africa and civil servants in Whitehall. There was formidable opposition in the late 1940s to the post-war policy of Creech Jones and Cohen. The production of the 1947 policy proved far easier than the task of securing its adoption in practice. The earliest opposition came from the Governors. Sir Philip Mitchell, Governor of Kenya since 1944, was a particularly trenchant critic. He had a robust faith in Western Civilization and in Britain's civilizing mission, and he did not believe that the African should develop on his own lines, sheltered from the impact of the

British presence. On the contrary, said Mitchell, 'there is but one civilisation and one culture to which we are fitted to lead the peoples of these countries – our own'.[40] In regarding the Western model as suitable for Africans, Mitchell was in sympathy with the post-war policy; but he was operating on an entirely different time-scale. Britain, he argued in 1946, would be doing her duty in Kenya 'tomorrow, and tomorrow and tomorrow'; the troubles of the future would take care of themselves provided Britain gave full rein in the present to her unerring instinct for leading others towards the 'liberty, justice, charity and good humour which are, in fact, the British way of living'.[41] He did not believe that in the foreseeable future Africans would be capable of governing themselves.

Mitchell entertained both Creech Jones and Cohen in Kenya in the summer of 1946 and was impressed. Cohen was 'a most intelligent and keen young man',[42] while the news that Creech had been made Secretary of State caused him much pleasure.[43] But the more Mitchell learned of the Government's policy, the more his criticisms grew. He was not against the local government policy as such: he believed a limited measure of democracy in the localities would prevent a premature access to the central institutions, while the new policy was, after all, simply grafting the conciliar policy, as practised in Kenya, onto traditional indirect rule. What Mitchell objected to was the overall political strategy. In his reply to the Local Government Despatch we see the challenge to Colonial Office and Labour thinking and a good example of the opposition that had to be overcome if the new policy was to become more than merely theoretical.

Mitchell argued that for generations to come the East African tribes could only enjoy civilized government if the Colonial Governments maintained their hold.

> The government of Kenya ... considers itself morally bound to resist processes which might be called 'political progress' by the misinformed or opinionated but would in fact, be no more than progress towards the abdication of its trust in favour of ... professional politicians. ... It may be difficult but will, for a very long time, be necessary to dispose of the moral courage and political integrity to say no to proposals for apparent progress of that kind.[44]

Mitchell's comments were the most outspoken, but other Governors were also critical. The Acting Governor of Tanganyika wrote to the Colonial Office to say that he had seen Mitchell's reply and was in substantial agreement with it.[45] An exasperated Creech Jones then tried to impress on the Governors that the demand for responsible self-government would inevitably grow and that Britain could not wait until Africans emerged of an ideal standard of responsibility and competence before allowing constitutional development.[46]

The first major confrontation between the Colonial Office and its critics took place at the Governors' Conference held in London in November 1947. As his diary reveals, Sir Philip Mitchell was dissatisfied with the Colonial Office and its new strategy from the start to the finish of the Conference. On 8 November Creech Jones made the opening speech – 'prosily and dully and with little relation to realities'.[47] This belief that the Office was simply not facing facts was the main burden of Mitchell's argument. He was bewildered by the doctrinaire and prejudiced attitude that was being taken. 'We conferred all day', he wrote two days later,

> largely on dry theoretical ideas of Colonial self government totally divorced from the realities of the present day. The C.O. has got itself into a sort of mystic enchantment & sees visions of grateful, independent utopias beaming at them from all around the world, as if there was – yet – any reason to suppose that [an] African can be cashier of a village council for 3 weeks without stealing the cash. ... There is really no understanding whatever of contemporary realities in the C.O. – Creech blathered a good deal.[48]

Hilton Poynton seemed to Mitchell 'a very typical bureaucrat without guts or understanding',[49] while Caine and Clauson, who discussed economic matters, were 'ignorant schoolboys' talking 'childish nonsense' with 'incredible naivete'.[50] Mitchell, of course, made it his duty to instil some appreciation of reality into these men and succeeded, to his own satisfaction, in bludgeoning them pretty severely. He was dismayed that the West African Governors were 'a silent lot', but the Governor of Nigeria, Lord Milverton, played up well.[51]

Milverton, as Sir Arthur Richards, had been responsible for the Nigerian constitution of 1946. This had done little for the educated Africans and was, according to its author, 'very little more than a continuation of Lugard's own outlook on the future'.[52] Milverton had been anxious to avoid undue haste: the constitution had been expected to last for nine years, a period he considered a very short time in the history of a nation. Small wonder, then, that at the 1947 conference he had no sympathy for the new ideas that were put forward. He called for an assurance that nothing would be done to derogate from the authority of the chiefs: and, since his tenure as Governor was up, Cohen gladly gave it.[53] Since a successor sympathetic to the new strategy had already been found in the person of Sir John Macpherson, Milverton's criticisms failed to ruffle the Colonial Office unduly. Indeed it was to the good fortune of Cohen and Creech Jones that all three of the major West African Governors, as well as the Governors of Northern Rhodesia and Nyasaland, were on the point of retiring.[54] Lord Milverton, however, remained an intransigent critic in the years that followed.[55]

The Governors' conference was not as successful, from the Colonial Office point of view, as the Summer School had been. The response of the East African Governors to the Office's new pan-African approach was a call for the proposed 1948 Conference of Unofficials to be divided into two separate bodies – one for East and the other for West Africa. The Colonial Office managed to forestall this demand, but only by agreeing that certain subjects at the Conference would be discussed separately by the East and West African delegates.[56] Disagreements tended to be glossed over in the official conclusions of the Governors' meeting. While it was noted that certain Governors did not agree with all the statements and implications of the Colonial Office memoranda that were submitted to them, the conclusions of the Cambridge Summer School on local government were generally endorsed. It was also agreed that

> Colonial Governments in Africa should be built up to the maximum possible extent as entities of their own, adapted to a gradual evolution towards the ultimate stage of self-government and with the maximum possible participation of local people on the executive side of both central and local government.[57]

The Governors, following Cohen's lead, endorsed the Office's recommendations on education in Africa, but they were far more cautious in reaction to the proposal that the Member System should be introduced wherever possible. This was an important aspect of Cohen's constitutional proposals; but whereas the Governors of those territories which had already adopted the system spoke in its favour, the other Governors opposed its use. No general agreement was therefore reached, and each Colonial Government was free to consider the issue on its merits in the future. The Office had obviously failed to achieve its objective on this point, and further propaganda and persuasion would have to be employed.

The 1947 Report had been originally prepared for presentation to the 1948 Africa Conference, but in fact it was revealed only in outline to the delegates. The Governors' criticisms had been such that the Colonial Office decided that the adoption of the plan would be more likely if its details were not known. Nevertheless Creech Jones certainly referred to the Colonial Office strategy in his speeches:

> There is a pattern in all this reform and development. It is not just a patchwork of happy improvisations in unrelated fields. It aims at being planned social development. We are trying to create the conditions of free nationhood and societies that are responsible and democratic.[58]

He closed the Conference by reiterating that

> There is ... a plan. We know what we are doing. We are not fumbling, we are organising things at this end to help. We are making great demands on you, but do believe that we have some conception of the overall picture, the kind of thing we want to reach.[59]

Andrew Cohen stressed at the Conference the new urgency that was informing British policy.[60] But to reassure the delegates from the settler territories, he emphasized not constitutional development at the centre but reforms in local government. He argued that the speed of the development of the local bodies would determine the speed at which the territories of East and Central Africa moved towards responsible self-government. He also made a significant emendation to the Local Government Despatch:

> I believe the key to success lies in the development of an efficient and representative system of local government. I wish to emphasise the words efficient, representative and local.[61]

Questioned by J.B. Danquah whether this semantic difference was deliberate or accidental, Cohen declared that it was a deliberate choice by the Colonial Office. The word 'democratic', he argued, had a 'rather coloured connotation', while 'representative', which had been suggested by one of the Governors in reply to the Despatch, seemed more applicable.[62] Obviously the criticisms

voiced at the Governors' conference on the inapplicability of western democracy for Africa led the Colonial Office to reassure the
Colonial Governments that change would be gradual. The alteration in terminology was simply a tactical move designed to find
favour with those on whose support the success of the policy
depended.

Cohen believed that, due mainly to the affection and confidence
the delegates had for Creech Jones, the Africa Conference had been
a real success. 'I have now seen the dry bones of papers transformed
so dramatically by personal contacts & speeches into something real
and human.' The theoretical policy, he believed, was beginning to
bear fruit.[63] Not only was the Conference on the whole sympathetic
to the broad policy that was put before it, but there were signs that
the persuasion of the Colonial Office was beginning to generate real
enthusiasm among some of the Africans. Danquah, one of the
leading politicians of the Gold Coast, was especially attracted to
what he heard at the Conference. He supported the change from
'democratic' to 'representative' on the grounds that local government was concerned with the vested interests of those who owned
property in a locality, while political democracy had nothing to do
with the ownership of property.[64] This notion, though perhaps caus-
ing misgivings among the Whitehall contingent at the Conference,
was no doubt treated with indulgence in view of Danquah's almost
lyrical affirmation of the 1948 meeting and of Britain's colonial good
faith.[65] Danquah henceforth stood for 'sweet reasonableness' with
the British.[66]

There were thus encouraging signs that the British strategy as
revealed in the 1947 Report could be implemented in Africa. The
Colonial Office had embarked upon the long and arduous process of
convincing the Colonial Service and Colonial Governments of the
wisdom and necessity of its policy. The results of this campaign were,
as we shall see, paradoxical: progress was uneven between the
central and local councils, as well as varying widely between the
different regions of Africa. Despite the vast amount of opposition to
be overcome, the policy was quickly put into operation in West
Africa on the mistaken assumption that mass nationalism had
already arrived and was able to insist on extensive concessions.
African progress was affected significantly by the 1947 policy, but
not in the precise way that had originally been intended.

NOTES

1. By Professor R.E. Robinson, whose biography of Cohen is eagerly awaited. I am particularly indebted to Prof. Robinson for letting me see a copy of the 1947 Report.
2. Sharwood Smith, *But Always as Friends*, p.170.
3. *Ibid*. pp.184-5.
4. Interview with Professor Kenneth Robinson, 30 July 1976.
5. CO 847/36/47238. Minute by Ivor Thomas, 18 Jan. 1947.
6. *Ibid*. 'Report of the Committee on the Conference of African Governors', Appendix I.
7. *Ibid*. Preliminary.
8. *Ibid*. Secretary of State to African Governors. Drafted by Cohen, 9 June 1947.
9. *Ibid*. Minute by Ivor Thomas, 30 May 1947.
10. *Ibid*. Cohen to L.N. Helsby, 6 June 1947.
11. *Ibid*. 'Report of the Committee on the Conference of African Governors'. Appendix I.
12. *Ibid*. Appendix VII. 'Education Policy in Africa'. Written by Cohen.
13. *Ibid*. Appendix V. 'The Colonial Service.'
14. CO 847/36/47238/1. Minutes of the Second Meeting of the Committee on the African Governors' Conference, 11 Feb. 1947.
15. CO 847/36/47238. Appendix VI. 'The Economic Development of Agricultural Production in the African Colonies'. Written by Monson and Clay.
16. *Ibid*. Appendix IV. 'Memorandum on Marketing Policy for Colonial Export Products'. Written by Melville.
17. *Ibid*. Appendix II. 'General Political Development of Colonial Territories'.
18. *Ibid*. Appendix III. 'Constitutional Development in Africa'.
19. *Ibid*. Appendix III. Part 3.
20. *Ibid*. Appendix III. Part 2.
21. FCB 69/5 72. Buscot Conference on the Transfer of Power, 10-11 May 1947.
22. FCB 49/1 14. Cohen to Hinden, 7 Apr. 1947.
23. African No.1176. 'Minutes of the Africa Conference'. Minute 6. (ACJ 23 Item 4.)
24. ACJ 10/5 12. 'Notes on Colonial Constitutional Changes, 1940-50'. Colonial Office Memo N.4, n.d.
25. African No.1174. Summer School on African Administration, 19 Aug.-2 Sept. 1948.
26. *J.A.A.*, vol.1, no.3, 1949. 'The Modern Conception of Government in British Africa', by Lord Listowel.
27. CO 795/133/45375. Minute by Cohen, 8 Jan. 1946.
28. *Ibid*. Minute by Creech Jones, n.d.
29. *J.A.A.*, vol.1, no.3, 1949 Article by Listowel.
30. *Parl. Debates* (Commons), vol.467, col.1407. 20 July 1949.
31. *Ibid*. col.2911.
32. R.E. Robinson, 'Andrew Cohen and the Decolonisation of Africa'. Seminar paper.
33. *The Colonial Territories (1947-1948)*. Cmd.7433. pp.1-2.
34. *The Colonial Territories (1947-1948)*. Cmd.7715. p.17.
35. *J.A.A.* vol.1, no.3. Article by Listowel.
36. CO 847/36/47238. Minute by Cohen, 9 June 1947.

37. *Manchester Guardian*, 23 March 1947. Letter to the Editor from a 'Jamaican'.
38. R.L. Stone, 'Colonial Admin. and Rural Politics', pp.187 *et seq*.
39. CO 847/25/47234. Confidential Memo by T.R.O. Mangin, 1 Aug. 1946.
40. CO 847/20/47139. *East Africa and Rhodesia*, 2 June 1938. Speech by Mitchell in Kampala.
41. ACJ 7/3 47-50. Mitchell to Creech Jones, 5 Oct. 1946.
42. Mitchell diaries, 25 Aug. 1946. Rhodes House.
43. *Ibid*. 7 Oct. 1946.
44. Governor to Secretary of State, 30 May 1947. Quoted in Cranford Pratt, *The Critical Phase in Tanzania, 1945-1968* (Cambridge, 1976), pp.16-17.
45. *Ibid*. p.17.
46. *Ibid*. p.15.
47. Mitchell diaries, 8 Nov. 1947.
48. *Ibid*. 10 Nov. 1947.
49. *Ibid*. 11 Nov. 1947.
50. *Ibid*. 12 Nov. 1947.
51. *Ibid*. 10 Nov. 1947.
52. Typescript of Interview with Lord Milverton, Rhodes House.
53. 'Memorandum on Native Administration Policy', by R.E. Robinson, n.d. Minute 14 of the Governors' Conference.
54. CO 847/36/47238. Minute by Ivor Thomas, 18 Jan. 1947.
55. Milverton was soon casting scorn on 'Fabian theorising' and Socialist Ministers 'distilling emotional platitudes and sentimental generalisations' (*New Commonwealth*, Nov. 1951).
56. CO 847/36/47238. Cartland to Sabben-Clare, 25 Nov. 1947.
57. ACJ 15/3 18. 'Conclusions of African Governors' Conference, 1947'.
58. African No.1176. 'Minutes of the Africa Conference'. Minute 4. (ACJ 23 Item 4).
59. *Ibid*. Minute 21.
60. *Ibid*. Minute 6.
61. *Ibid*. Minute 9.
62. *Ibid*. Minute 6.
63. ACJ 7/1 82-3. Cohen to Creech Jones, 9 Oct. 1948.
64. 'Minutes of the Africa Conference'. Minute 9.
65. J.B. Danquah, *Friendship and Empire: Impressions of the African Conference held in London in September 1948*. (FCB Pamphlet, Controversy Series, no.5, 1949.)
66. Speech in Gold Coast Legislative Council, 12 Dec. 1949. G.E. Metcalfe (ed.), *Great Britain and Ghana: Documents on Ghana History*, p.698.

8

Reform at the Centre Overtakes Reform in Local Government

> There is, it seems to us,
> At best, only a limited value
> In the knowledge derived from experience ...
>
> – T. S. Eliot, 'East Coker'

Britain's African policy, as enunciated in 1947, provided an awesome task for the Colonial Office. 'Nation-building' had to be undertaken in conditions that were unpropitious. Despite increased recruitment to the Colonial Service, important posts remained vacant. Creech Jones revealed in July 1949 that 1,395 positions were unfilled:

> We are sometimes in despair as to when some of the work in the Colonies can be proceeded with at all, because of this shortage of the necessary skill and technical knowledge on the spot.[1]

Again we are made aware of the paradox confronting the Labour Government from 1945 onwards of the contradiction inherent in far-reaching, idealistic – perhaps utopian – objectives held at a time of tremendous economic scarcity and hardship.

The Local Government Despatch of February 1947 had been issued soon after the announcement of Britain's fuel crisis. In view of Britain's own economic straits there were soon calls in the Commons for a reduction in the 'lavish' amounts of money available under the Colonial Development and Welfare Act.[2] Yet even more debilitating for African development than the inadequacy of the money supply was the post-war shortage of capital equipment and consumer goods; as a result only £8 million out of a possible £16 million were spent during the first two years of the 1945 Act.[3] It was announced in 1947 that there was 'no aspect of economic activity in the Colonies which is not affected by basic shortages of imported materials'.[4] At the end of that year the colonies were asked to restrict their imports not only from hard currency areas, because of the dollar gap, but even from Britain.[5]

In view of these restrictions, the task of fostering economic development was doubly formidable. Despite the ten-year development programmes which the Colonial Governments had drawn up, the problems were enormous and rapid progress could not be expected. The Under-Secretary of State drew attention to this fact in the Commons:

> The physical condition of most of the countries in the Empire is that of under-development and very great work has to be done before any development can be started, farming undertaken or industries set up. ... The tsetse fly occupies an area which has been computed to be 75 times the size of Great Britain. ... I was asked what success we had had against it as yet. The success is small because we are only in the planning stage. ... Although there is a tremendous amount of work to be done, we know what we have to do when we get the machinery and other capital goods, and we know how to do it.[6]

Progress would inevitably be painfully slow. In order to attempt to increase the pace of African development, and also to counter the British economic slump, Development Corporations, first mooted during the war and included in the 1947 proposals, were finally formed.

In 1948 the Overseas Resources Development Bill went through Parliament. The first two clauses of the Act set up the Colonial Development Corporation. This had funds of £100 million and was to undertake every kind of development within colonial territory. Clauses three and four created the Overseas Food Corporation, a smaller body, provided with £50 million and directly responsible to the Minister of Food. It was confined to the production of food and other agricultural products but was not restricted to the British colonies. The first undertaking of the OFC was to be 'Operation Groundnuts'.[7]

Britain's economic needs were certainly paramount in the decision to create the OFC and to start the groundnuts scheme. After the Second World War there was a world shortage of fats and oils: hence the plan to produce groundnuts, which have a forty-fifty per cent oil content, in 3.25 million acres of bush land in Tanganyika,

Northern Rhodesia, and Kenya. In 1947 the decision was taken to extend the scheme to 2.75 million acres in West Africa. At the same time as producing oil, the project was also expected to help the development of a large part of Africa. It would clear land and provide employment and training in scientific agriculture; welfare and health schemes would be introduced; a new port would be built in southern Tanganyika at Mikindani; and a hundred-mile railway was to be built from the port to the groundnut area.[8] Socialists like Rita Hinden saw enormous possibilities: she hoped that the scheme could become an African Tennessee Valley Authority.[9]

In fact, Labour's vaunted showpiece of food production and colonial development proved an expensive failure. It had been estimated that 600,000 tons of groundnuts would be produced annually once the project was under way; but totals fell lamentably below this figure. With the Overseas Food Corporation making large trading losses, the groundnuts scheme was rationalized in 1951 and put on a smaller footing, with a limited commitment of £6 million being undertaken over a period of seven years.[10]

The post-mortem revealed that the venture had been impractical. The production drive had been undertaken at a time when only second-hand plant and machinery were available and before a balanced administrative, financial, and accounting system had been created.[11] The sense of urgency with which the project had been started had been its major disadvantage. The attempt to develop and perhaps exploit Africa had been unsuccessful in this instance. There was in some quarters a definite feeling of imperialism which might have conflicted with the Colonial Office intention of transferring political power. The press, and particularly the *Express*, was calling confidently for the exploitation of African resources:

If dollars are scarce, Africa is ample.
Immense the wealth of agricultural products
that her vast expanses will yield to those
who seek it with resolution in their hearts.
Out with the bulldozers, the tractors, the trucks,
forward with the railroads, the highways!
Let the scientist and the engineer go forth upon
their civilising mission.[12]

In fact, British attempts to encourage the development of the African territories amounted neither to exploitation in the interests of British capitalism nor even an adequate preparation for constitutional advance. The problems involved in economic progress were enormous, and the period of post-war shortages was not the best time for tackling them. At the same time, Britain's efforts failed to convince Africans that they would benefit from development schemes: and articulate Africans were soon criticizing the new 'super exploitation'.[13]

> Even a million pounds can work wonders among a people who identify themselves with the spending of it, add their voluntary labour and creative abilities, and make the project their own. But we have not found the way – except in the rarest cases – for evoking this response.[14]

As a result there was little adequate preparation in the economic field for the constitutional concessions that were soon to be granted in West Africa. The political scheme outlined by Cohen in the 1947 Report was put into operation much more quickly than had originally been intended and before the desired social and economic progress could be made. The post-war African policy had immediate effects.

The Accra riots of February and March 1948 were of seminal importance for the subsequent constitutional development of the Gold Coast. Yet their significance has often been misunderstood. It is suggested here that the events in West Africa, and British reactions thereto, must be seen in the light of the 1947 strategy.

It is sometimes suggested that 1948 saw the first major eruption of violent African nationalism which, in a 'progressive model colony' like the Gold Coast,[15] shocked the Colonial Office out of its complacency and resulted in the decision to transfer power. Nationalism thereby caused a sharp break in official policy. But this interpretation can now be seen to be untenable. First of all, the Gold Coast was not considered a model colony: Sir Frank Stockdale, adviser to the Office, commented scathingly on the 'apathy, lack of real interest, lack of policy, lack of co-ordination & lack of vision' which characterized the whole of the administration in the Gold Coast.[16] Secondly, as we can see from Cohen's proposals of 1947, the Colonial Office was well prepared to transfer power to the nationalists. In fact it was the British anticipation of nationalism which led to an over-reaction in 1948. Events in the Gold Coast were perceived through the distorting mirror of British expectations.

We can now see that the Accra riots were definitely not attempts to overthrow the Colonial Government. In fact, the involvement of the United Gold Coast Convention, six of whose leaders were arrested, was extremely tenuous. The riots were caused by the rise in the price of imported goods, while wages lagged behind, and by the plight of cocoa farmers in areas affected by the swollen-shoot disease. Violence broke out on February 28, when a march of ex-servicemen broke route, and was exacerbated by economic discontents.[17] The Colonial Government was ill prepared and taken by surprise. The Governor, Gerald Creasy, had only arrived from the Colonial Office in January and had a theoretical rather than a practical knowledge of West African administration. On superficial evidence Creasy believed that the UGCC had deliberately fomented the riots:

> Convention is certainly behind, and almost wholly responsible for, the bitterness and violence connected with the opposition to the swollen shoot cutting-out campaign. They attempted to impede settlement of the boycott by amicable agreement. The present riots which appear to have been very thoroughly planned, are no doubt designed to carry the campaign a stage further. Technique of organisers follows a recognisable pattern designed to obtain the greatest possible propaganda value from effect of Government counter-action. ... To parley with the Convention leaders would be a negation of Government and I will have none of it.[18]

The events of 28 February were, to Creasy, a deliberate attempt at a *coup d'état*.[19] Naturally the Colonial Office took its lead from the man on the spot. Confirmation of the political nature of the troubles seemed to arrive on 1 March, when the Secretary of the UGCC, Kwame Nkrumah ('well known to us all as a thorough-going Communist'[20]) attempted to use the riots as a lever for political change.

> Unless colonial government is changed and a new government of the people and chiefs installed at the centre immediately conduct of masses now completely out of control with strikes threaten in police quarters and rank and file police indifferent to orders of officers will continue to result in worse violence and irresponsible acts by uncontrolled people stop Working Committee United Gold Coast Convention declare they are prepared and ready to take interim government stop [sic].[21]

One newspaper in Britain reported that the riots saw the emergence of 'the Frankenstein monster in African nationalism'[22] –

and this was what Creasy's Government seemed to think. But they
had actually seen nothing of the sort. Another correspondent noted
that the great majority of the people were 'unaffected by the efforts
of the extremists to produce a state of chaos'.[23] Quite simply, Creasy
had over-reacted: a much more dangerous situation was dealt with
with ease in January by Creasy's well-prepared successor, Sir
Charles Arden-Clarke.

The Colonial Office itself, having already decided that African
nationalism would arrive in force at some time, also exaggerated the
importance of the Accra riots. Before sending out Arden-Clarke as
Governor in 1949, Creech Jones told him that 'the country is on the
edge of revolution'.[24] One historian has noted that Creech Jones was
unwilling to recognize that nationalism could affect Colonial Office
plans,[25] while another has argued that the outstanding feature of
Labour's colonial policy was its 'sensitive and imaginative appreciation of the emotional awakening of the colonial peoples'.[26] Both of
these views have to be rejected. Creech Jones was not slow to
recognize the force of nationalism: he saw it even before it existed.

Because of the mistaken assumption that nationalism on a mass
scale had arisen in the Gold Coast, the Colonial Office naturally
turned to the strategy it had constructed for just this eventuality. The
only thing to do with nationalism was to grant it concessions. The
Office could not dictate but only use its influence; and, as we can
clearly see, it used that influence consistently in favour of the
proposals worked out by the Colonial Office committee. It had not
been expected that any but the first stages would be put into operation so soon, but a pragmatic and flexible attitude had been taken to
the time-scale. Cohen himself had argued that 'internal political
pressure may radically affect both the pace and manner of political
advance'.[27]

The first move of the Office was to establish a Commission of
Enquiry to report on the causes of the disturbances and make
recommendations. By 24 March the three-man team had been
appointed:[28] Aiken Watson, K.C. (third choice, after Sir William
Fitzgerald and Sir Thomas Creed) was its head, while Andrew
Dalgleish, a trade union expert, and K.A.H. Murray, Rector of
Lincoln College, Oxford, also served. The resulting Watson Report
was a radical document which ensured that important constitutional
changes would follow.[29]

The Commission pointed out that general suspicion surrounded

Government activity of any sort. In particular there was a widespread belief that the chiefs were merely tools of Government designed to suppress the aspirations of the people. Most educated Africans, Watson pointed out, thought the chiefs should occupy an 'ornamental rather than useful' place in society. According to the Commissioners it was obvious that 'the star of rule through the Chiefs was on the wane'; native authority as a whole was declining, while the old religions were being undermined. The Commission endorsed local government on English lines, with local authorities rather like rural District Councils. They also recommended that a new constitution to last ten years should be drafted. The 1946 constitution was thought to have been 'outmoded at birth'. It advised a House of Assembly of forty-five elected and five nominated members, as well as *ex officio* ones, together with a board of nine Ministers, five of whom should be African members of the Assembly nominated by the Governor and approved by the Assembly.

The Watson Report created much controversy. Lord Milverton called it 'an essay in temerity by unqualified persons' and argued that the Government was being dazzled by prophets of pseudonationalism.[30] Hugh Thomas, formerly Secretary for Native Affairs in the Gold Coast, particularly objected to the remarks on indirect rule:

> Anyone with the slightest knowledge of the Gold Coast – and I have been there for over 30 years – knows that with the exception of some of the larger towns, which after all are more or less detribalized, the Gold Coast African is solidly behind his chief, and regards him as father, helper and adviser.[31]

Yet the British Government accepted the Watson recommendations in broad terms. A defence was, inevitably, made of the 1946 constitution, and it was noted that the chiefs still had an essential part to play in the Gold Coast. The Colonial Office was certainly looking to the demise of the political power of the chiefs but did not think this could be achieved at a stroke. A local committee was to be set up to look into Watson's proposals: 'His Majesty's Government for their part would regard them as broadly acceptable, and would be prepared to arrange for their early implementation ...'[32]

The Colonial Office noted that the constitutional concessions which were to be granted 'are not the fruits of an outbreak of disorder, but a further advance which had to a large extent already been envisaged'. How seriously should we take this statement? Certainly the riots had been of great importance; and the Minister of State's assertion in the House of Lords, that 'agitation in the Colonies makes no difference one way or the other to the pace of our constitutional advance',[33] cannot be taken seriously. Yet Britain had envisaged further concessions in the future and intended to grant them along the path laid down in 1947; and where the Watson recommendations differed from Cohen's proposals, the Colonial Office pressed for its own ideas. On the whole the Watson Report fitted in surprisingly well with the 1947 plan, but the official comments on the Report urged that the Executive Council should retain its formal advisory position to the Governor, while there was disagreement with the notion that Africans nominated by the Governor to sit on the Executive Council should have to be formally approved by the Legislature. The idea that the new constitution should last for a specified period of ten years was also deprecated.

In 1949 Creech Jones set up a Committee of Enquiry under Mr Justice Henley Coussey to examine the proposals for constitutional reform put forward by Watson and 'due regard being paid to the views expressed on them by His Majesty's Government, to consider the extent to which they can be accepted and the manner in which they should be implemented'.[34] The Coussey Committee was composed of thirty-eight African members, five of whom had been arrested during the Accra riots. The British Government was making no attempt to maintain the *status quo*: on the contrary, it was facilitating extensive constitutional advances in accordance with the strategy it had outlined in 1947. The Coussey report, which built on the basis of the Watson recommendations, was accepted in Whitehall, subject to minor changes to bring it more in line with Cohen's proposals.

The Coussey Committee agreed with the Colonial Office that the summary disappearance of the institution of chieftaincy 'would spell disaster'.[35] Nevertheless extensive local government reforms, well in line with the policy expressed by the British Government, were recommended. Indirect election to a central legislature was endorsed, except for the existing municipalities, though not in the manner the Office had anticipated. There was to be direct election by universal suffrage to an electoral college in each constituency, each college to consist of not less than 200 delegates. Then these colleges would elect representatives to go forward to the centre.

This two-stage process was expected to eliminate the 'charlatan and the demagogue'. The Committee decided by a majority of only one to have a bicameral legislature – a senate of thirty-six chiefs and a House of Assembly of seventy-eight members, including not more than three *ex officio*. The Executive Council was to include the Governor, not more than three officials, and eight African members chosen from the Assembly and to have the status of Ministers. The Executive was to be collectively responsible to the Legislative, though the Governor was to retain certain reserve powers.[36]

The British Government accepted these proposals in outline.[37] It advised in favour of a unicameral legislature and noted that it would have preferred that the electoral colleges be elected by the local authorities. Most important of all, Creech Jones was adamant that, since the Governor would admittedly require reserve powers, he would retain ultimate responsibility. As in Cohen's scheme, the executive would be responsible to the Governor, while the African Ministers would defend their policies in the Assembly.

The Colonial Office was by 1949 prepared to concede more than hitherto. In 1948 there had been objections to Watson's proposal that Ministers should be removable on a seventy-five per cent vote of censure. Yet in 1949 it was recognized that the Assembly should have the right to remove African, though not *ex officio*, members of the Executive Council. Nevertheless it was, on the whole, remarkable that the British Government was not obliged to depart further from its 1947 strategy. This was partly due to the Colonial Office's influence in West Africa and partly to the prescience of the 1947 draughtsmen. Stage three of Cohen's constitutional strategy had been reached with the new Gold Coast constitution. The new Legislative Assembly was to consist of members almost entirely elected, directly or indirectly, by popular vote. The Executive Council was to contain the Governor as Chairman, three *ex officio* members, and eight African members drawn from the Assembly, six of whom were to be Ministers with portfolio and two without. The Executive Council was to be the principal instrument of policy and was to take decisions by majority vote.[38] The Gold Coast was now set beyond recall towards responsible self-government. According to the Colonial Office's scheme, stage four, in which internal self-government would be achieved, would inevitably follow quickly after stage three. The radical politician Kwame Nkrumah was arguing that 'Freedom or Self-Government has never been handed over to any colonial country on a silver platter'.[39] This may have been so, but the British Government were making it surprisingly easy for the African nationalists.

Britain had hoped that the moderate leaders of the United Gold Coast Convention, including Danquah, would win the 1951 election under the new constitution. The Convention split after the Accra riots, Nkrumah and the radical 'young men' breaking away to form the Convention People's Party in June 1949. The intelligentsia now re-formed their alliance with the chiefs and seemed set, according to Colonial Office hopes, for electoral success. In fact, the CPP swept to victory, with exactly the majority that Government Intelligence predicted.[40] Nkrumah's Party won thirty-four of the thirty-eight seats contested on a party basis: in the absence of other organized blocs, this was enough for them to dominate a House of eighty seats. Nkrumah was released from prison and became Leader of Government Business. The British Government had given too much weight to the intelligentsia and the chiefs and had not realized that a social as well as a political revolution was taking place.[41] In the typology of Martin Kilson, Britain had sought to conciliate the neo-traditional and the upper-echelon elites and had failed to reckon with the sub-elites.[42] Elections under the new constitution had given the radicals a greater focus for their political activities: and thus, un-wittingly, the British helped to create the nationalism they were consciously trying to appease.

Concessions granted in the Gold Coast could scarcely be resisted elsewhere in West Africa. As a result, Milverton's constitution in Nigeria was scrapped and replaced by one formulated by Sir John Macpherson and an all-Nigeria Constitutional Conference. Twelve Nigerian Ministers were to take their places in the Executive Coun-cil.[43] The policy of rapid decolonization could not be stopped.

We can now see clearly that the Colonial Office mistook the force at work in the Accra riots for fully-fledged nationalism and, by the premature application of the 1947 strategy, helped create this very phenomenon. The Colonial Office did the work of the nationalists for them. It is remarkable how little agitation achieved in West Africa. Nkrumah started a 'positive action' campaign against the 'half-baked' proposals of the Coussey Committee, with the CPP calling for 'Self-Government Now'. But these efforts achieved nothing, except increased notoriety and popularity for Nkrumah. Having won the 1951 election, the leader of the CPP applied himself to working the proposals he had so vigorously condemned. In Nigeria the Zikist movement, though favouring violence, was of no great significance. Reprisals for the Enugu shooting incident, in which twenty-one strikers were killed in November 1949, were rejected at the last minute by Azikiwe himself.[44] (In Central and East Africa the 1947 policy was slower to have its effects; but after the ill-conceived Federation had precipitated mass nationalism, and after the trauma of Mau Mau, the strategy was broadly adhered to.)

But if the Office did the work of the nationalists for them, the nationalists – because the riots secured acceptance of the 1947 plan – did the work of the Office. The Colonial Office had been 'forced' to apply their proposals earlier than had been expected; but there were few signs of dismay that this had been found necessary. Cohen, for one, was happy at the way things had turned out. Constitutional progress had outstripped economic development, but the Report had implied that this might happen; and there was by this time a new emphasis on the notion that 'unless a favourable political climate is created, economic development will be hampered and delayed at every turn'.[45]

The fears engendered by the Accra riots did more than anything else to secure acceptance in Africa, and especially among the Colonial Service, for the 1947 strategy. The fortuitous misapprehension that nationalism had already arrived in force supplemented the Colonial Office's manful attempts to propagate its views. When Cohen became Assistant Under-Secretary, and head of the Africa Division, in February 1947, he released Cartland from routine duties and formed the African Studies Branch. Ronald Robinson was recruited to this in July 1947, and in 1949 the *Journal of African Administration* made its appearance.[46] Since political advance was well under way by this latter date, the African Studies Branch concentrated particularly on local government reform. It was often an uphill struggle.

LOCAL GOVERNMENT REFORM

There was general optimism in 1947-48 that native administration could be successfully transformed into local government on English lines and that the pivotal role assigned to local government in the 1947 strategy could be made a reality. It was confidently asserted that the principles of the English system were indeed exportable to

Africa: it had grown up haphazardly in England, and many mistakes had been made, but Africa could profit from this experience and the consequent pitfalls could be avoided.[47] Yet the subsequent history of the African territories showed that the expectations of these early years had been naively sanguine. The logical and consistent scheme adumbrated in Britain resulted in a confused and complex variety of structures in Africa, in much the same way as indirect rule issued in a diversity of local forms in practice. Enthusiasm for the new policy had largely evaporated by the end of the 1950s.

The attempt to introduce local government into Africa is an untidy story: there were great differences between the institutions used in different territories, and indeed between different areas in the same territory. There was little consistency in the functions performed by the local authorities or in the methods of financing them. This is partly explained by the fact that local government had to be built on the infra-structure of the NAs, which had been heterogeneous. Also of significance was the fact that the Colonial Office could not impose change: initiative had to come from the Colonial Governments, while Britain could only advise when called upon to do so. There was nevertheless an important utilization of British local government expertise. For instance, when the Lagos Town Council failed to function effectively, Bernard Storey, the Town Clerk of Norwich, was called in by the Government of Nigeria to make recommendations.[48]

Changes in the old system occurred relatively slowly. In general, legislation was introduced in the early or mid-1950s but had little immediate impact. The area of most rapid progress was Eastern Nigeria, where indirect rule had never been at all successful. One of the most important questions to be decided, in this as in other areas, was whether local government was to approximate to a 'pyramidal' or a 'horizontal' pattern – whether there was to be a hierarchy of authorities, each exercising powers delegated from the one above, or whether local authorities should have independent spheres of action, responsible only to the central Government.[49] The Regional House of Assembly in Eastern Nigeria decided on a horizontal pattern, with a Regional Authority at the highest level and below a three-tier system of County, District, and Local Councils, each effectively autonomous within its own field of activity.[50] The local authorities were made elective, the chiefs became titular figure-heads with no political weight, while the power of the District

Officers was removed. But it was soon found that change had been too sudden: staff problems arose, while most of the new councillors had little notion what they were supposed to do. In 1955, under the Local Government Ordinance, the central Government took a more direct responsibility for the local authorities, the Regional Authority was scrapped, a Local Government Inspectorate (the District Officers 'in disguise') was formally established, and in 1956 provision was made to co-opt up to one-fifth of the Council of Chiefs onto the local authorities. After over-rapid advances, there was thus a partial return to older forms.[51]

Changes in Western Nigeria were similar, though less hasty. In 1952 Awolowo introduced the Ordinance which substituted elective councils for the old NAs. Twenty-one Divisional, one hundred District, and ninety-five Local Councils replaced seventy-one NAs. Provision was made for up to one-quarter of the councillors to represent the chiefs, while the rest were to be elected.[52] In the North developments were far more gradual. Local government continued to centre on the Emirates, though the councils now became more important and contained a larger elected element. District and Village Councils grew within the Emirates, and each level of the hierarchy became more democratic.[53]

In the Gold Coast the Coussey Committee had recommended that the NAs be replaced by democratically elected councils, with a place retained for the chiefs. The Local Government Ordinance of 1951 set up a two-tier system of District Councils with local councils beneath them. Two-thirds of the members of all councils were to be elected, the remaining places being reserved for the traditional authorities. The CPP under Nkrumah used its powers against the chiefs and against the Regional Councils recommended by Sir Frederick Bourne in 1955, and so the Gold Coast Government retained a tight control over local government.[54] But as elsewhere in Africa an orderly structure belied considerable confusion. By 1953 only 'embryonic local government bodies' had been formed. There were uncontested elections, while only a small percentage of the electorate voted; the new councillors lacked experience and skill; and there were acute shortages of trained staff.[55] The situation was similar in Sierra Leone, where tax abuses led to serious riots in 1955 and where a three-tier system of local government in the rural area of the Colony lacked vitality.[56]

Outside West Africa, local government was often looked upon as an alternative to political developments at the centre, rather than as a preparation for them. It was in Kenya, which had no history of traditional indirect rule, that local government worked most effectively. Those areas containing settlers saw an easy implementation of British forms, with County and District Councils being formed in 1952. A similar scheme was introduced in the reserve areas, with the existing local native councils being replaced by African District Councils. Kenya introduced English local government principles to an extent unparalleled elsewhere in the dependent empire at that time.[57] Yet even here the policy was not fulfilling its designated role, since African progress in the central Government was severely limited.

In Tanganyika the legislation which marks the theoretical transition to local government came in 1953 with the Local Government Ordinance, which aimed at replacing NAs by fully elective, multiracial bodies at the District Council level.[58] This Ordinance was adaptive, and could only be introduced where there was a definite desire for it. Hence the old and the new systems existed side by side for some considerable time, and the new local government policy encountered many difficulties. Lethargy, dishonesty, and nepotism all provided obstacles, and so did 'multi-tribalism', owing to the existence of about 120 tribes in Tanganyika.[59]

In Central Africa progress in local government was generally slow. In 1950 R. S. Hudson recommended that local government bodies on the English model be created at district level in Nyasaland to take over, in time, the functions of the NAs, and in 1953 the Local Government (District Councils) Ordinance set up councils with appointed members, election being a long-term goal.[60] Developments in Northern Rhodesia were similar. In Barotseland, where no true local government existed and where there was very little demand for it, the councils were gradually made more representative. Elsewhere 'parish' councils were induced with some success within the districts. Nevertheless official policy in Northern Rhodesia, to a greater extent than elsewhere, developed local government round the chief.[61]

The 1947 Despatch had a cool reception in Uganda. The 1949 Local Government Ordinance did increase the elective element in the District Councils, but it did very little to increase their powers and was, on the whole, a conservative measure. Greater progress was made when Sir Andrew Cohen, one of the chief initiators of the post-war policy at the Colonial Office, was Governor from 1952 to 1956.[62] The crucial piece of legislation came in 1955 with the District Councils Ordinance. The District Councils were now given increased powers and were to be almost wholly elected by the lower councils. Cohen insisted that the size of the Councils be reduced and, by this proposed innovation, presented a threat to the jealously guarded traditional form of the institutions in Buganda. The deposition of the Kabaka provoked a major crisis; and despite the fact that he was restored on conditions including an acceptance of local government, particularism had been enhanced and the Buganda Districts were stillborn. Cohen's scheme, however, proved far more successful in the other Provinces of Uganda, which comprised three-quarters of the country's territory and population.[63] Nevertheless local government did not fulfil the crucial role originally assigned to it by Cohen in 1947. It was noted with justification in 1959 that

> Not until the constitutional future of Uganda is clarified and stabilized and the constituent elements of the state are re-defined will *local* government as normally understood be possible.[64]

In other words, only when constitutional development at the centre had been settled could local government reform be completed. The hope that local government would precede, or be conterminous with, the transfer of power had proved illusory. Local government was not the key to the growth of nation-states.

Can we give a final verdict on the local government policy? All judgments depend on one's perspective, but clearly the hopes entertained in 1947 were exaggerated. This was recognized at the Cambridge Summer School in 1958.[65] The benefits of the policy were pointed out at this meeting: it had broadened the base of representation in local bodies; it had provided a democratic system of checks and balances; it had contributed to economic and social development; it had assisted the separation of local judicial, executive, and legislative functions.[66] Yet attention was also drawn to the abuses that had grown up. There was an undue prominence of party politics in local government affairs; committees were often packed by the dominant party; there were instances of false registration, of elections held at the wrong time, and of the intimidation of electors. Chiefs often exercised a decisive influence on elections or so dominated a council 'as to render its proceedings a formality only'.[67] Nor did the local authorities have enough revenue to employ the staff to make social services effective.

It was recognized that local government had not fulfilled the early aspirations associated with it. Local bodies had contributed to development, but in most cases there had not been much success with economic projects of a long-term nature or which affected indigenous land rights. The political aspirations of groups such as the ex-servicemen had not been channelled into local government. Though there had been a diminution of chiefly power, this remained stronger than had been anticipated in many areas. 'Our general experience is that they [the chiefs] have, and will continue to have, an important part to play in local government'.[68] The Colonial Office was now forced to take a far more flexible – indeed Haileyan – attitude to local authorities. There was a remarkable change between objectives in 1948 and 1958. Cohen had called for the assimilation of local differences to the English model and had stressed that progress might have to precede an active demand for it. But a decade later it was emphasized that

> there should be no question of forcing native authorities into any preconceived Colonial or even territorial pattern, but that the particular approach should be dictated by the actual condition of each individual native authority as measured by its strength, popularity and efficiency.[69]

Lastly, local government had failed to provide a training-ground for African politicians. The attractions of local administration had proved insufficient.

> We think we are right in saying that in the immediate post-war years, those eager for power tended to concentrate on central government and to conclude that the quickest route to it was to appeal to, or stimulate, racial feeling. ... Local government institutions ... were too remote from the centre of power to attract the ambitious politician.

Yet if this original hope had proved abortive, there remained another and characteristic one to cling to:

> The purpose which was ... not achieved immediately is, however, coming closer to achievement in the long-run for it is only under the regime of a representative government rather than that of an official government that the politically-minded find service in local as well as in central government attractive.[70]

The policy of local government, like theoretical indirect rule, remained consistent and rigorous only on paper. Presented with the diversity of African conditions, the policy was stretched so far that it often ceased to be recognizable. A policy from which so much had been expected in fact produced so little. Nor should we exaggerate the importance of the Colonial Office and its policy for the changes that did occur. The 1947 Despatch had been widely resented in the Colonial Service, and the similarity between subsequent developments and the propaganda of the Office may have been due as much to an identity of thought as to direct or indirect influence. *Post hoc ergo propter hoc* is a dangerous formula.

Was local government therefore a complete failure? The policy did not transplant English local government in tropical Africa. It was often remote from the people; it was grossly inefficient by Western standards; nor was it totally representative. Yet some progress was made in the direction of 'efficient and representative local government'. 'Failure' is surely only a meaningful concept in relation to the possibility of 'success', and this was absent. The men of 1947, though over-optimistic and idealistic, had realized that they had an immensely difficult task ahead of them, and one moreover that could yield little kudos for the British. They were perhaps trying to achieve the impossible; but it is difficult indeed to see how the planners, by adopting a more down-to-earth Haileyan approach, could in fact have achieved anything more. Given their determination to foster effective nation-states in Africa, based on the assumption that nationalism would soon be able to insist on responsible self-government, there seemed no alternative policy to pursue. Cohen and Creech Jones had been fiercely realistic in their determination to provide the best conditions possible for the fledgling nations and in their recognition that ideal circumstances could not be insisted upon. The 'best' simply meant that which could be achieved in practice.

The 1947 policy for the empire in tropical Africa thus had unforeseen and paradoxical results. Progress at the centre was achieved far more quickly than had been anticipated, especially in West Africa, and this had been partly due to the strategy itself. Local government, intended to counterbalance constitutional developments and to ensure a genuinely democratic and responsible public opinion, had not kept pace with the centre. Instead of new states being developed from below, the impetus came – and would continue to come – from above. The ideals of 1947 had not become reality: in other words, the fears expressed in that year had been realized. Progress had surged forward at the centre (as if) inevitably, while the localities had been left behind. Yet if developments had been one-sided, and if the vaunted policy of local government had been unsatisfactory, at least there had been little bloodshed or repression, while the hope remained that popular nationalist governments would successfully induce reform in the future.

The post-war policy of Creech Jones and Cohen had materially affected subsequent developments in Africa in the direction of rapid decolonization, though not with the conditions they wished to see. British planning had been logical and consistent, balancing opposing concepts in high strategy. Yet the whole of the post-war policy had been built on a belief in the inevitability of African self-government. The balanced planning was in effect jettisoned, and all that remained was the initial assumption, which helped to create the very phenomenon that was regarded as inevitable. Perhaps the emergence of popular African nationalism was indeed predestined. But there can be no doubt that Britain's mistaken interpretation of the Accra riots, and the premature implementation of Cohen's constitutional proposals, significantly hastened its emergence. Possibly there was an element of wish-fulfilment by its creators in the premise on which the 1947 policy was based. If so, the wish was soon fulfilled. The initiative had passed with surprising rapidity to the African nationalists. Creech Jones had always been sceptical of what an alien government could do without massive local support, and such support had seldom been forthcoming. Now the Africans themselves would have their chance. British hopes for the formation of modern democratic states in Africa lay – even at the time of independence – with black Africans.

NOTES

1. *Parl. Debates* (Commons), vol.467. col.1395. 20 July 1949.
2. *Ibid.* vol.453, cols.663, 666, 668. 8 July 1948.
3. *Ibid.* vol.454, col.628. 22 July 1948.
4. *The Colonial Empire 1939-1947.* Cmd.7176, p.81.
5. *The Colonial Empire 1947-1948.* Cmd.7433, p.83.
6. *Parl. Debates* (Commons), vol.453, cols.700-703.
7. *Ibid.* vol.443, col.2020. 6 Nov. 1947.
8. *Plan for the Mechanised Production of Groundnuts in East and Central Africa.* Cmd. 7030. See also Alan Wood, *The Groundnut Affair* (London, 1950).
9. FCB 43/1 278-84. Article for the *New Statesman*.
10. *The Times*, 10 Jan. 1951.
11. *Manchester Guardian*, 10 June 1950.
12. *Daily Express*, 26 June 1947.
13. FCB 18/4 85. Hinden to Ian Mikardo, 24 Feb. 1948.
14. *Venture*, vol.2, no.8, Sept. 1950.
15. Goldsworthy, *Colonial Issues*, p.20. See also Austin, *Politics in Ghana*, p.49.
16. CO 96/757/31165/D. Minute by Stockdale, 16 Feb. 1940. O.G.R. Williams minuted, 16 Dec. 1938, that 'The Gold Coast is not a model of Colonial administration'. (CO 323/1616/7322/1).
17. See Austin, *Politics in Ghana*, pp.58, 72-4. See also R. Rathbone, 'The Government of the Gold Coast After the Second World War', *African Affairs*, LXVII, 1968, pp.213-14.
18. CO 96/795/31312/2 Pt.1. Creasy to Secretary of State, 29 Feb. 1948.
19. *Ibid.* Creasy to Lloyd, 9 Mar. 1948.
20. *Ibid.* Minute by J.K. Thompson, 1 Mar. 1948.
21. CO 96/795/31312/2 Pt.2. Telegram from Nkrumah to Creech Jones, 1 Mar. 1948.
22. *Daily Herald*, 15 Apr. 1948.
23. *The Times*, 6 Apr. 1948.
24. Rathbone, 'The Government of the Gold Coast', p.217.
25. Goldsworthy, *Colonial Issues*, p.20.
26. Haqqi, *Colonial Policy of the Labour Government*, p.272.
27. CO 847/36/47238. Appendix III, Part 2, of the Report.
28. CO 96/796/31312/2D Pt.1. Minute by Cohen, 24 Mar. 1948.
29. *Report of the Commission of Enquiry into the Disturbances in the Gold Coast.* Colonial no.231.
30. *Parl. Debates* (Lords), vol.165, cols.1070 and 1075. 30 Nov. 1949.
31. *The Times*, 13 Aug. 1948.
32. *Statement by His Majesty's Government.* Colonial no.232.
33. *Parl. Debates* (Lords), vol.165, col.1110. Listowel.
34. *Colonial Office Bulletin*, 1 Jan. 1949.
35. *Report by the Committee on Constitutional Reform.* Colonial no.248. See also *JAA*. vol.II, no.1, 1950, 'Constitutional Reform in the Gold Coast'.
36. *Ibid.*
37. *Parl. Debates* (Commons), vol.468. col.1316. 25 Nov. 1949. Creech Jones.
38. *Ibid.*
39. 'What I Mean by Positive Action'. Quoted in Metcalfe (ed.), *Great Britain and Ghana*, p.688.

40. Rathbone, 'The Government of the Gold Coast', p.218.
41. Austin, *Politics in Ghana*, p.22.
42. Gann and Duignan (eds.), *Colonialism in Africa*, vol.II, 'Emergent Elites of Black Africa'.
43. Olusanya, *The Second World War and Politics in Nigeria*, pp.127-38.
44. Interview with Hugh Elliott, 31 Mar. 1979.
45. Speech by Griffiths at a Labour Party and FCB Conference, 23 Sept. 1950. Quoted by H. Pelling (ed.), *The Challenge of Socialism* (2nd edn. London, 1968), p.361.
46. See the *Journal of Administration Overseas*, April 1966: 'The Journal and the Transfer of Power', by R.E. Robinson.
47. *JAA*, vol.I, no.2. 'The Application of English Local Government Principles in Africa', by R.A. Stevens.
48. *JAA*, vol.V, no.3. 'Lagos Town Council'.
49. *JAA*, vol.I, no.1. 'The Relationship of Major and Minor Local Government Authorities'.
50. *JAA*, vol.II, no.1. 'Local Government Reform in the Eastern Province of Nigeria'.
51. U. Hicks, *Development from Below* (Oxford, 1961), pp.169-74.
52. *Ibid.* pp.175-81. (See also *JAA*, vol.VII, no.4: 'Local Government in the Western Region of Nigeria'.)
53. *Ibid.* p.182. (See also *JAA*, vol.VII, no.2: 'A Review of the State of Development of the Native Authority System in the Northern Region of Nigeria on the 1st January, 1955'.)
54. *Ibid.* pp.186-91.
55. *JAA*, vol.IV, no.4. 'Supplement – A Survey of the Development of Local Government'.
56. Hicks, *Development from Below*, pp.196-203.
57. *Ibid.* p.214.
58. *JAA*, vol.VI, no.3. 'Changes in Local Government in Tanganyika'.
59. *JAA*, vol.VIII, no.3. 'Some Difficulties in the Democratisation of Native Authorities in Tanganyika'.
60. *JAA*, vol.VII, no.4. 'The Progress of Local Government in Nyasaland'.
61. L.H. Gann, *A History of Northern Rhodesia* (London, 1964), pp.379-87.
62. For Cohen as Governor, see C. Gertzel, 'Kingdoms, Districts, and the Unitary State: Uganda, 1945-1962.' Low and Smith (eds.), *History of East Africa*, vol.III.
63. Hicks, *Development from Below*, pp.206-10.
64. *JAA*, vol.XI, no.1. 'Some Problems of Local Government in Uganda'.
65. *Colonial Office Summer Conference on African Administration*. 'A general review of progress in local government in British African Territories'. African no.1193. 1958.
66. *Ibid.* p.18.
67. *Ibid.* p.11.
68. *Ibid.* p.21.
69. *Ibid.* p.13.
70. *Ibid.* p.11.

9

Conclusion

Deceptive dreams, abortive hopes, expectations
unfulfilled ...
– Jean-Paul Sartre, *Existentialism is a Humanism*

During the period covered by this book a revolution took place in
British African policy. Between 1938 and 1948 the whole rationale
and purpose of the empire in Africa changed: a defensive, static
conception gave way to a positive, dynamic one. On the eve of the
war, British ascendancy in Africa seemed unassailable, but in 1947
the door to rapid decolonization was unlocked. The magnitude of
this metamorphosis was not realized while it was happening and has
never received due recognition. The preceding chapters of this book
have attempted to describe the changes in attitude and policy that
occurred and to evaluate the forces that caused them.

The most fundamental novelty after the war was the assumption
that British methods and institutions were exportable to Africa. The
empire receded on the wave of this imperialist notion. The attempt
to conserve indigenous society behind the barrier of indirect rule,
and so to allow of gradual and 'organic' change, was abandoned in
the Colonial Office in 1947. Local government on British lines,
together with the development of Parliamentary institutions at the
centre, had finally been accepted as goals of policy. Democracy, in
the western sense of the word, was to be evolved in Africa. No
longer was the African to develop 'on his own lines' towards an
unknown destination.

> The solutions of the 'native problem' all lay somewhere between
> the two extreme ends of a spectrum, with the 'schoolmaster'
> concept of ultimate Europeanization at one end and the protec-
> tive 'game warden' outlook at the other.[1]

After the Second World War, the outlook of the 'schoolmaster' was in the ascendant, with Creech Jones and Cohen putting forward their plan for the end of empire.

Yet the paternalism of the policy-makers after 1947 was of the variety that wished to see initiative and enterprise from the colonial wards. Indeed the Africans were expected to reach full maturity and take over the government of new nation states. The schoolmaster, wisely realising that dependency stifles growth, would soon be out of a job. Suitable successors would inevitably be drawn from among educated Africans. In 1947 the intelligentsia had not organized powerful nationalist movements and did not have the power to force concessions from the British (and indeed they would first have to attract mass support before the transfer of power would be conceded). But the future was thought to lie ineluctably with the educated elite. The growth of nationalism seemed to many to be an automatic response to colonial rule, while the Labour Government's whole outlook favoured an elite based on education and intelligence rather than on the hereditary principle. Creech Jones in particular was sympathetic to the aspirations of the intelligentsia rather than to the chiefs. Furthermore, the British conception of government's role in society had, since the inter-war years, undergone a change which militated against the conservation of power in alliance with unprogressive chiefs. Government, partly owing to the Second World War, had now actively to promote the economic and social well-being of its citizens. 'Nowadays', wrote a correspondent of *The Times* in January 1945, 'the view that the final purpose of government is not the maintenance of order nor the increase of wealth but the general social betterment of the governed inspires both domestic and colonial policy.'[2] The vital question for Africa therefore became – who can best promote development and run social services? The answer led to a search for new educated collaborators, despite the fact that the cost would be the transfer of power.

The fostering of colonial self-government was itself thought to be necessary for a variety of reasons. Despite the increased usefulness of the empire to Britain, the moral and intellectual climate during and after the war was profoundly anti-imperialist, especially in international circles. Imperialism was tantamount to exploitation. The Labour Party had long called for eventual self-government in the colonies, and from 1945 onwards Attlee's Government, despite indifference and despite calls for the economic development of

Africa to help close the dollar gap, was concerned to devolve increasing measures of self-government to the colonial territories. The forward views of Creech Jones, and his identity of thought with Andrew Cohen, were vital for the formulation of a progressive and comprehensive policy towards Africa, while the political necessity for the Labour Government to construct and espouse a scheme distinct from previous Conservative statements made more urgent a radical reorientation. Even if the goal of self-government had not been stated before, the Labour Government would have made such a commitment.

As it was, the Coalition Government had already defined its policy in 1943 as the fostering of the fullest possible measure of self-government for the colonies. This meant that after the war the Labour Government had to go one step further. The Second World War had been of vital importance in the re-definition of colonial principles. Because of the ideological requirements of a war against Nazi imperialism and because of American pressure, Britain liberalized the theory of her colonial policy. American imperial involvement gave a profound shock to the officials in the Colonial Office, and all complacency was removed. In 1943 one official judged that

> He would be a bold man who would sit down now to draw the map of the British Empire as it may appear in 1950. Possibilities which would have seemed fantastic five years ago cannot be excluded.[3]

The policy of self-government, together with the doctrine of Colonial Development and Welfare, meant that the empire was now morally rearmed, while the Colonial Office itself was preparing for a more dynamic and authoritative role. Yet the empire had in effect been mortgaged by liberal promises during the war, and major repayments would soon be necessary.

During the war the Colonial Office constructed plans not only in economic but also in political matters. The Office was under the sway of Lord Hailey. He advised cautious developments both in the sphere of native administration and of the central councils. His was essentially a pragmatic attitude, more concerned with the effectiveness of the institutions of local government than with their theoretical composition. Insofar as indirect rule was a system, Hailey helped to destroy it. Yet his advice on constitutional development was soon overruled. He wanted to avoid an irrevocable commitment to institutions of the British type and advised that Africans should not be admitted to the Executive Council, while unofficial majorities on the Legislative Councils should also be resisted. By the end of the war, however, initiatives from the Colonial Governments had destroyed this strategy. Once Burns and Bourdillon had overcome considerable Colonial Office resistance to their call for Africans on the Executive Council, Hailey's conception of political advance had been ruined. Yet by the end of the war a pattern of development was becoming discernible, and it was one which utilized the existing organs of government. The African Governors unwittingly provided the embryo of a scheme for the transfer of power, and as a result there was to be no development of indigenous institutions and no new political forms.

By 1945 Africans had taken their place on the Executive Councils of West Africa, and the problem to be solved was how to remove their constitutional irresponsibility. The answer was to make them responsible to the Governor and thereafter to the Legislature. On the Legislative Council, unofficial majorities existed in 1947 in the Gold Coast, Nigeria, and Northern Rhodesia, and they had been accepted in theory in Sierra Leone, Kenya, and Nyasaland.[4] Though the diversity of colonial conditions and constitutions had always been stressed in the past, these differences were now seen to exist 'within a common form'.[5] Hence the 1947 Report could produce a uniform scheme for the constitutional development of Africa.

Thus we can see that the Second World War had played an important part in the construction of the post-war policy. Ideas of closer union or amalgamation had been resisted, *laissez-faire* and the idea of colonial self-sufficiency had been abandoned, native administration had been criticized by Hailey and was beginning to be modified, while the development of the central councils was slowly being undertaken. Moreover, Britain was now committed to developing responsible self-government within the empire. Policy-makers after the war did not operate from a *tabula rasa*: they built on the changes in policy that had occurred during the war. Nevertheless significant innovations were introduced after 1945. Democracy was to be fostered in Africa to an extent unparalleled hitherto. There was a new urgency and a further telescoping of the time-scale. British policy became much more systematic and more rigorous, even doctrinaire. Indeed the changes introduced in 1947 appear even more revolutionary if compared with war-time practice rather than theory.

We have seen that a revolution in African policy occurred between 1939 and 1947, but it may reasonably be argued that in fact two revolutions took place. Imperial practice during the war was very different from that before or after. Politicians and officials talked and wrote at length during the war about the liberalization of imperial policy and the fostering of self-government, about the good future intentions of the Mother Country. Yet this disguised the fact that Britain was acting more imperialistically than ever before. In a sense this was the heyday of the empire. During the war the British empire really existed for the first time! Imperial control at last became a reality. Colonial troops were conscripted and played an important part in the war effort. Colonial production was increased and used to Britain's best advantage, without proper payment being made. Forced labour became a common feature in Africa and elsewhere during the war. Discontent in the colonies produced no redress of grievances: instead all 'agitators' were summarily imprisoned. Britain tightened her grip on the dependent territories and used them remorselessly to help the war against the Axis Powers. At last the imperialism against which the critics of empire had railed so long actually existed. The empire was now of substantial worth to Britain: small wonder that there were many during the war who wanted to make the relationship between Britain and the colonies permanent.

There was thus a remarkable contrast between imperial theory and practice during the war. Little publicity was given to the growth of imperialism during the hostilities, and instead it was focused on Britain's good intentions. After 1945 practice had to be brought more into line with these intentions. The upsurge of imperialism could be no more than a temporary aberration. Yet many people in Britain felt that they had been fighting to keep the empire intact and had no intention of liquidating it. This makes even more remarkable, and revolutionary, the work of Creech Jones and Cohen at the Colonial Office. Though building on the legacy of the past, they constructed a strategy which few believed desirable in itself. In 1947 Britain was prepared to concede self-government within a generation, and there was no thought of repression: yet the plan could be interpreted as actually slowing down the rate of political change. Cohen had ensured that his proposals were attractively packaged.

The effects of this policy on Africa were complex but significant. It proved impossible to convert native administration into English-style local government, though some progress in this direction was made, while constitutional development outstripped both economic and all other forms of progress. Thus anti-imperial pressure from the United States, the formulae of the politicians, the increasingly strident cries of African nationalists, Hailey's recommendations, the initiatives of the Governors, the influence of the Labour Government, together with the important work of the civil service – all these factors produced results which no one intended or even surmised.

NOTES

1. Gann and Duignan, *Burden of Empire*, p.215.
2. *The Times*, 10 Jan. 1945.
3. CO 847/27/27265/33A. 'Memorandum on Post-War Training'. R. Furse, 26 Feb. 1943.
4. CO 847/36/47238. 1947 Report: 'Constitutional Development in Africa'.
5. Martin Wight, *The Development of the Legislative Council, 1606-1945* (London, 1946), p.136.

Bibliography

A. Manuscript Sources

Public Record Office, London

The Colonial Office Papers
The Cabinet Papers

Rhodes House, Oxford

The Fabian Colonial Bureau Papers
The Arthur Creech Jones Papers
The Hailey Papers
The Diaries of Sir Philip Mitchell

Churchill College, Cambridge

The Attlee Papers
The Bevin Papers
The Swinton Papers

The British Library of Political and Economic Science, London

The Dalton Papers

University College, Oxford

The Attlee Papers

Nuffield College, Oxford

The Cripps Papers

University of Sussex

The Leonard Woolf Papers

Institute of Commonwealth Studies, London

Sir John Shuckburgh, 'Colonial Civil History of the War'. Unpublished, 4 Vols.

Unpublished Theses

Henderson, Ian, 'The Attitude and Policy of the Main Section of the British Labour Movement to Imperial Issues, 1899-1924'. (Oxford B.Litt. 1964)

Nordman, C.R., 'Prelude to Decolonisation in West Africa: The Development of British Colonial Policy, 1938-1947'. (Oxford D.Phil. 1976)
Stone, R.L., 'Colonial Administration and Rural Politics in South-Central Ghana, 1919-1951'. (Cambridge Ph.D. 1974)
Tumasi, E.Y., 'Aspects of Politics in Ghana, 1929-1939: A Study of the Relationships between Discontent and Nationalism'. (Oxford D.Phil. 1971)
Wylie, D.S., 'Critics of Colonial Policy in Kenya with special reference to Norman Leys and W. McGregor Ross'. (Edinburgh M.Litt. 1974)

B. Published Sources

GOVERNMENT PUBLICATIONS

Parliamentary Debates (House of Commons), Official Report
Parliamentary Debates (House of Lords), Official Report

Nutrition in the Colonial Empire, cmd.6050 of July 1939
West India Royal Commission, 1938-39: Recommendations, cmd.6174 of Feb. 1940.
Statement of Policy on Colonial Development and Welfare, cmd.6175 of Feb. 1940
Speech by the Late Marquis of Lothian, cmd.6239 of 1940
Colonial Development Advisory Committee: Eleventh and Final Report, cmd.6298 of July 1941
Certain Aspects of Colonial Policy in War-Time, cmd.6299 of June 1941
Colonial Development and Welfare Act 1940: Report on the Operation of the Act to 31st October, 1942, cmd.6422 of Feb. 1943
Report of the Commission on Higher Education in the Colonies, cmd.6647 of June 1945
Report of the Commission on Higher Education in West Africa, cmd.6655 of June 1945
Colonial Development and Welfare: Despatch dated 12th November, 1945, from the Secretary of State for the Colonies to Colonial Governors, cmd.6713 of Dec. 1945
The Colonial Empire, 1939-1947, cmd.7167 of July 1947
Colonial Office Summer School on African Administration, African no.1173 of Aug. 1947
The Colonial Empire, 1947-1948, cmd.7433 of 1948
Partners in Progress: the Africa Conference, 1948
Report of the Commission of Enquiry into Disturbances in the Gold Coast, Colonial no.231 of 1948
Statement by His Majesty's Government on the Report of the Commission into Disturbances in the Gold Coast, Colonial no.232 of 1948
Colonial Office Summer Conference on African Administration, Aug.-Sept. 1948, African no.1174
The Colonial Territories, 1948-1949, cmd.7715 of 1949

The Colonial Territories, 1949-1950, cmd.7958 of 1950
The Colonial Territories, 1950-1951, cmd.8243 of 1951
Colonial Office Summer Conference on African Administration, Aug.-Sept.
    1951. African no.1178
Colonial Office Summer Conference on African Administration, Aug.-Sept.
    1957. African no.1190
Colonial Office Summer Conference on African Administration, Aug.-Sept.
    1958. African no.1193

NEWSPAPERS AND PERIODICALS

A Digest of African Local Administration (Dec. 1947–Sept. 1948)
The Journal of African Administration (Jan. 1949–Oct. 1961)
Empire, the Journal of the Fabian Colonial Bureau (1941-48)

The press-cuttings, from British and African sources, at Chatham House

ARTICLES

Crowder, Michael, 'Indirect Rule – French and British Style'. *Africa,* xxxiv
    (1964)
Jones, Arthur Creech, 'Colonies in War'. *Political Quarterly,* xi (1940)
— 'The Colonial Office'. *Political Quarterly,* xiv (1943)
Lee, J.M., ' "Forward Thinking" and War: The Colonial Office during
    the 1940s'. *Journal of Imperial and Commonwealth History*, vol.vi, Oct.
    1977
Lonsdale, J., 'The Emergence of African Nationalism: an historiographical
    analysis'. *African Affairs,* lxvii (1968)
Pearce, R.D., 'Governors, Nationalists, and Constitutions in Nigeria,
    1935-51'. *Journal of Imperial and Commonwealth History*, May 1981.
Rathbone, R., 'The Government of the Gold Coast after the Second World
    War'. *African Affairs,* lxvii (1968)

BOOKS AND PAMPHLETS

Ajayi, J.F.A. and Crowder, Michael (eds.), *History of West Africa*, vol.2
    (London, 1974)
Akpan, Ntieyong U., *Epitaph to Indirect Rule* (London, 1956; repr. Cass,
    1967)
Albertini, R. von, *Decolonization* (New York, 1971)
Amery, L.S., *The Forward View* (London, 1935)
Anti-Slavery and Aborigines Protection Society, *An International Colonial
    Convention* (London, 1943)
Attlee, C.R., *The Labour Party in Perspective* (London, 1937)
— *As It Happened* (London, 1954)
— *Empire Into Commonwealth* (1960 Chichele Lectures)

Austin, Dennis, *Politics in Ghana, 1946-1960* (Oxford, 1964)
Awolowo, Obafemi, *Path to Nigerian Freedom* (London, 1947)
— *Awo: The Autobiography of Chief Obafemi Awolowo* (Cambridge, 1960)
Azikiwe, N., *My Odyssey* (London, 1970)
Barnes, Leonard, *The Future of Colonies* (Day to Day pamphlet, 1936)
— *Empire or Democracy?* (London, 1939)
— *Soviet Light on the Colonies* (Penguin Special, 1944)
Bartlett, C.J., *The Long Retreat: A Short History of British Defence Policy, 1945-1970* (London, 1972)
Bello, Alhaji Sir Ahmadu, *My Life* (Cambridge, 1962)
Bennett, George (ed.), *The Concept of Empire: Burke to Attlee, 1774-1947* (London, 1962)
— *Kenya: A Political History* (Oxford, 1963)
Bertram, Sir Anton, *The Colonial Service* (Cambridge, 1930)
Brockway, A. Fenner, *Inside the Left* (London, 1942)
— *Outside the Right* (London, 1963)
— *The Colonial Revolution* (London, 1975)
Bullock, Alan, *The Life and Times of Ernest Bevin*, 2 vols. (London, 1960, 1967)
Burger, John, *The Black Man's Burden* (London, 1943)
Burns, Sir Alan, *Colonial Civil Servant* (London, 1949)
— *History of Nigeria* (London, 4th edn., 1951)
— *In Defence of Colonies* (London, 1957)
Campbell, Alexander, *Empire in Africa* (London, 1944)
Chandos, Viscount, *The Memoirs of Lord Chandos* (London, 1962)
Cohen, Andrew, *British Policy in Changing Africa* (London, 1959)
Communist Party, *The Colonies: The Way Forward* (C.P. Pamphlet, 1944)
Conservative and Unionist Central Office, *Imperial Policy: A Statement of Conservative Policy for the British Empire and Commonwealth* (June 1949)
Cooke, Colin, *The Life of Richard Stafford Cripps* (London, 1957)
Crowder, M., *West Africa Under Colonial Rule* (London, 1968)
Crowder, M., and Ikime, Obaro (eds.), *West African Chiefs* (Africana Publishing Corporation, 1970)
Dalton, Hugh, *High Tide and After* (London, 1962)
Danquah, J.B., *Friendship and Empire: Impressions of the African Conference* (FCB Pamphlet, Controversy no.5, 1949)
Donoughue, B., and Jones, G.W., *Herbert Morrison: Portrait of a Politician* (London, 1973)
Emerson, Rupert, and Kilson, Martin (eds.), *The Political Awakening of Africa* (New York, 1965)
Fabian Colonial Bureau, *Downing Street and the Colonies* (1942)
— *Domination or Co-operation?* (Controversy no.1, 1946)
— *Kenya Controversy* (Controversy no.4, 1967)
Fiddes, Sir George V., *The Dominions and Colonial Offices* (London, 1926)

Fieldhouse, D.K., (ed.), *The Theory of Capitalist Imperialism* (London, 1967)

Foot, Michael, *Aneurin Bevan*, 2 vols. (London, 1962, 1964)

Gann, L.H., *A History of Northern Rhodesia* (London, 1964)

Gann, L.H., and Duignan, Peter, *Burden of Empire* (London, 1968)

— (eds.), *Colonialism in Africa, 1870-1960*, vol.II (Cambridge, 1970)

Goldsworthy, David, *Colonial Issues in British Politics, 1945-1961* (Oxford, 1971)

Gunther, John, *Inside Africa* (London, 1955)

Hailey, Lord, *An African Survey* (Oxford, 1938; Revised edn., 1957)

— *The Position of Colonies in a British Commonwealth of Nations* (Oxford, 1941)

— *The Future of Colonial Peoples* (Oxford, 1943)

— *Native Administration in the British African Territories*, 4 vols. (London, 1951)

Haqqi, *Colonial Policy of the Labour Government, 1945-1951* (Aligarh, India, 1960)

Hargreaves, J.D., *The End of Colonial Rule in West Africa* (Historical Association Pamphlet, 1976)

Hatch, John, *A History of Postwar Africa* (London, 1965)

Hetherington, P., *British Paternalism and Africa, 1920-1940* (London, Cass, 1978)

Hicks, U.K., *Development from Below* (Oxford, 1961)

Hinden, Rita, *The Colonies and Us* (Fabian Special Pamphlet, 1942)

— (ed.), *Fabian Colonial Essays* (London, 1945)

— *Socialists and the Empire* (Fabian Special Pamphlet, 1946)

— *Empire and After* (London, 1949)

— *Local Government and the Colonies* (London, 1950)

Huxley, Julian, *Africa View* (London, 1931)

— *Memories* (London, 1970)

Jackson, Robert J., *Rebels and Whips* (London, 1964)

Jeffries, Sir Charles, *Whitehall and the Colonial Service: an Administrative Memoir, 1939-1968* (London, 1972)

Jones, A. Creech, *Labour's Colonial Policy* (FCB pamphlet, Controversy no.3, 1947)

— (ed.), *New Fabian Colonial Essays* (London, 1959)

Kiernan, V.G. *Marxism and Imperialism* (London, 1974)

Kirk-Greene, A.H.M., (ed.), *The Principles of Native Administration in Nigeria: Select Documents, 1900-1947* (London, 1965)

Koebner, Richard, and Schmidt, H.D., *Imperialism* (Cambridge, 1964)

Labour and Socialist International, *The Colonial Problem* (London, 1928)

Labour Party, *The Empire in Africa: Labour's Policy* (n.d. but 1921)

— *Labour and the Empire in Africa* (n.d. but 1926)

— *British Imperialism in East Africa* (1926)

— *The Colonial Empire* (1933)

— *The Demand for Colonial Territories and Equality of Economic Opportunity* (1936)

— *The Colonies: the Labour Party's Post-War Policy for the African and Pacific Colonies* (1943)

Lee, J.M., *Colonial Development and Good Government* (Oxford, 1967)

Listowel, Judith, *The Making of Tanganyika* (London, 1965)

Louis, W. Roger, *Imperialism at Bay, 1941-1945* (Oxford, 1977)

Low, D.A., *Lion Rampant: Essays in the Study of British Imperialism* (London, Cass, 1973)

Low, D.A., and Smith, Alison, *History of East Africa* vol.III (Oxford, 1976)

Lugard, Lord, *The Dual Mandate in British Tropical Africa* (London, Cass, 5th edn, 1965)

Macmillan, Harold, *The Blast of War, 1939-1945* (London, 1967)

Mansergh, N., *Survey of British Commonwealth Affairs: Problems of Wartime Co-operation and Post-War Change* (1958; repr. Cass, 1968)

Martin, Kingsley, *Harold Laski* (London, 1953)

Metcalfe, G.E. (ed.), *Great Britain and Ghana: Documents on Ghana History, 1809-1957* (London, 1964)

Morrison, Herbert, *An Autobiography* (London, 1960)

Mosley, Sir Oswald, *My Life* (London, 1970)

Nkrumah, Kwame, *The Autobiography of Kwame Nkrumah* (Panaf edn., 1973)

Norman, Dorothy (ed.), *Nehru: The First Sixty Years*, 2 vols. (London, 1965)

Obituaries from The Times, 1961-1970 (Newspaper Archive Developments Ltd, 1975)

Oliver, Roland, and Atmore, Anthony, *Africa Since 1800* (Cambridge, 2nd edn., 1972)

Olivier, Sydney, *White Capital and Coloured Labour* (London, 1929)

Olusanya, G.O. *The Second World War and Politics in Nigeria, 1939-1953* (London, 1973)

Orwell, G., *The Collected Essays, Journalism, and Letters of George Orwell*, 4 vols. (edited by Sonia Orwell and Ian Angus, Penguin, 1970)

Padmore, George, *History of the Pan-African Congress* (London, 2nd edn., 1963)

Pandey, B.N., *Nehru* (London, 1976)

Parkinson, Sir Cosmo, *The Colonial Office from Within, 1909-1945* (London, 1947)

Pelling, H. (ed.), *The Challenge of Socialism* (London, 2nd edn., 1968)

— *A Short History of the Labour Party* (London, 4th edn., 1974)

— *Winston Churchill* (London, 1974)

Perham, Margery, *Native Administration in Nigeria* (Oxford, 1937)

— *The Colonial Reckoning* (London, 1960)

— *Colonial Sequence, 1930-1949: A Chronological Commentary upon British Colonial Policy especially in Africa* (London, 1967)

Porter, Bernard, *The Lion's Share* (London, 1975)

Pratt, Cranford, *The Critical Phase in Tanzania, 1945-1968* (Cambridge, 1976)

Pritt, D.N., *The Labour Government, 1945-1951* (London, 1963)
Roosevelt, F.D., and Churchill, W.S., *Roosevelt and Churchill: Their Secret Wartime Correspondence* (edited by F.L. Loewenheim, H.D. Langley, and M. Jonas, London, 1975)
Robinson, Kenneth E., *The Dilemmas of Trusteeship* (Oxford, 1965)
Rotberg, Robert I., *The Rise of Nationalism in Central Africa* (Harvard, 1965)
Shiels, Sir Drummond, *The Colonies Today and Tomorrow* (London, 1947)
Short, Philip, *Banda* (London, 1974)
Silberman, L., *Crisis in Africa* (FCB Pamphlet, Controversy no.2, 1947)
Sithole, Ndabaningi, *African Nationalism* (Oxford, 2nd edn., 1968)
Smith, Sir B. Sharwood, *But Always As Friends* (London, 1969)
Strachey, *The End of Empire* (London, 1959)
Taylor, A.J.P., *English History, 1914-1945* (Oxford, 1965)
Thomas, Hugh, *John Strachey* (London, 1973)
Thornton, A.P., *Doctrines of Imperialism* (London, 1965)
— *The Imperial Idea and its Enemies* (London, 1968)
— *For the File on Empire* (London, 1968)
Toynbee, Arnold, *Experiences* (Oxford, 1969)
Wight, Martin, *The Development of the Legislative Council, 1906-1956* (London, 1946)
— *The Gold Coast Legislative Council* (London, 1947)
Williams, Francis, *Ernest Bevin: Portrait of a Great Englishman* (London, 1952)
— *A Prime Minister Remembers* (London, 1961)
Wilson, Henry S., *The Imperial Experience in Sub-Saharan Africa since 1870* (Oxford, 1977)
Wood, Alan, *The Groundnut Affair* (London, 1950)
Woolf, Leonard, *Sowing* (London, 1960)
— *Growing* (London, 1962)
— *Beginning Again* (London, 1964)
— *Downhill All the Way* (London, 1967)
— *The Journey Not the Arrival Matters* (London, 1969)

C. Oral Testimony

Mr Ivor Bulmer-Thomas – interview on 9 Oct. 1976
Sir Alan Burns – interview on 31 Mar. 1979
Mr Aiden Crawley – interview on 26 July 1977
Mr Hugh Elliott – interview on 31 Mar. 1979
The Earl of Listowel – interview on 30 July 1976
Sir Frederick Pedler – interviews on 25 Apr. 1977 and 30 Mar. 1979
Dame Margery Perham – interview on 18 July 1977
Professor Kenneth Robinson – interview on 14 July 1977

Index

Achimota College, 65
Acland, Sir Richard, 18
Accra, 80, 103, 133
Accra riots (1948), 188-90, 192, 194,
  195, 202
Adams, D., 137
Africa Conference (1948), 125, 158,
  164, 176, 181-2
African Governors' Conference (1947),
  179-80
African Studies Branch, 195
African Survey, 3, 42-4, 156
Anderson, Sir John, 66
Arden-Clarke, Sir Charles, 190
Ashanti, 80
Asquith Commission on Higher
  Education, 64
Atlantic Charter (1941), 24-6
Attlee, Clement R., 24, 84, 91-3, 94,
  95, 117, 176, 206
Australia, 37
Awolowo, Obafemi, 136, 197
Azikiwe, Nnamdi, 103, 116, 135,
  137-8, 195

Baldwin, Lord, 119
Balliol College, 73
Banda, Hastings, 121, 136, 139, 140
Barnes, Leonard, 12-14, 108
Barotseland, 9, 198
Bevan, Aneurin, 18, 91, 96
Bevin, Ernest, 94-6, 120
Bledisloe Commission, 63
Boer War, 110
Bofo of Bamfe, 49
Bourdillon, Sir Bernard, 7, 15, 57,
  76-8, 80-3, 84, 135, 208
Bourne, Sir Frederick, 197
British Centre Against Imperialism,
  138
Brockway, Fenner, 124
Brooke, Gerald, 117
Buganda, 199
Bullock, Alan, 95

Burma, 22, 25, 93, 115, 134
Burns, Sir Alan, 57, 76-80, 83, 84, 113,
  118, 135, 147, 173, 208
Burt, Cyril, 3

Caine, Sydney, 58, 86, 164, 167, 179
Calabar, 82
Cambridge Summer Schools (on
  African administration), 150-3, 163,
  199
Cameron, Sir Donald, 8, 55, 154, 155
Campbell, Roy, 162
Camus, Albert, 17
Cape Coast, 80
Cape Colony, 4
Carlton Hotel, 46-7, 50
Carnegie Corporation, 43
Carrow, J.H., 88
Carstairs, C.Y., 143
Cartland, G.B. 141-3, 195
Cary, Joyce, 1
Casement, R., 98
Ceylon, 34, 105, 120
Chief Secretary's Office, 172
Churchill, Winston, 22, 24, 25, 37, 71,
  90, 115
Clauson, Gerard, 86, 179
Cohen, Andrew: early career, 15, 61-2,
  67, 75, 81-2, 119-20, 163; local
  government policy, 142, 145-53,
  157-8, 195, 198-9, 200-2; 1947
  Report, 162-4, 167-74, 177-8,
  180-2; Governor of Uganda, 198-9;
  Coussey Constitution, 192-3, 195
Cold War, 90
Colonial Development Act (1929), 3,
  20
Colonial Development and Welfare Act
  (1940), 19, 20, 38, 43, 65, 100, 162
Colonial Development and Welfare Act
  (1945), 65-6, 100, 166, 185
Colonial Development Corporation,
  186

Colonial Service, 1, 25, 70, 118-19, 142, 145, 158, 162, 165-6, 175-7, 182, 185, 195, 201
Congress Party (Indian National), 29
Convention People's Party, 194, 197
Council on African Affairs, 138
Coussey Committee, 192-4, 197
Cranborne, Lord, 25, 26, 72, 92
Creasy, Gerald, 75, 86, 138, 189
Creed, Sir Thomas, 190
Cripps, Stafford, 29, 96-7, 137
Crowder, Michael, 151
Cummings, Ivor, 66
Curtis, Lionel, 95
Cyrenaica, 93

Daily Comet, 137
Daily Express, 187
Daily Telegraph, 49, 123
Dalgleish, Andrew, 190
Dalton, Hugh, 91, 93-4
Danquah, Joseph B., 103, 110, 136-7, 181-2, 194
Davies, H.O., 136
Dawe, Sir Arthur, 19, 76, 119
Decolonization, 2, 174
Devonshire, Lord, 5
Dickens, Charles, 70
Dodds-Parker, 114
Donner, Squadron-Leader, 123
Douglas, F.C.R., 119
Dual Mandate, 7, 43
Dugdale, John, 117
Dundas, Sir Charles, 42, 73
Durham Report, 4, 162
Dutton, A.H., 143

East African High Commission, 72
Eastwood, Christopher, 33, 35
Economic policy, 85-7, 96-7, 99, 158-9, 166-7, 186-8
Eden, Anthony, 37
Education, 64-5, 165-6
Edwards, Talbot, 77
Eliot, T.S., 2, 185
Elliott, Hugh P., 140
Elliott Commission 65, 99, 103
Emirs, 80
Enugu shooting incident (1949), 195

Fabian Colonial Bureau, 98, 109-12, 116, 122, 125, 144-5, 149, 164
Fenton, J.S., 10
First World War, 2, 42, 97
Fitzgerald, F. Scott, 40
Fitzgerald, Sir William, 190
Footman, C.W.F., 143
Fourah Bay College, 65
Freetown, 138
Freud, Sigmund, 2
Furse, Sir Ralph, 118-19

Gambia, 29, 65
Gammans, Mr., 117
Gandhi, M.K., 29, 43, 96
Gater, Sir George, 76, 119
George, David Lloyd, 17
Gold Coast, 11-12, 22, 47, 57, 62, 65, 76, 78-9, 83, 141, 145, 151, 168, 172, 175, 177, 182, 188, 190-1, 193-4, 197, 208
Gordon, Dr. H.L., 3
Gore-Brown, S., 74
Griffiths, James, 92, 117
Grigg, Sir Edward, 12
Grosz, George, 12
Groundnuts, 94, 96, 186-7
Guest, Dr. Haden, 18, 27, 108
Guggisberg, Sir Gordon, 47

Hailey, Lord, 3, 20, 27, 29, 33, 42-67, 71, 73, 76-9, 83, 142, 155-7, 171, 200-1, 207-8
Haldane, Lord, 3
Halifax, Lord (formerly Lord Irwin), 31, 43
Hall, George, 91, 101, 121-3
Hall, Hathorn, 139
Harlech, Lord, 70
Hayford, Casely, 133-4
Hinden, Dr. Rita, 109-12, 123, 125, 144-5, 148, 187
Hobson, J.A., 12-13, 105
Hodson, Sir Arnold, 10-11, 47, 83, 137, 145
Hong Kong, 22
Houston, George, 144
Hudson, R.H., 198
Huggins, Godfrey, 74
Hull, Cordell, 31
Huxley, Julian, 3, 6, 65

Ibadan, 65
India, 29, 43, 77, 93, 96, 105, 113, 115, 124, 132, 139, 169
Indirect rule, 7-11, 13, 44-6, 50, 53-4, 56-7, 102-3, 107-8, 135, 141, 144, 147, 154-8, 174, 177, 196, 198, 201, 205, 207
Institute of Journalists, 138
Intermediate Administrative Service, 53
Inter-University Council for Higher Education, 64
Irwin, Lord, see Halifax, Lord
Israel, 120

Japan, 36-8, 96
Japanese Mandated Islands, 36-8
Jeffries, Sir Charles, 20, 139, 166
Johnson, Carol, 151
Jones, Arthur Creech, summary of early career, 97-104; as critic of empire, 17, 18, 26-8, 65, 72, 74, 91-2, 94, 114; and Fabian Colonial Bureau, 98, 109, 112, 116, 122, 125, 145, 149, 164; as responsible Minister, 113, 116-27, 136-8, 140, 142-3, 157-8, 162-5, 170-5, 177-82, 185, 190, 192-3, 201-2, 206-7, 209
Journal of African Administration, 195

Kabaka of Buganda, 199
Keith, J.L., 47
Kenya, 4, 6, 17, 62, 71-3, 86, 99, 101, 121, 172, 177-8, 187, 198, 208
Kenyatta, Jomo, 136, 140
Kikuyu, 98
Kikuyu Central Association, 101
Kilson, Martin, 194
Korea, 91
Krishnamurti, Jiddu, 90
Kumasi, 80

Labour Party, 51, 56-7, 141-59, 195-202, 205, 210
Lagos, 82, 196
Laski, Harold, 138
League of Coloured Peoples, 66, 138
League of Nations, 5
Leeward Islands, 19
Lenin, V.I., 12, 13, 105

Lennox-Boyd, Alan, 127
Lewis, Dr. Arthur, 110, 112
Leys, Norman, 108
Life magazine, 28
Listowel, Lord, 176
Lloyd, Lord, 74
Lloyd, T.I.K., 118-19
Local government, 51, 56-7, 141-159, 195-202, 205, 210
Local Government Despatch (1947), 146-51, 162, 178, 181, 198, 201
Lugard, Lord, 7, 43, 46-7, 154-5, 157-8, 179

MacDonald, Malcolm, 17-20, 23, 46-8, 99
MacDonald, Peter, 18, 122
Macmillan, Harold, 26-7, 86
Macpherson, Sir John, 180, 194
Makerere College, 64
Malan, Dr. Daniel, 94
Malaya, 2, 22, 24-5, 64, 134
Malta, 119, 163
Manchester Guardian, 109, 124
Mandalay, 2
Mandates, 5, 37, 113
Mangin, T.R.O., 177
Marris, Sir William, 43
Marshall Plan, 90
Mathu, E.W., 73
Mau Mau, 195
Member System, 172, 180-1
Mercury, 27
Mikindani, 187
Milverton, Lord (formerly Sir Arthur Richards), 81-4, 137-8, 145, 173, 179-80, 191, 194
Ministry of Information, 21
Mitchell, Sir Philip, 118, 150, 177-9
Mombassa, 2
Montagu, Edwin, 43
Moody, Dr. Harold, 66, 121
Moore, Sir Henry, 58, 72
Morel, E.D., 98
Morgan, Dr., 123
Morrison, Herbert, 94
Moyne, Lord, 17, 20-1, 24, 56
Murray, K.A.H., 190

Natal, 4
National Congress of British West Africa, 133

National Council of Nigeria and the Cameroons, 135
National Peace Council, 102
Nationalism, 1, 52, 104, 111, 133-41, 162, 167, 169, 170, 172, 188, 194, 201-2, 206, 210
Native Administration, 7, 10-11, 48, 60-1, 134, 141-2, 147, 156, 159, 205, see also Indirect rule
'Native Administration and Political Development' (Hailey), 49-58
Nehru, Jawaharlal, 126
New Statesman, 123
New Zealand, 37
News Chronicle, 123
Nkrumah, Kwame, 110, 136, 138, 140, 189, 193-4, 197
Nietzsche, F., 42
Nigeria, 2, 22, 45, 53-4, 67, 76, 78, 80-1, 83, 116, 135-8, 140, 143, 145, 151, 172, 194-7, 208
Nigerian Youth Movement, 135
Noel-Baker, Philip, 18, 94
Norman, Montagu, 3
Northern Rhodesia, 4, 9, 54-5, 62-4, 74, 163, 172, 174, 180, 187, 198
Norwich, 196
Nyasaland, 8-9, 54-5, 63-4, 75-6, 121, 144, 180, 198, 208
Nyasaland Congress, 139

Observer, 113
Ogaden, 93
Orde-Browne, Major, 12
Overseas Food Corporation, 186-7
Overseas Resources Development Bill, 186

Pakistan, 115
Palestine, 120-1
Paling, W., 98
Pan-African Congress (1945), 136
Parkinson, Sir Cosmo, 6
Partnership, 27
Passfield, Lord (formerly Sidney Webb), 6, 91
Pedler, Frederick J., 45, 48-9, 77, 82, 119, 135, 143
Perham, Margery, 7, 23, 46, 109
Placentia Bay, 24
Poynton, Hilton, 119, 179

Queens' College, Cambridge, 150-1

Rankin, C., 143
Read, Margaret, 65
Rees-Williams, David, 125
Richards, Sir Arthur, see Milverton, Lord
Robinson, Kenneth, 6
Robinson, Ronald, 195
Roosevelt, Franklin D., 24, 29
Rotberg, Robert, 10
Royal African Society, 102
Royal Empire Society, 102
Russell, Sir Alison, 109
Russell, Bertrand, 14

Samuel, Lord, 18
Sarawak, 117
Sartre, Jean-Paul, 161, 205
Schuster, Sir George, 43
Second World War, 1, 21-2, 28, 57, 70, 99, 133-4, 186, 205-9
Seel, G. F., 63-4
Sekondi-Takoradi, 80
Selwyn-Clarke, Dr., 119
Seychelles, 119
Sherbro, Chief Bai, 10
Shinwell, E., 90, 94
Shuckburgh, Sir John, 84
Sierra Leone, 10, 54, 65, 79, 134-5, 197, 208
Simon, Sir John, 47, 92
Singapore, 22-3, 25
Sithole, N., 133
Skinnard, Mr., 124
Slater, Sir Ransford, 10
Smuts, Jan Christian, 43, 71
Somaliland, 93
Sorenson, Rev. R., 137-8
South Africa, Union of, 4, 64, 71, 75, 98, 110
Southern Rhodesia, 4, 63-4, 74-5
Soviet Union, 30, 38, 95
Standing Central African Council, 75
Stanley, Oliver, 34-7, 58, 63, 65-6, 74-5, 114, 122, 127
Stevenson, Sir Hubert, 138-9
Stockdale, Sir Frank, 188
Storey, Bernard, 196
Strachey, John, 90, 96
Sunday Times, 123
Swinton, Lord, 70, 79

Tanganyika, 8-9, 22, 54-5, 71-3, 144, 179, 186-7, 198
Teita Hills Association, 101
Temple, C.L., 177
Tennessee Valley Authority, 187
Thomas, Hugh, 144, 191
Thomas, Ivor, 125, 165
Thomas, J.H., 91
The Times, 23, 27, 36, 38, 206
Toynbee, Arnold, 2
Transport and General Workers' Union, 94-5, 97
Trenchard, Lord, 67
Tribune, 91, 114
Trusteeship, 4-5, 14, 27, 37, 99, 106, 113, 126

Uganda, 42, 64, 71-3, 139, 151, 198-9
Ukamba Association, 101
United Africa Company, 67, 99
United Gold Coast Convention, 189, 194
United Nations (Organisation), 31-2, 36, 38, 92, 113, 126, 169
United States, 24, 28-38, 84, 210

Varvill, M.H., 143

Wallace, O.S., 143
Wallace-Johnson, I.T.A., 103, 116, 134-7
Watson Commission, 190-2
Webb, Sidney, *see* Passfield, Lord
Wedgwood, Josiah, 108
West African Pilot, 137
West African Students' Union, 24, 134-6
West African Youth League, 137
West Indies, 17, 24, 28, 78
Wilkins, P., 143
Williams, J.B., 143
Williams, O.G.R., 47, 58-63, 76-7, 136
Woolf, Leonard, 12, 57, 105, 107
Wum of Bum, 49

Yalta, 37
Young, Sir Hubert, 9

Zikist Movement, 195